TH
P

DATE DUE			

THE INDUSTRIAL POLICY DEBATE

Edited by

CHALMERS JOHNSON

ICS PRESS

Institute for Contemporary Studies
San Francisco, California

338.973
In 2
133029
Feb. 1986

Inquiries, book orders, and catalog requests should be addressed to ICS Press, Suite 750, 785 Market Street, San Francisco, California 94103—(415) 543-6213.

Library of Congress Cataloging in Publication Data
Main entry under title:

The Industrial policy debate.

    Includes index.
    1. Industry and state—United States—Addresses,
essays, lectures.   2. Industry and state—Japan—
Addresses, essays, lectures.   3. Industry and state—
Europe—Addresses, essays, lectures.   I. Johnson,
Chalmers A.
HD3616.U47I45   1984   338.973   84-6741
ISBN   0-917616-65-0
ISBN   0-917616-64-2 (pbk.)

CONTENTS

II
Foreign Models and the American Experience

III
Current Problems

IV

Government Policies and Reforms

V

Conclusion

PREFACE

Since the late 1970s, the term "industrial policy" has come to figure more and more prominently in American political debate. The apparent decline of America's competitive position in the world economy, widespread concern over the deterioration of such basic industries as steel and automobiles, and increasing uneasiness about the potential of the United States to maintain its preeminence in high technology have led to many calls for a broad reappraisal of government's role in economic life.

In many cases, "industrial policy" has clearly become little more than a new label for old, ideologically inspired programs of government intrusion in the marketplace. On the other hand, many legitimate, even urgent, questions have been raised about the effectiveness of American business and government in shaping a dynamic response to the challenges of external competition and internal economic change.

In the fall of 1983, the Institute for Contemporary Studies asked Chalmers Johnson of the University of California at Berkeley, author of the widely acclaimed *MITI and the Japanese Miracle,* to gather together a group of the nation's leading economists and political scientists for a thorough assessment of the issues in the industrial policy debate. The contributors to this volume share a concern that the label of industrial policy not be used as a cover for economically unsound, politically inspired programs. There is also general agreement on a number of fundamental issues—e.g., the hazards of protectionism, the need for a more sensible tax structure. But within this broad consensus, there is considerable disagreement as to how to proceed. On the one hand, a number of authors argue that any effort to initiate large-scale, coordinated reforms of government policies will only make matters worse. On the other hand, some authors see a pressing need for such efforts, especially in light of concern with such issues as America's requirement for a sound industrial base for national defense.

This is the latest of several books on economic policy published by the Institute for Contemporary Studies; earlier volumes include *The Economy in the 1980s: A Program for Growth and Stability,* edited by Michael J. Boskin; *The Federal Budget: Economics and Politics,* edited by Michael J. Boskin and Aaron Wildavsky; and *Reaganomics: A Midterm Report,* edited by Wm. Craig Stubblebine and Thomas D. Willett.

In addition to Professor Johnson and the distinguished contributors to this volume, I wish particularly to express my appreciation to Patrick Glynn and Walter J. Lammi, who conceived the idea for this project and, working closely with Professor Johnson, guided it to completion.

Glenn Dumke
President
Institute for Contemporary Studies

I

The Issues

1

CHALMERS JOHNSON

Introduction: The Idea of Industrial Policy

The essays in this volume will strike some American readers as perfectly timed for 1984, with their Orwellian implications of more "bureaucrats, scientists, technicians, trade union organizers, publicity experts, sociologists, teachers, journalists, and professional politicians" (one wonders why Orwell left out economists). Other Americans will find in this collection a gratifying, if belated, recognition that the government-business relationship in the United States has become a serious, costly drag on American economic competitiveness in the world, and they will welcome the beginnings of a broadly based, nonpartisan discussion of how to improve the situation. Whatever one's preconceived opinions, almost everyone recognizes that the subject of this book—the industrial policies of the advanced industrial democracies and whether or not the United States needs an industrial policy of its own—is intensely controversial. There are several reasons for this: political, doctrinal, and conceptual.

First, and most obviously, the issue of industrial policy is politically controversial because 1984 is a presidential election year. Many Republicans think the Democrats are planning to throw money at the northern Midwest "Rust Belt" states and to disguise what they are doing under the elegant term "industrial policy." And the Republicans are almost surely right about this; it is a good and logical way for the Democrats to win trade union votes and to respond to the American public's worries about deindustrialization, unemployment, and industrial relocation to the Sun Belt or abroad. But rather than saying so directly, many Republicans are painting themselves into a corner by attacking the very concept of industrial policy, arguing that its importance in Japan and other countries has been exaggerated, that it won't work in America, and that it violates the sacred principles of private enterprise and free trade.

At the same time, serious observers understand that the Republicans' own policies—so-called Reaganomics, a version of supply-side economics—are in fact a first step toward an American industrial policy and that the popular contrast between Reaganomics and a properly conceived American industrial policy is a false distinction. President Reagan has actually set the American political agenda for the rest of this century—jobs, high technology, saving and investment, world competitiveness, orderly change of industrial structure—and the Democrats have, in a sense, paid him a compliment by trying to go him a step better.

President Reagan himself has not backed away from these issues. During August 1983, he established a new Commission on Industrial Competitiveness, headed by the president of the Hewlett-Packard Company, and his missile defense speech of March 23, 1983—the so-called "Star Wars" speech—has profound industrial policy implications. If Japan's industrial policy has been implemented by its Ministry of International Trade and Industry (MITI) and for purposes of economic defense, then America's industrial policy (to the extent that it already has one) has been implemented by the Department of Defense and for purposes of its own military defense and that of the Free World. But if the United States is not to become the world's leading producer of ICBMs and soybeans, while Japan produces everything in between these two extremes, then it is clear that we must do more in terms of rethinking our basic economic policies.

Sources of Controversy

The subject of industrial policy is controversial on doctrinal grounds for two reasons. First, although it is an economic concept and Americans have won more Nobel prizes in economics than any other nationality, they did not happen to come up with this one. Second, the idea of industrial policy calls into question many of the economic beliefs that Americans have popularly used since the end of World War II to explain their own economic preeminence—such things as their commitment to the market mechanism as the supreme arbiter of economic decisions, their reliance on adversarial rather than cooperative public-private relations, and their greater devotion than other peoples to free trade. American-sponsored institutions such as the General Agreement on Tariffs and Trade, the International Monetary Fund, the Marshall Plan, fixed exchange rates until 1971, and the use of the U.S. dollar as an international medium of exchange to replace gold were all critically important to the prosperity and growth that the Free World enjoyed for the postwar generation. But these institutions may be more accurately understood as examples of ingenious American industrial policies rather than as suprapolitical arrangements dictated by economic laws. It is, in fact, necessary to understand them this way in order to modify and improve them as new economic conditions arise.

The contemporary idea of industrial policy is of Japanese origin (although the Japanese claim to have gotten it long ago from the Americans, a topic to which we shall return). This paternity is as disturbing to American *amour propre* as is the realization that Japan beat Detroit at its own game to become in 1980 the world's largest manufacturer of automobiles. Such an achievement, moreover, required a degree and form of cooperation between the Japanese public and private sectors that is comparable only to the American Manhattan and Apollo projects.

American economists, in particular, are irritated by these developments. When Charles Schultze tells us that "we actually know precious little about identifying, before the fact, a 'winning industrial structure,'" one wants to reply that Japan's techniques of bottom-up decision-making and extensive public-private consultation offer some important clues as to how to go about it. When Richard McKenzie writes, "In the industrial policy debate, there is

no dispute over whether or not government policies affect industrial development in this country; the dispute is over whether
or not industrial development and stability can be, and should be,
enhanced through voluntary or coercive institutions," one wants
to point out that Japan's high-speed economic growth occurred
only *after* that country shifted from coercive to voluntary institutions. When Melville Ulmer asks rhetorically, "How can bureaucrats tell, more accurately than private investors, which are the
'most promising' firms or industries?" one wants to insist that no
Japanese economic bureaucrat thinks he can and that modern
Japanese industrial policy has shown a greater reliance on the
wisdom of the market than many of its American critics.[1]

The domestic controversy over industrial policy is not going to
go away. Claims of revolutionary new discoveries and charges of
abominable heresy will doubtless continue to punctuate the debate
since well-established interests and reputations are involved. But
if the challenge of Japan does nothing more than let a little fresh
air into the doctrinaire discussion of economic life in America, it
will be one of the best things that ever happened to the United
States. It may also be recalled that when presidential candidate
Reagan offered his supply-side challenge to the then-prevailing
Keynesian demand-management set of policies, he was assailed as
a purveyor of "voodoo economics"—until his policies stopped inflation and laid the foundations for the economic recovery of 1983
and 1984. But the partial success of Reaganomics has not so much
ended the debate as escalated it. Which leads us to the next area of
controversy: what, exactly, is industrial policy?

Industrial policy is conceptually controversial because, as
Hiroya Ueno, one of Japan's leading theorists of the concept, puts
it, "Unlike traditional fiscal and monetary policies, industrial
policy demonstrates no clear relationship between its objectives
and the means of attaining them. Its conception, content, and
forms differ, reflecting the stage of development of an economy,
its natural and historical circumstances, international conditions,
and its political and economic situation, resulting in considerable
differences from nation to nation and from era to era."[2] This contingent nature of industrial policy must be stressed; it helps to explain why Japanese industrial policy in the 1950s and 1960s was
protectionist and why today it is oriented toward free trade and

the internationalization of the Japanese economy. The concept's contingent nature also makes clear at the outset that the United States cannot and should not copy Japan's industrial policies. The responsibilities, endowments, and political institutions of the two countries differ too much for that. Japan cannot be a model, at least not for the United States. Nonetheless, Japan's priorities in economic policy, its long-range perspective, its market-conforming methods of governmental intervention, and its government-business relationships pose a challenge to the United States to match and excel them. Such organizational inventiveness is what competition among capitalist nations is all about.

Defining Industrial Policy

Industrial policy is a summary term for the activities of governments that are intended to develop or retrench various industries in a national economy in order to maintain global competitiveness. As a set of policies, industrial policy is the complement, the third side of the economic triangle, to a government's monetary policies (money supply, attitude toward inflation, cost of capital, interest rates, exchange rates) and fiscal policies (government spending, public investment, tax burden). Industrial policy is first of all an attitude, and only then a matter of technique. It involves the specific recognition that all government measures—taxes, licenses, prohibitions, regulations—have a significant impact on the well-being or ill-health of whole sectors, industries, and enterprises in a market economy.

Industrial policy may be positive or negative, implicit or explicit. Put negatively, industrial policy refers to the distortions, disincentives, and inequities that result from uncoordinated public actions that benefit or restrain one segment of the economy at the expense of another. Bruce Bartlett, executive director of the Joint Economic Committee of Congress, had this aspect in mind when he wrote, "We ought to be dismantling our existing industrial policy, not enhancing it."[3] Calls to "get the government off the back of the private sector" are natural responses to an implicit industrial policy, one that fails or refuses to recognize that government is also a player in the global competitive scramble and that some governments provide their services more cheaply and more effectively than others. As Frank Weil, former assistant secretary of commerce, has noted, "We have an industrial policy in this country; the policy is that we do not want an industrial policy."[4]

In a positive, explicit sense, industrial policy means the initiation and coordination of governmental activities to leverage upward the productivity and competitiveness of the whole economy and of particular industries in it. Above all, positive industrial policy means the infusion of goal-oriented, strategic thinking into public economic policy. It is the attempt by government to move beyond the broad aggregate and environmental concerns of monetary and fiscal policy of the market system. At the very least it involves the understanding that in advanced industrial democracies, in which economies of scale alone dictate huge investments and the employment of thousands of individuals, changes of industrial structure are only poorly accomplished through the market mechanism. Equally to the point, in democracies the workings of the market are commonly preempted by political action. Rather than leaving such political interventions solely to pressure groups and other well-organized interests, industrial policy seeks to solve problems before they arise. Industrial policy does not mean the nationalization of industries, the spending of more government money, or greater bureaucratism; if these things occur it merely means that a nation has chosen a poor industrial policy.

In more abstract terms, industrial policy is a logical outgrowth of the changing concept of comparative advantage. The classical or static notion of comparative advantage referred to geographical differences and various natural endowments among economies that were supposed to produce a global division of labor. The newer dynamic concept of comparative advantage replaces the classical criteria with such elements as human creative power, foresight, a highly educated work force, organizational talent, the ability to choose, and the ability to adapt. Moreover, these attributes are not conceived of as natural endowments but as qualities achieved through public policies such as education, organized research, and investment in social overhead capital. This newer concept helps explain why 18 million Taiwanese export about the same amount as 130 million Brazilians and about four times as much as 75 million Mexicans, even though Mexico is located next door to the world's largest market and Taiwan is 6,000 miles away.

At various times and places industrial policy has emerged to fulfill many different goals of nations—such things as overcoming late development, securing national defense, and managing scarce natural resources. But today in the United States, its primary purpose must be to secure a dynamic comparative advantage in the global economy for American enterprises. International industrial competitiveness depends, of course, on several factors, including macroeconomic conditions (capital costs, fiscal deficits), the structure of international trade (cartelization, import and export incentives), and the qualities of management (mastery of foreign marketing techniques, ability to gather and use information about the global economy). But the key elements in the long run are economic growth, productivity, and the avoidance of structural rigidities that block change. This is where industrial policy comes in.

With regard to facilitating growth, industrial policy has its own macro and micro aspects. At the macro level it provides governmental incentives for private saving, investment, research and development, cost-cutting, quality control, maintenance of competition, and improvements in labor-management relations. At the micro level it seeks on the one hand to identify those technologies that will be needed by industry in twenty to thirty years and to facilitate their development, and on the other hand to anticipate those technologies that will decline in importance and to assist in their orderly retreat or to support them as a matter of social necessity (food supply, munitions, and so forth). Macro- and microindustrial policies are both important, but the micro aspect —so-called "industrial targeting"—has often been stressed to the exclusion of the first, even though targeting cannot succeed without favorable macro conditions and is best evaluated as a matter of batting averages, not in terms of absolute successes or failures.

Industrial Targeting

Industrial targeting is a much maligned concept. It does not depend on the displacement of the market by bureaucratic fiat, but

instead reflects cooperative efforts by the public and private sectors to understand the nature of technological change and to anticipate its likely economic effects. In some cases targeting will be
undertaken because of gross changes in inputs or the unantici-
pated consequences of other industrial developments—e.g., the
targeting of new and alternative energy sources in light of the
Arab petroleum cartel or the targeting of pollution control devices
in light of environmental damage and new medical information.
Industrial targeting or, more accurately, the dynamic anticipation
of the economically efficient allocation of resources for the future,
is in a sense little more than a new name for the selective public
support of research and development projects. Government does
not so much make these decisions as ratify and underwrite them.
Industrial policy becomes a way to evaluate their economic as well
as their scientific significance. Targeting thus does not mean the
promotion of technologies that are unlikely to develop at all on
their own; it means, rather, helping them rapidly to achieve the
necessary economies of scale and manufacturing efficiency without which they can never become internationally competitive.

Any country's record on targeting is hard to evaluate because
the failures are obvious to all (e.g., the Concorde), whereas it can
never be shown that a successful industry would have failed to
develop without governmental support. Japan's alleged failures in
energy-intensive industries such as aluminum refining and
petrochemicals only became failures after world oil prices quad-
rupled. Until then they were very successful and were, moreover,
indispensable to other of its industries such as automobiles.
Similarly, the Japanese government's schemes for reducing the
number of competitors in the automobile industry in order to
achieve scale economies did not succeed, but this does not mean
that the targeting of the automotive industry itself was a failure.
In fact, the government's aid to smaller subcontracting companies
and its structuring of them into families of suppliers to large-scale
assemblers was one of the important measures that lowered car
costs and promoted their export.

It is sometimes thought that now that Japan has caught up with
the advanced industrial economies, microindustrial policy is no
longer possible (because there are no more advanced economies
for it to use as models) and no longer desirable (because private in-

dustry does not want or need assistance any more). A 1982 Hudson Institute study commissioned by the U.S. Department of State came to this conclusion.[5] My own impression is that while Japan's industrial policy is certainly changing as its national capabilities and those of current and future competitors change, it is not declining. I agree with the World Bank study group on this issue: MITI is today "exploring technological frontiers with the same vigor it has shown earlier in the search for ways to catch up with advanced countries."[6] In addition to its well-known fifth-generation computer project, MITI is also operating research consortia in fine ceramics, biotechnology, space satellites, and ultra-high-precision technology, and it is providing tax incentives for the rational grouping of high-technology and venture capital enterprises in new research cities — so-called technopolises.

Industrial policy is a complex and controversial subject because it *can* mean anything from economic warfare to the ad hoc consequences of uncoordinated governmental regulatory decisions. But it need not be understood in such a broad sense. *By industrial policy I mean the government's explicit attempt to coordinate its own multifarious activities and expenditures and to reform them using as a basic criterion the achievement of dynamic comparative advantage for the American economy.* Such an industrial policy would work on the supply side and would be long-term in outlook. It would seek to produce aggressive investment behavior by reducing risks, providing information, promoting R&D, removing irrational antitrust barriers (joint research by American auto makers in developing emission control technology would have saved millions of dollars but was prevented by governmental regulations), and encouraging the appropriate education and reeducation of the labor force. Louis Mulkern's observation is apropos: "I would suggest that there could be no more devastating weakness for any major nation in the 1980's than the inability to define the role of the government in the economy."[7] Overcoming that lack of definition in the American case would be the first task of an American industrial policy.

The United States government's expenditures in 1981 as a percent of gross domestic product were 18.1 (Japan 10.1), public sector employment as a percent of the labor force 16.5 (Japan 6.6), defense expenditure as a percent of gross domestic product 4.9

(Japan 1.0), and income taxes and social security payments as a percent of gross income 30.1 (Japan 22.3). Many Americans believe that the U.S.'s proportions should be reduced as well as reoriented and given a strategic industrial policy focus. Others believe that a precipitate move to try to implement an industrial policy will merely compound the problems of the public and private sectors. Some maintain that the American government itself is structurally and philosophically unable to deliver what its critics are asking of it. To them a better solution would be to concentrate on improving the macroeconomic environment (easier said than done), leaving change and adjustment to the private sector. One way to get a little more specific on this subject is to focus on the problems, precedents, and proposals for an American industrial policy.

Long-Term Trends

Does the United States have a problem in its international competitiveness? Many prominent Americans who have established through their careers the right to hold an opinion on the subject think so. For example, Sol Chaikin, leader of one of America's most internationally oriented unions, the ILGWU, writes: "Broadly speaking, this country has been following policies which can only lead to intensified deindustrialization. Unrestricted import penetration (during more than a decade of economic stagnation and retrogression) and insufficient new investments have played a vital contributing role in this process."[8] W. J. Sanders, III, chief executive officer of Advanced Micro Devices, asks, "Does the U.S. need a national industrial policy? No discussion required. The answer is yes. . . . What is missing in economic policy is a focus — an international competitive strategy."[9] And Malcolm Baldrige, the secretary of commerce, testifies: "Our trade deficit for 1983 is expected to exceed $50 billion — a figure that is all the more dramatic as the value of oil imports has fallen off so sharply during the past several months. . . . The major policy and operational programs on trade are scattered about the federal system. . . . Foreign governments enjoy the benefits that are available from 'shopping' around the agencies as they seek to pursue their own ends."[10]

In such a recitation of grief, we want to identify the long-term structural problems, not those associated primarily with either the recession of 1981–82 or the recovery of 1983–84. Everyone has his or her own list. My own includes the following:

1. Both management and labor in this country have so far failed to address seriously and overcome their traditional adversarial relationships. New ways are needed to avoid shut-downs and to adjust wage levels to changes in world market conditions. Such recent innovations as give-backs, the appointment of union officials to boards of directors, and the sale of obsolete factories to workers are short-term gimmicks and so understood by both sides. Japan has invented effective ways to replace layoffs with wage cuts through such practices as a career employment system, a mix of fixed monthly wages and variable semiannual bonuses, and enterprise unionism. These ideas derive from the Japanese conception of labor as a form of capital, one that differs from physical capital in that its value increases rather than decreases over time, and not as a separate input into production. Japanese workers are loyal to their enterprises, strike them rarely and only for short periods of time, and accept wage cuts to keep their products competitive (as well as to keep their jobs), not because of some cultural predisposition but because of explicit incentives that make such behavior rational. American management and labor must meet the competition on this score.

2. U.S. government policies and regulations to deal with economic problems are commonly contradictory and self-defeating. For example, even though the government recognized that the domestic auto industry needs a new infusion of capital to produce energy-efficient, high-quality, price-competitive products, its policy of restricting Japanese competition has hardly done the job. Instead, the Japanese are filling their import quotas with their more expensive, upscale models, and the smaller supply of inexpensive, fuel-efficient cars is leading some American dealers (of both Japanese- and American-made models) to raise their prices. Protectionism never increases competitiveness, and this kind of protectionism has served primarily the interests of our competitors.

3. As the superpower responsible for the defense of the Free World, the United States cannot be indifferent to erosion or loss of its basic industrial infrastructure. The popular notion that a nation must move from low-technology, capital-intensive industries of the past into high-technology, knowledge-intensive industries of the future is both false and impossible for a superpower. It is false because whereas the products of capital-intensive industries are not high-tech, the modern processes to make them are. It is impossible because the United States must continue to have both kinds of industries. Steel is an obvious example. The closing in 1982 of Bethlehem Steel's 82-year-old plant in Lackawanna, New York, with the loss of 10,000 jobs, was undoubtedly justified on grounds of efficiency, but the fact that the United States had been relying for some of its steel on an 82-year-old facility indicates a need for strategic input—in the military sense—into our economic policies. (This issue is addressed at length in chapter 10 by Paul Seabury.)

4. The public educational system has for too long been burdened with achieving virtually every imaginable social goal except education. Japanese pupils go to school 5.5 days per week for 220 days per year, whereas American students meet only 5 days per week for 180 days per year. By the completion of high school this means that Japanese students have a net gain of four full years of education. When American students are not going to school, they are looking for temporary jobs, often supplied to them by the public sector at the full minimum wage for adults. A macroindustrial policy in this area would mean no innovations but rather the consolidation of welfare and employment funds now spent on youth into the educational system.

5. Americans must increase their awareness of the markets that exist outside their national boundaries and of the growing dependence of the American economy on these markets. Total U.S. exports in 1980 were 8.2 percent of gross national product, compared with only 4.3 percent in 1970. More important, some 80 percent of all new manufacturing jobs created in the U.S. between 1977 and 1980 were linked in some way to ex-

ports. People living in a continent-sized country and speaking the world's only international language find it difficult to imagine the export challenge. But that is precisely what their competitors have been doing. All of the postwar high-growth capitalist economies of Asia—Japan, South Korea, Taiwan, Hong Kong, and Singapore—have been externally oriented in calculating their economic strategies. The economic concept of efficiency has become meaningless if it is not measured by world prices and costs.

There are still other well-known distortions in the American economy. Coordination and the reconciliation of conflicts among federal economic programs are increasingly entrusted to ninety-four federal district courts, ten appellate courts, and one Supreme Court. These institutions are ill-equipped to understand or respond to the dynamics of international competition, even though their preeminence in the American system contributed to what Derek Bok has called a "massive diversion of exceptional talent into the law." Japan gets by with one lawyer and three accountants per 10,000 people, whereas the United States employs twenty lawyers and forty accountants for the same number. The Japanese have avoided this misallocation of resources partly because their history and culture differ from that of the United States; but, equally important, the Japanese have built into their modern capitalist system formidable disincentives and even barriers to litigation in commercial affairs.[11] Perhaps symbolic of the U.S. problem is the fact that even though the government finally relaxed its antitrust barriers against semiconductor firms' pooling their research funds and entering into R&D consortia, smaller firms not included in the groups are now suing the consortia.

Would an American industrial policy be a logical and intelligent way to address some of these problems? For those who doubt that industrial policy can make a difference, it might be noted that today commercial aircraft account for the biggest single category of U.S. manufactured exports, and aviation has long been the beneficiary of U.S. government-supported research and development via the Department of Defense and of government-supported export financing via the Export-Import Bank. It does not seem accidental that the impressive National Aeronautics and

Space Museum is located only a few blocks from the capitol and across the street from NASA.

The Problem of Politicization

On the other hand, one obvious objection to a U.S. industrial policy is its likely politicization. David Smith, an aide to Senator Edward Kennedy of Massachusetts who is a prominent advocate of industrial policy, maintains that "Congress is not going to invest any group with the authority to make policy" because this would cut into the prerogatives of the professional politicians.[12] (I am reminded of a recent Southern California bumper sticker: "Don't steal! The government doesn't like competition.") There is no question that one of the prerequisites for the success of Japanese industrial policy has been its depoliticization to the greatest degree consistent with a democratic government.[13] The Japanese case may thus be less relevant to the United States than many more homely examples of what happens when the Congress takes an interest in the economy. As Murray Weidenbaum puts it:

The sad fact is that in the United States many laws and regulations limit our exports. In many ways—and often without considering the effects— we have enacted statutes and promulgated rules that prohibit U.S. exports or make it more difficult for American companies to compete in foreign markets. For example, the Trans-Alaskan Pipeline Authorization Act prohibits exporting oil from North Slope fields. A provision that was added to an appropriations act for the Interior Department bans exports of timber from federal lands west of the 100th meridian. When the injunction becomes that specific, one can detect that pressures from special interests are at work.[14]

A major danger is that in attempting to implement an industrial policy, we will get more self-defeating protectionism instead.

In my view the United States needs an industrial policy and has the political creativity and experience not to allow it to be sabotaged by special interests. I do not deny that American business through its own efforts has begun to regain some world competitiveness—that is, once it recovered from the shock of discovering that its postwar strength was not based on any comparative advantage supplied by its own managerial capabilities but rested instead on an absolute advantage enjoyed by the United States because the war had weakened all of its competitors. Today global industrial competition is fierce, but the effects of that competition are reviving some American businesses without public assistance.

I also do not deny that the shift from demand management to supply-side stimulation in American macroeconomic policy cooled inflation and fueled a strong recovery from recession. More important than either of these effects, it provided new incentives to save, produce, and consume. However, Reaganomics without an accompanying industrial policy to guide it has also been costly to America's external sales. The Japanese Economic Planning Agency (actually not a "planning" agency but a bureau for econometric analysis) calculates that the strengthening of the dollar vis-à-vis the yen because of Reaganomics contributed almost a third (c. $7 billion) to Japan's 1983 current account surplus of about $20 billion.[15] A real international commercial consciousness in this country would have signaled both public and private sectors about this unintended consequence of a particular mix of domestic monetary and fiscal policies. Providing such an early warning could be a major function of an industrial policy agency, similar to that which the National Security Council performs in the area of foreign policy.

History of U.S. Industrial Policies

The United States is actually neither as innocent of nor as unskilled at industrial policy as many Americans seem to believe. In his "Report on Manufactures" of 1791, Alexander Hamilton gave classical expression to what is today a commonplace of industrial policy theory: the understanding that market prices are important and effective signals for adjusting supply and demand in the short run but that they are quite inadequate as guides for investment decisions about new technologies, choice of products, and scales of production ten to fifteen years hence. Hamilton wrote, "Capital is wayward and timid in lending itself to new undertakings, and the State ought to excite the confidence of capitalists, who are ever cautious and sagacious, by aiding them overcome the obstacles that lie in the way of all experiments."

During the late nineteenth century the Japanese learned about and came to accept Hamilton's ideas through the works of

Friedrich List, who contrasted favorably the "American system" of protective tariffs and support of industry with British laissez faire and imperialism. On almost any given day in contemporary Tokyo, the Hamiltonian perspective is repeated back to us. Thus, for example, Sadanori Yamanaka, MITI minister during 1983, began a formal defense of his country's industrial policy with these words: "One of the most important functions of the state is to facilitate economic development and to enhance the popular welfare. Since industrial activity is the cornerstone of national economic development, all states practice a wide variety of industrial policies, albeit under different names and in different forms."[16]

Not just American doctrine but also American practice, for example, in providing public education for an industrial work force, are well known in Japan. In 1862, just before the Meiji Restoration of 1868, which marked Japan's debut as a modern nation, President Lincoln signed the law written by Congressman Justin Morrill of Vermont that has become famous as the Morrill Act. It created the system of public land-grant colleges and universities "to provide instruction in the science of agriculture and the industrial arts." Needless to say, the Japanese also know that agriculture (together with defense) has been among the longest targeted and most successful objectives of American industrial policy. The public-private collaborative relationships that exist in the American defense and agriculture industries are models of the similar relationships that prevail in the Japanese steel, automotive, and computer industries. For example, MITI's Iron and Steel Policy Council has met every Monday since the 1950s so that government officials and industry representatives could discuss world market conditions and their own strategies in relation to them.

Closer in time to the present, the U.S. government has continued to provide for the educational foundations of economic growth through the GI Bill of 1944 and the Sputnik-inspired National Defense Education Act of 1958. It should be noted that Americans in the past and still today seem to be more comfortable with a national security rationale for macroindustrial policies than with a purely economic one. Postwar public assistance for the housing and automotive industries, for example, was provided under the guise of the National Defense Highway Act of 1956. Similarly, many Americans seem happier to have the new Microelectronics and Computer Technology Corporation (MCC) of 1982 headed by an ex-admiral and former deputy director of central intelligence than by an industrialist or a scientist. No one questions Admiral Inman's qualifications; it is just that in its long battle to get started, the "MCC was struggling up mountains that wouldn't even be molehills in Japan" until he came on board.[17] Even so, the MCC has a budget of only $50 million per year and has yet to begin operations.[18]

There are other precedents for a U.S. industrial policy in such institutions as the Reconstruction Finance Corporation of the 1930s and 1940s, the Tennessee Valley Authority, and the World War II government-business relationship that spawned such industries as synthetic rubber and helped win the war without nationalizing a single industry. American industrial policy failures should not be glossed over; the gropings for a national energy policy during the 1970s and numerous urban renewal schemes are the most obvious examples. But the cases of failure in genuine, consensually based, depoliticized industrial projects are not as numerous as the critics of industrial policy like to assume. The United States has as much trial-and-error knowledge in this area as most of its competitors, and congressional staffs would be as well advised to read some history as to draft new laws.

Perhaps the best example, even if one of the least well known, of a very successful, developmentally oriented American industrial policy is that of the Texas Railroad Commission and the domestic petroleum industry from about 1930 to about 1970. For forty years the commission supported American oil prices by keeping a lid on Texas production. It also devised a system of spacing and allocation among wells that favored small producers and kept the business highly competitive. Producers were given incentives to conserve natural gas at a time when it was practically useless, thus providing the United States with a secure source of energy throughout the wartime and postwar eras. As David Prindle writes:

> The domestic petroleum industry was enmeshed in a web of state regulations specifically designed to shield it from the ravages of the market. . . . The system was a creature of the state rather than of the

federal government, but that does not make it a free-market system. . . .
This system was run by persons actively sympathetic to the industry,
rather than neutral or hostile, as was the case with the federal government in the 1970's. . . . Because of the Commission, there was no free
market for oil in Texas after 1935. . . . The unrestrained pursuit of individual profit in oil production leads both to industry self-destruction
and to enormous waste of the nation's resources. . . . Despite the state
regulations, most of the decisions about investment, organization,
growth, and competition in the industry are made privately. Although
the Railroad Commission and related agencies have created an artificial
environment in which the industry has functioned, within the specific
confines of that environment private choices have predominated. . . . For
half a century, Texas Railroad Commissioners have chosen petroleum
policies that have been, in the main, intelligent and public-spirited. Yet
they have made these choices in a political atmosphere dominated by private rather than public concerns and subject to a constituency that
barely includes the broad citizenry that must live with their decisions.
The substance of Commission policies has been generally admirable, but
the process that produced them must be disappointing to friends of
democracy.[19]

On Prindle's own evidence, I am not quite as disappointed a
friend of democracy as he is. Among other things, Texas railroad
commissioners were elected, as federal bureaucrats assuredly are
not. Nonetheless, he has offered a compelling case of an American
government-business relationship based on cooperation rather
than confrontation and one that produced outstanding results.
Given the nature and organization of the United States' major competitors in the world today, devolution of industrial policy to the
states does not seem indicated. But if the federal government were
unwilling or unable to do the job, that would be one alternative. On
the evidence from Texas, it would not necessarily be disastrous.

Current Proposals

Many different proposals are circulating in the country today to
create new governmental agencies to administer a national industrial policy. Most of them are premature, in my opinion,
because they emphasize the techniques of industrial policy to the
exclusion of its content and face severe dangers of politicization.
Before we begin to implement an industrial policy there are
several issues to be clarified and debated. These include govern-

mental reorganization, money, protectionism, and the winners vs. losers debate. Until we have clarified our goals in each of these areas, an attempt to implement industrial policy will fail.

The issue of tinkering with the government's organization involves the explicit recognition, regardless of the interests of professional politicians or office seekers, that the government *is* much of the problem, even though it *may* turn out also to have some of the answers. Reorganization alone will not make any difference unless there is also an infusion of the spirit of industrial policy and an attack on bureaucratism. By the spirit of industrial policy, I mean a determination to include the criterion of enhanced competitive ability along with any other criteria that might apply in the determination of policy. Tax laws, for example, should be modernized to favor entrepreneurship (Japan has no capital gains tax except on the sale of land) and to avoid incentives, shelters, and loopholes that are unintended from the point of view of industrial policy. Our tax system's current reluctance to target narrowly—leading, for example, to the investment in cattle ranches purely as a form of tax shelter—generates many undesirable side effects.

Bureaucratism develops whenever the basic unit of any organization does not compete for the right to exist. The fact that half of the seventeen-year life of an American patent is often dissipated in complying with bureaucratic regulations and governmental testing procedures before a product can even be marketed is unfortunately typical of the bureaucratism that impedes American economic policy.[20] In Japan, by contrast, the patent office is part of MITI. No human institution is perfect, but the issue is not perfection, it is competitiveness. Performance tests must be applied to government agencies responsible for industrial policy, just as they are applied to its beneficiaries. As George Gilder notes, "For some three decades Japan has been the world's cheapest producer of governmental goods and services."[21] How to meet the competition on this score must be addressed before the U.S. government can be entrusted with implementing an industrial policy.

Reorganization is actually a much misunderstood process, and the principles involved are often contradictory. Take, for example, the consolidation of agencies, which is usually promoted in the

name of cost-cutting and greater accountability. The end result
may instead be a possible sophistication of functions. Japan has
some of the world's strongest consumer protection standards, but
because these standards are enforced by the Economic Planning
Agency, they are also subjected to serious cost-benefit evalua-
tions. By contrast, a dispersal of agencies can produce desirable
intrabureaucratic competition, something that is common among
Japanese economic bureaucracies and American intelligence
agencies. The greatest threat to a bureaucrat's security and complacency, it must never be forgotten, comes not from the public or
politicians, but from other bureaucrats.

Having a great deal of money to expend tends to exacerbate both
bureaucratism and politicization in government agencies. The principle in all cases should be to look first at ways to achieve objectives
without expenditures. Announcement effects are often all that is
needed. The Japan Development Bank, for example, has never supplied all the money needed by a targeted industry, but a small loan
is an effective signal to the private sector that a national consensus
has been reached to promote that industry. Similarly, as the U.S.
International Trade Commission writes, "If a government an-
nounces its intention to underwrite losses of its local producers in a
selected industry, competing producers in other countries may be
discouraged from investing in the industry, but local producers in
the industry are encouraged to invest more, even though no actual
government payments may occur. The government announcement
removes the risk to domestic firms, but in so doing, increases the
risk to its foreign competitors."[22]

Japan has long relied on such techniques in preference to direct
subsidies. This has led many non-Japanese critics of industrial
policy to conclude that Japan's industrial policy does not amount
to much since the Japanese government spends so much less
money on industry than the American government. No public
money changed hands in Japan's bailout of Mazda Motors during
the mid-1970s, for example, in contrast to the Chrysler case in this
country. But this was possible only because Mazda was beholden
not to shareholders but to the Sumitomo Bank, which ultimately
took over and reorganized Mazda, and because the principle of
public guarantees to designated national banks has long been implicit in the Japanese system.[23]

The basic funding techniques of microindustrial policy include: (1) home-market protection (discussed below); (2) tax policies, including special depreciation rules, exemptions for export earnings, tax deferral for export earnings, and grants; (3) antitrust exemptions, including mergers, price-fixing cartels, rationalization cartels, export cartels, joint research and development, and restrictions against domestic competition; (4) science and technology assistance; and (5) financial assistance, including loan guarantees, loans at preferential terms, export financing, and preferential access to investment funds. In general, tax incentives are always preferable to subsidies because subsidies are paid before and often without any performance, whereas a tax incentive becomes useful only upon some performance.

Americans should avoid protectionism, in the sense of import substitution, at all costs. It is possible to imagine intelligent protectionist policies in a developing country that would be aimed at developing an industry for eventual export (the infant industry argument). And of course one can make a case for defending critical technology from purchase or theft by hostile nations. But the usually stated conflict between jobs and imports is both false and static. The real issue is jobs today versus jobs tomorrow. Nations that have relied primarily on import-substitution strategies in the past are in trouble today (e.g., the Philippines), and Japan's own protection of its domestic agriculture for political reasons has produced one of the world's most high-cost, inefficient farming sectors outside the Communist bloc. Japanese agricultural protection is also a drag on the growth of Japan's large domestic market since too much is spent on food and not enough on income-elastic goods. As a result Japan has not played as large a role as a locomotive of growth for the global economy as it should. Protectionism does not work. Industrial policy is the specific antidote for it—the only way to maintain both competitive domestic industries and free trade.

The debate over whether industrial policy should discriminate between winners and losers, supporting winners only, or conversely supporting losers only, is also misconceived. As we have already seen, the United States needs both capital-intensive and knowledge-intensive industries as a prerequisite to fulfilling its global role. Support for research and development in high tech-

nology therefore does not mean that we intend to replace older industries with newer ones. It does mean that the high-tech sector is
where the United States could and should command a comparative advantage in international trade. We are never again going to
produce domestically all the steel we consume, but we cannot
afford to be without a significant domestic capacity. At the same
time, it is very unlikely that we can export any domestically produced steel in the face of external competition. To pay for the steel
we import, we must export high-tech products. High technology
should also be used to make our residual capital-intensive industries more cost competitive. Industrial policy is necessary to ensure that we have the high-technology industries today and in the
future.

Support for industrial R&D is not just a matter of funding. It
also includes a needed reorientation of our science and technology
apparatus to develop production technology. As is well known,
Japan pursues a policy of promoting "engineering R&D." Japan's
orientation toward R&D is to take basic scientific discoveries
made elsewhere and commercialize them, to engineer cost reductions and quality controls into them, and to concentrate on innovative design. Reflecting this orientation, Japan graduates annually more engineers than the United States does—in 1980
almost 87,000, 46 percent of them electrical engineers, versus the
U.S.'s 63,000—even though its population is only half that of
the U.S.

By contrast the United States concentrates on "Nobel Prize
R&D," graduates more chemists and physicists than Japan, and
institutionally isolates its basic R&D from industrial and commercial pressures. One must not overstate this dichotomy between
Japanese engineering and U.S. pure science R&D, since Japan is
going more and more into basic science and U.S. engineering
schools are beginning to receive significant private support. But
the distinction does reflect important differences of emphasis between the two countries.

However, there is one exception to this generalization, and that
exists in the area of U.S. national defense. Here the United States
lavishes its engineering talent every bit as much as its basic
science talent, and this concentration of American engineering in
the defense industries is an added strain on American interna-

tional competitive ability. Over time, as the United States draws more and more of its limited engineering resources into the defense sector, while Japan keeps its big engineering establishment working on the civilian commercial front, the industrial capabilities of the two nations must diverge.

Proposals for the international sharing and joint research and development of high technology are warranted, and both sides are cooperating toward putting them into effect. But such projects are only palliatives. The bottom line of mutual access R&D activities will still be which country's firms come up with the best, cheapest, and most reliable products from the basic science that is available at any given time. The answer must involve an American industrial policy that addresses the educational and engineering needs of American civilian industries, in addition to the other goals that such an industrial policy must meet. This is what the so-called Merrifield Plan of 1983—the scheme of Assistant Secretary of Commerce R. Bruce Merrifield to stimulate private funding of innovative research and development—is intended to do. It or its equivalent is a mandatory element in any American industrial policy.

In recent years the United States has undertaken many experiments with protectionism, wage and price controls, ad hoc targeting (Lockheed, New York, Chrysler), draconian monetary policies, out-of-control fiscal policies, and subsidies (milk, tobacco, and so forth), none of them very effective and all of them deleterious to overall American economic competition in the world. Industrial policy aims to clear out the costly and ineffective residue left by governmental attempts to displace the market and to put the government into the market as a strategic, competitive actor. Critics of industrial policy are complacent about the problems of the American economy and alarmist about the implications of industrial policy. They seem to hold the view that if there is no solution to a problem—and industrial policy is thought not to be one—then, like the weather, it must simply be endured. Positive public action versus benign neglect is what the debate is all about.

Our purpose in presenting these essays is not necessarily to resolve this debate but to throw some light on it. Ortega y Gasset once wrote, "We do not know what is happening to us, and that is precisely the thing that is happening to us—the fact of not knowing what is happening to us." To know what is happening to us economically and industrially is a necessary first step to appreciating what the proposed remedies are worth.

2

AARON WILDAVSKY

Squaring the Political Circle: Industrial Policies and the American Dream

Both of the terms in "industrial policy" are suspect. There may not be any deep defect in industry that requires repair or restructuring.[1] And, if there is, we may not know what it is or how to do better. The economy may be producing as many jobs as can be; there may be sufficient investment in industry; plant closings may be an opportunity as well as a difficulty—normal, not abnormal. For every policy proposed under this rubric there is also its diametrical opposite: Industry is to be coerced; industry is to be coddled. Labor is to be protected; labor is to be disciplined. Old restrictions on private markets are to be eliminated; new restrictions are to be imposed. Neither the condition of industry nor the direction of policy are agreed-upon. On the contrary, "industrial policy" is a contested concept.

Suppose, however, instead of taking industrial policy as a solution, we consider it as a problem. Instead of being an answer, industrial policy would pose its own question: Why, at this time, have so many politicians and theoreticians turned their attention to policies ostensibly designed to improve the condition of industry? What do their prognoses about what is wrong and their proposals for setting it right tell us about American politics?

Benchmarks

Looking for benchmarks against which to appraise proposed departures in public policy, I begin with three propositions. Existing governmental policy for economic management, first of all, is practically pure Keynesianism: higher spending with lower taxation combine to create larger deficits with which to reduce unemployment. Note that I did not say that this was President Reagan's or Speaker O'Neill's preferred Republican or Democratic party policy. Ours is a political system in which Republican desire for lower taxes and higher defense outlays may meet up with Democratic demands for higher domestic spending to produce a combined Keynesian result. Perhaps "the system" is wiser than its parts, no party previously having suggested taking resources out of the economy in order to counteract a depression.

So long as unemployment remains high, a *de facto* Keynesian policy of putting resources into the economy is likely to outlast whichever party is in power. This means huge deficits. Having preached the opposite for so long, Republicans are dismayed. Nor are Democrats overjoyed; if their spending constituencies advance at even a modest rate, they will absorb all available resources, leaving nothing left for new initiatives. No wonder, then, that politicians of both parties are looking for an inexpensive policy to liberate themselves from spending all their time on the budget.

The second benchmark is almost a truism: there is no such thing as not having an industrial policy. Action and inaction alike affect the condition of industry. Prices are also plans. To the extent that market competition exists, it sends out signals to which management and labor must respond. To the extent that there are burdens placed on competition—with over $500 billion in loan guarantees outstanding, not to mention other subsidies, restrictions on banking, and varieties of regulation too numerous to mention—that, too, in its own disjointed way, is a policy of sorts.

Whatever it means, our third benchmark goes, industrial policy is an elite phenomenon. There is no visible public groundswell of support for any version of industrial policy.[2] Asked whether they want more government planning of the economy, 21 percent of Americans said about the same, 28 percent favored more, and 45 percent less. "American workers," William Schneider reports, "were more hostile to government planning than workers in any of the other countries."[3] While the American public was opposed to bailing out major companies in important industries 48 percent to 33 percent (with disapproval rising to 56 percent in a later survey), Australian and British workers favored such rescue plans. Overwhelming majorities of the American people are in favor of free enterprise for generating economic growth.

What is it that does find support in the general public? Majorities or large pluralities favor cutting government spending (78 percent); encouraging cooperation among labor, business, and special interests (59 percent); cutting taxes (58 percent); providing incentives to increase consumer spending (52 percent); relocating and retraining workers in failing industries (49 percent); and educating people about business economics (47 percent). By far the most popular items would reduce the size of government, hardly the sort of thing to gladden the heart of an interventionist. Indeed, when Harris asked which institution was most responsible for productivity's not being better, 61 percent chose government. And when Gallup asked whether big labor, big business, or big government posed the greatest threat to the nation's future, 51 percent picked big government, the highest proportion since 1959. It is, then, clear that a national plan for industrial policy would run counter to existing citizen preferences.

Aside from their well-known opposition to governmental planning of the economy, business executives are overwhelmingly opposed to government aid for financially troubled companies (89 percent to 4 percent), or special benefits to industries deemed to be the wave of the future (92 percent to 7 percent). Direct loans, federal subsidies, and higher tariffs on competing goods are opposed by more than two-thirds of executives. What kind of help would they like? Lower taxes (69 percent), special tax breaks (61

percent), aid for consumer spending (71 percent), easier access to
the tax-exempt bond market (57 percent), and relaxing safety and
environmental rules (57 percent) were favored. These executives
do not want direct government intervention but they do support
indirect help to lower their tax burdens and the costs of doing business, as well as enabling consumers to buy their products. Help for
business as a whole rather than selective intervention is their
preference. In a phrase, business executives want government to
do more for them by taking less from them.

I am not aware of polls of labor executives or of politicians in the
conservative and liberal wings of the Democratic party. As far as
labor is concerned, it can, depending on how its unions are situated, be expected to favor higher tariffs, legislation to make plant
closings more costly, and aid to ailing industries. If one were to
imagine a conversation between Lane Kirkland, the head of the
AFL-CIO, and the next president, were he a Democrat, it would
undoubtedly include two things: a presidential request for
restraint on wages and welfare spending and a Kirkland counter
for protection against adversity, including tariffs, quotas, restrictions on plant closings and anti-union activities, safety measures,
higher minimum wages, stimulation of the economy, and the like.

Turning to liberal Democrats, the best evidence we have is the
bills they have introduced in Congress and the books and articles
they write. I shall consider all proposed legislation. In order to
reveal traits of industrial policy that would otherwise remain
obscure, I shall classify these bills according to the instrument of
public policy they propose to employ, how these instruments would
appear in the budget, whom they are supposed to help or are
directed against, and whether these instruments are punitive
(sanctions) or offer incentives (inducements).

Credit

The essence of the various bills to establish a Reconstruction Finance Corporation (RFC) is that the government would provide
something like $5 billion of capital stock, allowing up to ten times
that amount to be granted as loans or loan guarantees to individuals or companies who would otherwise be unable to secure
financing. The obligations of the corporation would be guaranteed

by the United States government. Bills sponsored by Democratic Representatives Claude Pepper and Jaime Whitten would prohibit credit to companies that are sufficiently profitable to raise money on their own. But this prohibition is not widely shared. Democratic Representative John P. Murtha's bill, in addition to providing credit for those who cannot raise it or who are in financial distress, would allow the RFC to issue debentures, bonds, or notes to facilitate a given plant's expansion or modernization. Apparently, only businesses that are entirely static would be excluded—but not really. What Democratic Senator Robert Byrd takes away with one hand—projects must have some reasonable probability of paying back the loan—he gives with the other—projects may be supported if they are in regions suffering severe, long-term unemployment, or can be sources for future economic growth, or promote new technologies, or enable existing industries to significantly increase their productivity. With Byrd's National Investment Corporation, though he would limit its obligations to $25 billion rather than the usual $50 billion, there would be an institution that could lend long or short term at or below market interest rates for virtually any purpose.

Well, not quite every purpose. Democratic Representative Joseph G. Minish adds to his National Development Bank (NDB) the additional task of providing job training for semiskilled and unskilled workers who are either underemployed or unemployed. His wrinkle is that the United States Treasury would appropriate the difference between the interest paid by the bank on its obligations and the interest received on its loans as well as make up any capital loss through defaults.

Some RFCs and NDBs give out money without expecting much back in return and others want a *quid pro quo*. There is some talk in various bills about plans or reports or auditing so as to compare promises with performance, but this is a minor theme. Professor Robert Reich, however, in his well-known proposal for regional development banks to provide interest rate subsidies to companies that would retrain workers and, in his view, increase social justice, adds a kicker: these business firms would have to reorganize themselves so as to become more competitive. Poor countries like India often face a similar dilemma in that the regions where the poorest people are located are not those that offer the best economic opportunities. The state governments involved walk a tightrope in trying simultaneously to argue that they are more needy and more capable. Reich would make these criteria compatible by compelling companies to be more efficient, assuming that the regional development banks know how to do so. Investment banker Felix Rohatyn is more blunt: his RFC would allocate sacrifice directly. He wants to use "money as a tool or a weapon . . . to leverage concessions from unions, suppliers, banks, management, legislatures."[4] Whether the problem were high wages, old-fashioned management practices, or the unwillingness of legislatures to provide sufficient investments for "infrastructure," loans would be given and withheld to induce changes in business behavior.

If these RFCs are going to use sanctions as well as rewards, it is important to understand how they would be run or, at least, who is supposed to control them. The management of this corporation, whatever it is called, is generally designed to include the secretaries of the treasury, of labor, and of commerce, as well as people representing industry, corporate finance, and unions; sometimes the chairman of the Council of Economic Advisers, the chairman of the board of governors of the Federal Reserve System, and representatives of the general public are also to be included. Control is to be vested in a microcosm of the macrocosm—namely, a representative group of people. If they did prove to be representative, of course, there is little reason to believe they would behave differently than the other representative body, the Congress of the United States, that heretofore has made whatever might be called industrial policy.

Tax Preferences

Almost anything that can be done by direct appropriations can also be accomplished indirectly through the use of tax preferences. Increasing or decreasing taxes can provide individuals or businesses with incentives to engage in certain activities and sanctions against following other lines of endeavor. I shall begin with proposals designed to provide positive inducements, go on to other devices implying negative sanctions, and conclude with larger-scale plans for overhauling the tax system.

When it comes to positive inducements, Republicans and conservative Democrats make their appearance. Republican Representative Bobbi Fiedler would like to use tax credits (not deductions but dollar-for-dollar reductions) to induce employers to hire the long-term unemployed, defined as employees who have exhausted their unemployment benefits. By offering credits of between $500 and $1000 per position, Republican Representative Claudine Schneider hopes to encourage employers to add new full- or part-time positions in areas of high unemployment. She would also give tax preferences to firms that trained skilled laborers for industries that were short of qualified employees. Wherever there were a labor shortage or surplus, therefore, tax concessions would be offered. A variety of bills by both Democrats (Senator Gary Hart and Representative Parren J. Mitchell) and Republicans (Senator Rudy Boschwitz and Representative Barber Conable, Jr.) would, like the others, amend the internal revenue act to provide tax relief for businesses locating in what are considered to be economically distressed or depressed areas, sometimes called "enterprise zones." When introduced by Republicans, these bills provide for regulatory relief and, when sponsored by Democrats, they include provisions specifying that employment in a particular area or business must be increased by a certain percentage in order to qualify.

There is a difference between a little help and a lot. Arguing that the United States is losing out to Japan because the real rate of interest there is one-third that paid by business in the United States, George Hatsopoulos, chairman of the Thermo Electron Corporation, proposes a substantial change in the tax code that would treat dividends from cumulative preferred stock in the same way that interest on debt is now treated, i.e., as a deduction. He believes, no doubt correctly, that if this were done (a big "if"), a lot of equity capital would flow into companies.

Not to be outdone, the authors of a new book called *A Business Plan for America,* Joel Kotkin and Dan Gevirtz, wish to encourage economic growth by eliminating the capital gains tax and the corporate income tax on profits of less than half a million a year, by expanding the research and development credit so as to enable small businesses to make more use of it, and by encouraging banks to give loans to new companies beyond the usual rules relating debt to equity.[5]

Not to be outdone, Senator Hart would have capital expenditures treated as an expense for tax purposes so as to reduce the bias he believes exists against new firms that do not have even a minimal depreciation allowance to deduct from taxable profits. To pinpoint his concern, Senator Hart would create "new capacity stock" that would be used to finance new equipment, research, and plants and therefore, assuming the new can be distinguished from the old, would be exempt from taxes on capital gains. In addition, Hart would not only reduce the income tax for small businesses but would enable their stockholders to deduct the business losses of the companies from their personal income tax.

It would not be entirely correct to say that these inducements harm no one. If it were possible to understand fully the opportunity costs of these tax benefits, so that the alternatives foregone were as visible as those encouraged, it might be found that overall efficiency or even equity had been reduced. What can be said with reasonable confidence is that the direct beneficiaries are offered advantages and are in a position to consider whether incurring costs of employment or of plants is worth what they are receiving.

There are other measures whose purpose is to deny existing benefits to firms that do not behave as desired. Legislation introduced by Democratic Representative Charles E. Bennett, for example, would deny any business that does not expand the number of its employees access to the provisions of the Internal Revenue Code governing the accelerated cost recovery system. To reduce what he calls "paper entrepreneurship," Robert Reich would invoke sanctions against mergers, acquisitions, and various devices to reduce taxes, such as purchasing tax losses, by permitting deductions for interest on loans only when modernizing old plants and equipment or buying new ones. Since it is evidently not easy to distinguish modernization from more of the same or the new from what was planned years before, Democratic Representative James R. Jones would require businesses to pay back what they received in the form of investment tax credits if they did not invest in new equipment and plants.

Now taxation is a protean subject and there is no end of ingenuity in expanding its reach. In order to stimulate investment in both human and physical capital, for instance, Senator Hart has suggested not only exempting savings from taxation but also moving to a progressive expenditure or consumption tax. Whether a tax on consumption would provide a substitute for the income tax or an addition to it, as is true everywhere in Western Europe, is a subject that cannot be discussed here. But it would represent a radical change and might encourage people to consume less (because they are taxed on consumption) and invest more (because investment is untaxed).

A more straightforward approach is taken by Democratic Representative Timothy Wirth, who would fund the various industrial programs he has in mind by increasing taxation on higher incomes. Felix Rohatyn would finance his version of an RFC through a tax on oil imports. And Robert Reich would straighten out the difference in treatment of investment in human versus physical capital by creating a "human capital tax credit" so as to encourage business to do more employee training. Whether bills seek targeted tax preferences to achieve a particular aim, or a root-and-branch revision of the tax code, all but the few that call for tax increases would reduce the revenue flowing to the Treasury. These reductions would not show up in the budget per se, because taxes that are not collected do not appear there.

Regulation

If one adopted a neomercantilist view, in which there was only a limited amount of employment in the world, more employment abroad would mean less employment at home. What is more, competition from abroad, based on low-wage labor, would drive out high-wage labor in the United States.[6] The remedy is tariff barriers. Because tariffs would undoubtedly lead to retaliatory measures, and because of considerable sentiment in favor of free trade, these proposals are commonly phrased in terms of opening access to markets abroad in return for permitting goods to enter the United States.

Concern over distributional equity within America is based on the premise that the United States' economy is in decline due to a transition from mass-production industrial goods to high-technology, information-based activity. In order either to spread the cost of decline and/or to gain consent for measures necessary to reorient the economy, regulation is required: government is to intervene to allocate more equitably the costs of economic change.

For over a decade, there have been proposals to curb the "runaway shop" by inhibiting firms from leaving one place and going to
another and by making it more difficult to close plants. The National Employment Priorities Act of 1983, introduced by Democratic Representative William Ford, would discourage firms from
leaving the United States by forcing them to pay the local communities in which they were located three times their annual tax
payment in the three years prior to closing down. To discourage
plants from closing, in addition to similar restitution payments,
they would be required to give one year's notice, continue the
employer's contribution to employee benefit plans for up to a year,
and pay severance to workers equivalent to 85 percent of a year's
pay, not, however, exceeding $25,000 per worker. Note that the fi-
nancial costs are imposed on the firm. In addition to regulatory
measures, moreover, the Ford bill would attempt to keep plants
from closing by a variety of interest subsidies to business and to
employees who wanted to buy out the firm. It would even require
that government buy the firm's products.

Plant-closing legislation is directed at business mobility. Other
proposals are directed at restricting labor unions. Felix Rohatyn,
for instance, would have government require one-year contracts
without cost-of-living escalators to reduce labor's temptation to
benefit from inflation or to gain from strikes. To give labor and
management a greater stake in cooperation, he would have a
larger part of the compensation package be negotiated by means
of profit-sharing arrangements. Obviously, such measures would
restrict the scope of collective bargaining. Reich would force a
marriage of labor and management by requiring firms to act as
their employees' agents in bargaining with the federal government. Since management would be acting on behalf of labor, it
would be appropriate, then, for workers to elect representatives
who would participate with management in making investment
decisions as well as selecting the combination of governmentally
supported benefits available to employees.

This is not far from the basic idea of corporatism through the
direct representation of labor, management, and other affected
groups in national policymaking. There are a variety of proposals,
especially those by Barry Bluestone and Bennett Harrison, calling
for some combination of economic democracy at the workplace

and national economic planning.[7] Agreeing in principle with Representative Ford's legislation to restrict plant closings, Bluestone and Harrison would like laws enabling workers to buy out failing companies, coupling government bailouts for failing industry with a substantial voice in management decisions for employee councils. Excluded would be agreements on planning between government, workers, and management on such matters as automation, prices, environmental protection, health and safety, affirmative action, and experimentation with forms of worker participation. Should any or all of this prove insufficient, Bluestone and Harrison also advocate selective nationalization.

As with other aspects of industrial policy, there are two sides to antitrust legislation. Walter Mondale, former vice-president, is only one of many who have complained about "wasteful mergers and acquisitions." At the same time, he has suggested changing the antitrust laws to permit joint research and developmental ventures to "enhance international competitiveness without reducing domestic competition."[8] Senator Ernest Hollings, another Democrat, has come out simply for higher protective tariffs. Going in the opposite direction, Senator Hart wishes the president to enter negotiations to open foreign markets to United States' exports of high technology, including strengthening the General Agreement on Tariffs and Trade (GATT). This strengthening would include eliminating export subsidies used by other countries to make their goods cheaper.

Appropriations

It may seem strange to have come so far in discussing industrial policy while barely mentioning the most direct way of supporting federal activities, which is through the annual appropriations process. A fifth or a tenth of support for RFCs would come from appropriations. Under the rubric of industrial policy, Senator Hollings includes a lot more governmental money for education, including an across-the-board pay hike of $5,000 for all teachers in the United States, student loans, on-the-job training, nutrition, community health centers, child care, and other things that could be said to improve the capability of "human capital." Much the same spirit is expressed in Senator Hart's suggestion that the

federal government pay one-half of the cost of training for people
unemployed longer than three months as well as the whole cost of
retraining vouchers, redeemable at universities, for people unemployed for more than two years. Since discrimination imposes economic costs, Professor Reich would have the federal government
give grants to firms that employ the handicapped, unemployed, or
generally those groups that may be deemed to have been discrimi-
nated against. There are many proposals for increasing federal
support of programs in science, engineering, computing, and other
subjects deemed to be on the rise rather than in decline. Though
cost estimates are hard to come by, Representative Wirth is precise in setting a goal of 3 percent of gross national product that
should be spent on research and development, involving such
things as assisting universities and improving their research
equipment.

Everyone understands that one cannot have an industrial
superstructure without a viable substructure of roads, bridges,
sewers, and other underpinnings of modern life. Mondale is
straightforward in suggesting federal appropriations for infrastructure, especially for areas that are hurting from plant closings or are otherwise certified as suffering from particularly high
economic distress. Roughly comparable purposes could be accomplished through legislation amending the Defense Production
Act of 1950 in order to revitalize the defense industrial base of the
United States by training skilled personnel and providing financial assistance to modify the industries related to defense.[9] We
know that this is a Republican initiative, not merely because it is
about defense but because it limits appropriations for four years to
a total of only one billion dollars.

Research is relatively cheap. Representative Wirth would like to
establish a National Economic Cooperation Council as an early
warning system to monitor the health of domestic industries in
order to ward off dangers at an early stage. Toward this end there
would be an evaluation of economic trends, improvement in the
collection of data, the creation of forums involving business, labor,
and government to identify national economic problems and
develop strategies to solve them, and above all a massive effort to
let everyone know that the revival and expansion of America's
economy is the number one national priority. Democratic Repre-

sentative Albert Gore, Jr., would establish an "Office of Critical Trends Assessment" in the executive office of the president to advise the chief executive about alternative futures and to produce, every four years, an "Executive Branch Report on Critical Trends and Alternative Futures." Considering that it might be difficult to implement an industrial policy without having first formulated one, Representative Stanley N. Lundine, a Democrat, introduced legislation to establish a National Industrial Development Board to advise congressional committees and governmental agencies about national industrial development priorities. The board would be composed of 32 members chosen equally from Congress or federal agencies, heads of national or international unions, presidents of major corporations, and representatives of sectors of society who are otherwise not represented. This is a large board, considering that total appropriations per year are not supposed to exceed $8 million. Evidencing a greater sense of urgency, Republican Representative Charles Pashayan, Jr., proposes to establish a National Commission on Technological Innovation and Industrial Modernization that would evaluate federal legislation about industrial policy and submit a report by mid-1984 containing a national industrial strategy. To be on the safe side, this strategy is to assure not only the economic vitality but also the national security of the United States. The Service Industry Development Program proposed by Democratic Representative James J. Florio costs even less, being authorized at $5 million per annum, basically to conduct studies of U.S. service industries and to develop policies designed to increase their industrial competitiveness. Much is said about a new partnership between government, industry, and labor, sometimes called an "economic cooperation council" (rather than an "economic conflict council," presumably because there is enough of that already).

Any reader familiar with the discussion about industrial policy may have expected to hear something about "picking winners" and ending up with "losers" or some variants thereof. The bulk of the bills leave that sort of thing to some version of the Reconstruction Finance Corporation. In an admirable display of bipartisanship, however, Representative George E. Brown, Jr., a Republican, and Senator Paul E. Tsongas, a Democrat, provide for a forum composed of people from government, academia, and industry to

decide which technologies, brought up in the study to be performed by the director of the Office of Science and Technology
Policy and the National Academy of Sciences and the National
Academy of Engineering, should be developed further. While
Brown's bill does not specify an upper limit, Senator Tsongas' legislation would authorize a sufficient appropriation to implement
the programs envisaged.

Contradictions

Is the problem that American-based multinational corporations
are dominating the global economy, so that the solution consists of
weakening their hegemony, or is it that the United States can no
longer compete in world markets, therefore requiring protection
against loss of jobs and income to Japan and assorted Third World
nations? Is the problem that American industry adapts too
rapidly to changing economic conditions—in which case the solution may be to legislate against plant closings—or does the
difficulty consist rather of industrial rigidity—thus requiring
governmental intervention to foster more change (hopefully from
"sunset" to "sunrise" industries) than market relationships would
spontaneously produce? Is the problem a mania for economic
development damaging to the physical environment and human
relationships, so that the solution involves restricting growth and
sharing the remainder more equitably, or is there not enough to go
around due to a decline in economic productivity, implying that
the economy should expand more rapidly? Under the umbrella of
industrial policy, solutions are suggested based on all these sup-
positions—slowing and speeding economic change, freer trade
and more protectionism, more and less economic growth. Why
these contradictions?

When political parties (and other responsive institutions) are
beset by contradictory demands to move left and right, they often
seek to evade their dilemma by going first one way and then
another. This phenomenon is well known.[10] It is not entirely evident, however, that movement in one direction may alter the
situation sufficiently to facilitate movement in another direction.
These two-step strategies require a bit of elucidation. Since I will
end up with an application to the strategy of industrial policy on

the left, it is only fair to begin with a two-step strategy on the right.

It would hardly be an exaggeration to say that a favorite remedy for economic ills proposed by market-oriented conservatives is an across-the-board reduction in marginal tax rates. Like everyone else, these strategists know that the progressive income tax is modified by many numerous tax preferences, called "loopholes" by those who object to them. Rather than recognize the exceptions as part of the price for progressivity, however, our conservative strategists seize upon liberal concern about loopholes to advocate a flat-rate tax. And it takes a while for liberals to understand that though these infamous loopholes would indeed be much diminished, progressive taxation would be abolished in the process. Although they do not like to say so out loud, the rotten progressive tax, riddled with loopholes, actually is moderately progressive. Yet once the first step is taken—denigration of the existing progressive tax—the second step—replacement of a more progressive by a less progressive tax—can hardly be far behind.

Utilizing a similar strategy, proponents of industrial policy argue that there is already a great deal of governmental intervention in the economy. Examples (viz. the Reagan administration's limitation of imports of large motorcycles) are readily available. Therefore, they call for rationalizing the existing haphazard interventions by formally acknowledging the desirability of intervention as a matter of principle.[11] Once the principle of governmental intervention is legitimized, i.e., treated as the desired rule rather than the regrettable exception, step one is complete. If government is supposed to be part-and-parcel of decisions by business, however, strategists on the left claim that relationships appropriate to democratic decision-making in government be mandated. Enter the second step—industrial democracy and worker control.

Efficiency is one thing and sharing is another. The broad left would like to believe that the two criteria are mutually reinforcing. This can be accomplished, in theory at least, by arguing that unless people feel they are being treated fairly, however "fair" is defined, they will be unwilling to make whatever sacrifices are necessary to improve economic productivity. Amitai Etzioni, in his *An Immodest Agenda: Rebuilding America Before the 21st Century,* has this in mind when he advocates intensification of economic growth now in order to provide more for redistributive and environmental purposes later. But if economic redistribution and industrial reconstruction can be made compatible, why wait?

Visions

In a perceptive essay, William A. Schambra explains why Robert Reich's *The Next American Frontier* has become so popular among contenders for the Democratic party presidential nomination:

He shows them how to reconcile two competing visions—the visions of growth and community—that have split the party into bitterly warring factions, causing them to lose three of the last four presidential elections to the minority party Republicans. This reconciliation is possible, Reich claims, because economic growth in the high-technology future will be driven—not by central planning, or by supply-side economics—but by workplaces reorganized into small, intense, participatory democracies.[12]

Where Thurow and Rohatyn call for sacrifice, in Reich's formulation, as Schambra has it, the New Left's participatory democracy "becomes not only compatible with growth [but] it becomes essential to it."

Elsewhere on the left, however, there is an alternative view, exemplified by Tom Hayden's *The American Future*, in which growth is given up for fellowship. Competition will be replaced by cooperation, self-interest by community. I think it is worth pursuing these alternative visions of the good life further.

There are two major sources of left-liberalism: the *noblesse oblige* of hierarchies and the egalitarianism of sects. A sectarian political culture seeks to diminish social differences—between black and white, rich and poor, male and female, parents and children, experts and laymen, man and nature, old and young, humans and animals, and even, if recent movies are a harbinger, earth people and extraterrestrial beings. Economic growth threatens to exacerbate the very invidious distinctions that lead to inequality of result. Yet it is not easy to ameliorate the condition of the worst off without additional resources.

What are those who embrace the sectarian vision to do? If their anger at inequality is great, they may move toward an alliance with hierarchy in order to secure redistribution of material resources. This is the route of European social democracies. If their opposition to authority is greater, sectarians may give up part of their preference for equality of outcomes so as to remove restrictions on their way of life. This alliance between markets and sects, recognizable as part of the noncentralist, "small is beautiful" movement, is quintessentially American. It is also, I maintain, responsible for the special aura that industrial policy has in the United States.

During the era of Jacksonian democracy, broadly from the 1820s through the 1850s, a remarkable cultural coalition was born—a coalition, so far as I know, without historical parallel. Jacksonian social theorists, as well as, so far as is known, substantial sectors of public opinion, believed that pure equality of opportunity would actually lead to substantial equality of results. (Here it is necessary to recall that in a nation that not long before had fought a revolution against a British hierarchy under the leadership of King George III, the federal government was widely regarded as a source of "corruption" or "fraud" by introducing artificial inequalities.) If only the government would stop chartering banks, awarding franchises, fostering monopolies, creating privileged classes of debt holders, and otherwise interfering with economic life, Andrew Jackson and his supporters argued, the natural, rough equality of men, bolstered by blessed American circumstances, would lead to as close an approximation to equality of condition as human differences would allow. The exceptional American belief was that the competitive individualism of markets, pursued without fear or favor, would lead to something like equal outcomes.

Were it deemed desirable to abolish market enterprise as incompatible with substantive political equality, a dozen European programs would be cut to measure and ready to wear. But not in America. Such programs are unpopular with the electorate— hence the existing haphazard industrial policy, where interference with enterprise is justified by exceptional circumstances. America is different. Here a genuine desire to make use of the autonomy, energy, calculating power, and incentives for productivity conveyed by markets leads liberal Democrats to try to tame markets so as to make them serve equality.[13] When Democrats gather for their Jefferson-Jackson Day dinners, industrial policy, partly despite and partly because of its contradictions, may help them convey their version of the American dream of a nation of producers whose pure competition brings them closer to genuine equality.

Industrial policy also solves a short-run problem: how to craft a substantial-sounding policy without allowing public spending to grow visibly. The solution lies in predominant use of instruments of public policy—credit, tax preferences, regulations—that do not appear in the budget. And, should all else fail, Democrats can join Republicans in the one approach that has always appealed to America's diverse policy cultures—namely, education, research, and commissions to create the sense of unity that everyday experience tells us is incompatible with our differing visions. In this respect as well, the issue of industrial policy reaffirms the classic American formula of unity in diversity.

II

Foreign Models
and the
American Experience

3

ROBERT S. OZAKI

How Japanese Industrial
Policy Works

Industrial policy has been an object of considerable attention as
well as confusion in the U.S. over the past five years or so. No
doubt one reason for its greater visibility is America's frustration
with the apparent inadequacy of the conventional Keynesian-type
monetary and fiscal policies in generating and sustaining the
dynamism of the nation's economy. The conventional macroeconomic policy mix seemed to work reasonably well in achieving
economic growth and high employment with price stability for
about two decades after World War II. However, after the
mid-1960s the overall performance of the U.S. economy began to
deteriorate. In search of new approaches to coping with the nation's economic problems, government leaders have tried incomes
policy (wage-price controls or guidelines), monetarism, and
supply-side economics, all with mixed results.

Discovery of Industrial Policy

Then America "discovered" that other industrial countries practice something with the unfamiliar name of "industrial policy,"
which seems to vitalize their domestic industries and enhance the
international competitiveness of their products. With its internal
and external economic conditions worsening, America's curiosity
naturally was aroused. Books and articles on the subject began to
proliferate.

The American debate on industrial policy has been clouded by a
good deal of confusion. One source of the confusion is conceptual
ambiguity. In contrast to monetary and fiscal policies, which are
well defined and whose means and ends are clearly identifiable,
industrial policy has a broad scope and loose boundaries. It can
mean different things to different people. Sometimes it is used to
refer to a "picking-the-winners policy" or a "positive adjustment
policy"; to some discussants it is protectionism pure and simple, be
it to foster an infant industry or to rejuvenate a senile sector.

What, then, is industrial policy? The most generally accepted
definition today is that it is whatever the government does vis-à-
vis private industry or individual firms to achieve a variety of objectives. These objectives include promoting the nation's economic
development and growth, accelerating the structural transformation of domestic industry in a desired direction, improving the international competitiveness of designated products, encouraging
the development of new technologies, smoothing the phasing out
of chronically depressed industries, assisting the rationalization
and reorganization of a weakened industry that is judged to have
a chance for recovery, protecting domestic employment, and programming regional development. The means to achieve these ends
may be tax incentives, subsidies, special government procurement, grants, low-interest loans, government-guaranteed loans,
credit rationing, tariffs, quantitative import restrictions, administrative guidance, and the like.

At times industrial policy pertains not only to these directly
industry-related measures but also to policy actions concerning
social capital and infrastructure, environmental protection, housing, and urban development. The central premise of industrial
policy is that the nation's welfare and interest cannot be optimized
by the private market alone.

Given this all-encompassing definition, it follows that each nation's policy in one way or another inevitably reflects its history,
culture, and tradition, and that the specific content and form of
that policy are subject to change over time, depending upon stages
of economic development, geopolitical circumstances, and shifts in
a nation's political ideologies and aspirations. Nonetheless, while
specific names and designs may vary, practically all nations have
practiced and continue to practice industrial policy of one kind or
another. Laissez-faire, or a total absence of industrial policy, has
never existed except in the realm of ideological imagination.

The United States may only recently have discovered the ter-
minology of industrial policy, but in fact the country has long been
an unwitting practitioner of it. Its nineteenth-century protectionism against British manufactures is a case in point. The New Deal,
the Manhattan Project, oil depletion allowances, agricultural and
housing subsidies, the adjustment assistance program for trade-
displaced workers, the Chrysler bailout, the trigger price mechanism (to protect the steel industry), orderly marketing agreements
(e.g., to restrict imports of color televisions), and voluntary export
restraints (to help revitalize the automobile industry) can all be
construed as instances of industrial policy.

Notwithstanding the often-mentioned stagnation of the American economy, the U.S. still holds a position of supremacy in the
world market in weapons, aircraft, advanced computers, space
technology, nuclear energy, and agriculture. The items on this list
have one thing in common: they owe their comparative advantage
largely to long-term deliberate developmental assistance provided
by the Defense Department, NASA, the Atomic Energy Commission, and the federal and state departments of agriculture—all
governmental agencies. Current American interest in Japan's industrial policy often overlooks these quite successful home-grown
examples.

Discussions of Japan's industrial policy as a possible model for
the U.S. also tend to labor under numerous misperceptions about
the Japanese economy in general and Japanese industrial policy
in particular. In my view, these misperceptions stem mainly from
two sources: the overuse or abuse of the "cultural model" to explain Japanese success, and the inadequacy of the Western economic paradigm.

It has been fashionable for Western observers to approach the Japanese economy from a sociological or anthropological perspective. Presumably Japanese culture is unique and so different from Western culture that Western economics cannot possibly explain the Japanese economy. The trouble with such a cultural view is that it tends to deteriorate quickly into stereotype or caricature, overemphasizing the differences between Japan and the West and ultimately boiling down to a kind of tautology. To argue that "the Japanese save a lot because they are frugal," or that "the Japanese work hard thanks to the value their culture places on diligence" is not particularly revealing. According to this model, Japan's economic dynamism is sustained by her people's industriousness, self-discipline, work ethic, team spirit, and the like. If so, the model fails to explain why the same Japanese apparently lose these cultural attributes once they are employed in petrochemical, shipbuilding, and aluminum smelting industries—all of which have in recent years been severely depressed. The model encourages the misconception that since Japan is different so too must be her industrial policy.

The second problem has to do with thinking about economics. The conventional Western paradigm classifies economic systems into "capitalist" or "socialist" or "mixed" economies that fall somewhere in between. If an economy's public sector expands, according to this paradigm, it moves closer to socialism. There is the strong impression in the West that in Japan the state is big, powerful, and pervasive, as symbolized by the notorious MITI (Ministry of International Trade and Industry) and its infamous industrial policy, which promotes the growth and efficiency of Japanese firms to the terror of their Western rivals. Some think that Japan is a private enterprise economy in name only and a Soviet-style command economy in fact.

All this is bewildering. Actually, the public sector in Japan is comparatively the smallest among the advanced industrial democracies. The notorious MITI happens to be the smallest of the economic ministries of the Japanese government. It is the conventional wisdom of conservatives and an increasing number of liberals in America that government represents inefficiency; anything the government puts its hand to becomes a mess. How this wisdom can be reconciled with the observation that in Japan the (same) government's industrial policy is an agent of industrial growth is left unclear.

The confusion results from the inadequacy of the Western economic paradigm, which associates socialism with big government, a weak market, and inefficiency, and capitalism with little government intervention, private enterprise, and efficiency. The truth of the matter is that the Japanese government is small but effective and "more developmental than regulatory," to borrow Chalmers Johnson's terms—a fact that the Western paradigm fails to reveal with clarity.

Background

A nation's industrial policy is inseparable from its history. In order to understand Japan's contemporary industrial policy, it is useful to bear in mind the following observations.

A late starter in economic development, Japan began her modernization in the late nineteenth century. The slogan of the day in a country determined to catch up with the West was "prosperous nation, strong military." Accelerated industrialization was the means to achieve the objective shared by both the state and private business. Under the unequal treaties imposed by the Western powers, Japan was forced to practice free trade, with a 5 percent maximum permissible tariff rate. Instead of accepting the fate of forever remaining an agrarian society engaged in monocultural trade, the government built and managed the first generation of pilot factories, later sold to private firms at considerable discounts.

Japan adopted capitalism from the West in the nineteenth century, but it was a capitalism without the Western ideology of individualism and economic freedom. The notion that the state and individuals necessarily form an adversarial relationship is at odds with the traditional Japanese concept of nation-family. The state and the market are interwoven parts jointly constituting the nation's economy. The state may make errors but is neither good nor bad per se; it is an entity with its own functions to serve vis-à-vis the private sector. Just as the head of a household is expected to manage the affairs of a biological family, the task of the state is to manage the affairs of the nation-family, including its economic affairs. Industrial policy in Japan is generally viewed as a developmental supplement to the market, not as an act of unwanted "intervention" or "interference" with private business.

Japan has a long tradition of competent bureaucracy. Many of the nation's best minds enter the national civil service, which is considered a prestigious profession. Without this tradition, the character of Japanese industrial policy in all probability would have been significantly different. Japanese bureaucracy (if not her politics) has been remarkably free of (major) corruption. After their early retirement, usually at age fifty-five, many Japanese bureaucrats run for political office or become senior executives of public corporations or large private companies. This convention contributes to good working relationships between the bureaucracy and the Diet (parliament) on one hand, and the bureaucracy and private business on the other.

Group Orientation

The Japanese are said to be group-oriented, but their group orientation, as it affects Japanese industrial behavior, requires careful interpretation. It is neither a collectivism with strong ideological overtones nor a communalism that leans toward peace and the warm comfort of the status quo. Rather, it operates most effectively at the level of a firm and an enterprise group (the Japanese term for the latter is *kigyo shudan,* meaning a grouping of firms affiliated through mutual stockholding and long-established business relations). The typical firm in the advanced sector of the Japanese economy is free of capitalist-owner control of management and does not suffer from adversarial relations between management and labor, since both parties identify themselves with their company, sharing a common interest. The absence of internal conflicts of interest enhances the "synergy" of the firm. At the same time the firm-specific group identity does not degenerate into complacency and stagnation because fierce competition prevails among firms as well as enterprise groups. The Mitsubishi group's archrivals are not so much its American competitors as Mitsui and the other Japanese enterprise groups constantly struggling for a greater market share.

Network of Institutions

Many institutions are involved in the implementation of industrial policy in Japan. While some are more important than others, it is not easy to pinpoint where the various spheres of policymaking begin and end.

Contrary to the impression that an uninitiated observer might form, the Economic Planning Agency is not directly associated with industrial policy. The agency drafts a series of economic and social plans that express the official economic outlook for the future, but these plans bear little resemblance to those of a Soviet-type command economy. At most, they indicate what the government is thinking about the direction in which the economy is moving and the problems the nation will likely be facing. Information thus provided is useful to firms and the general public for anticipating in broad terms what sort of economic policy the government will be pursuing. However, the plans in no way oblige firms to behave in a prescribed manner. The agency also publishes an annual Economic White Paper, a voluminous, in-depth review and discussion of the Japanese economy that is packed with statistics on all sectors. The agency's research institute, meanwhile, conducts sophisticated, mainly empirical studies of the economy.

The Diet approves the budgets that include appropriations for industrial policy measures, and passes the laws to provide the legal base for implementing them. As a rule, these laws are written in general language, and the statutory authority to put into effect specific policies is delegated to the competent ministries, which in turn issue more detailed decrees, recommendations, notices, and the like.

The Ministry of Finance plays an important role in industrial policy, in two ways. First, unlike the U.S. Federal Reserve System, the Bank of Japan (the nation's central bank) does not hold a position of independence but operates under the supervision of the Ministry of Finance. The ministry is ultimately responsible for the nature, extent, and direction of selective credit control, monetary policy, foreign exchange policy, banking regulations, and so forth, that have had significant bearings on industrial policy, especially in the early postwar years. Second, the ministry oversees the Fiscal Investment and Public Loan Program, which moves voluminous funds—mainly supplied by Postal Savings (whose total deposits are three times as large as those of the Bank of America)—toward a multitude of public corporations, many of which act as instruments of industrial policy.

The Role of MITI

The focal point of Japanese industrial policy is MITI because the majority of industries come under its jurisdiction.[1] Yet for all its fame and prestige, the ministry is surprisingly small; it took only 1.6 percent of the initial fiscal 1983 national budget, and its total staff numbers only about 2,500. (Its elite corps of career officials—those who passed the senior civil service examination and were assigned to the ministry—is much smaller in number.)

MITI's functions are comprehensive and far-reaching. It is responsible for shaping the structure of industry and making necessary adjustments for industrial dislocations as they occur, properly guiding the development of specific industries and the production and distribution of their products, managing Japanese foreign trade and commercial relations with other nations, ensuring an adequate supply of energy and raw materials to industry, and managing particular areas such as small business policy, patents, and regional development. To achieve these diverse goals, MITI plays many roles ranging from that of broad policy architect to ad hoc working-level problem-solver, and from formal regulator to regional policy arbiter or informal administrative guide. In some areas MITI holds strong statutory authority; elsewhere it has only a broad and weak influence.

The ministry's organizational structure is well suited for its diverse functions. Besides the Secretariat, it has four so-called "horizontal" bureaus—Industrial Policy, International Trade Policy, International Trade Administration, and Industrial Location and Environmental Protection—which develop and coordinate policy across industries. Along with these horizontal bureaus, there are three so-called "vertical" bureaus—Basic Industries, Machinery and Information Industries, and Consumer Products—which develop programs and address problems at the level of individual industries. In addition, nine regional bureaus reconcile national policy to local concerns and help MITI develop its extraordinary data base on the various industries that come under its purview.

One unique feature of Japanese industrial policy is MITI-sponsored "vision-making." The ministry has attached to it many deliberation councils (*shingi kai*), the most important of which is the Industrial Structure Council. This group's membership is all-inclusive, with participants representing big and small business, government, consumers, academia, mass media, labor, and local interest groups. The council and its subcommittees are asked to examine diverse industry-related issues—general or particular, national or regional—with the aim of formulating a vision of what lies ahead. Specifically, the council is charged with the task of identifying the nature and direction of changes taking place in the overall economic environment, determining what sort of new industrial structure is most desirable for the nation, and indicating what are the most effective policy means to carry out the desired structural transformation of industry, and how and where those means should be applied.

The "vision" that results from council deliberations is published and widely circulated in the nation.[2] Vision-making is the Japanese version of indicative economic planning, intended to build a consensus among all segments of society concerning the country's industrial structure, to ensure continuity and stability of industrial policy, to provide information useful for firms' long-term strategic planning, and to contribute to the optimal allocation of resources for the good of everyone. It merely indicates what is desirable. Actual decisions are left to the individual firms.

MITI also stays in continual close contact with industry groups such as steel, automobiles, and chemicals, and with major business-management associations such as Keidanren (Federation of Economic Organizations, representing big business), Shoko Kaigi Sho (Chamber of Commerce and Industry, representing small and medium-size firms), Keizai Doyukai (Committee for Economic Development, concerned with broader social issues), and Nikkeiren (Japan Federation of Employers Associations, concerned with a common labor policy for big business). The dialogues are maintained to share information, identify emerging problems, and build a consensus toward their solution.

Postwar Industrial Policy

It is actually not possible to speak of *the* industrial policy of postwar Japan because its character and specific contents have kept
changing with time, reflecting the shifting needs dictated by the
environment in which the Japanese economy has operated.

In the years immediately following World War II (1945–52), the
government was faced with the overwhelming task of reconstruct-
ing the war-torn economy. In the context of an absolute shortage
of goods and services, price control and rationing of basic commodities were routinely invoked as a matter of necessity. The core
of industrial policy then was the "preferential production system"
(*keisha seisan hoshiki*), under which resources were systematically
and preferentially allocated toward the coal, steel, and electric
power industries for the purposes of accelerating the simultaneous
and complementary redevelopment of these interdependent key
industries and rehabilitating the allied sectors.

The Japanese economy remained highly protected and regu-
lated during the following decade or so, a period during which the
image of so-called "Japan, Inc." fit the reality fairly closely.[3] Most
domestic industries were still too fragile to compete effectively in
the international market. The nation's economy, overpopulated
and resource-poor, was hardly capable of "self-support," to use the
then-fashionable expression. Under the interrelated Foreign Exchange and Foreign Trade Control Law and the Foreign Investment Law, priority was given to the importation of vitally needed
industrial materials and Western technologies at the expense of
consumer goods, and to foreign loans as against foreign direct
investment involving managerial and equity control by foreign
enterprises.

During these early postwar years the Ricardian doctrine of comparative advantage was summarily dismissed, for to apply it would
have meant that Japan would have to concentrate on the production and export of labor-intensive goods—labor being the only
abundant input then domestically available. But instead of selecting toys, matchsticks, and sandals, the government chose important industries to be developed under state guidance and assistance. The criteria for selection were anticipated worldwide income elasticity of demand for certain products, the high value-

added nature of the products, and the long-term income- and employment-creating effects of these same products on the domestic economy. Accordingly, heavy and chemical industries (steel, automobiles, shipbuilding, and petrochemicals) were targeted for guided growth.

These industries all require enormous financing, large-scale plant and equipment investment, long lead time, and advanced technologies. Developmental efforts were made on all fronts. The Japan Development Bank and the Long-Term Credit Bank supplied preferential loans. The Bank of Japan practiced credit-rationing (so-called "window guidance") to channel voluminous city bank credit toward designated industries. A series of special laws was passed to provide a statutory framework for tax incentives, export subsidies, and other means to execute the developmental plans.

This was the period in which private industries by and large closely cooperated with the government, since the two shared a common interest in the accelerated growth of the strategic industries, and the former still depended on the latter for their survival. There was a widespread consensus in the nation that laying a solid foundation of the key industries was the first step toward achieving durable growth of the economy. What was remarkable about this period was not so much the elaborateness of the industrial policy as the fact that somehow the firms in the protected industries did not lose their keen competitive spirit.

Liberalization and Rapid Growth

From 1960 on, the slow and cautious liberalization of trade and capital began, a process designed to open and expose the Japanese economy to the world market. In 1963 Japan assumed Article 11 status within the General Agreement on Tariffs and Trade (GATT). In 1964 she joined the OECD and agreed to comply with Article 8 of the International Monetary Fund (IMF). These steps meant that she was now obliged to dismantle quantitative import restrictions and direct foreign exchange control for balance-of-payments reasons. Trade liberalization started in 1960, capital liberalization in 1967. Quantitative import restrictions were removed from steel in 1961 and from color televisions and automobiles in 1965. By the mid-1960s most of the direct export subsidy measures had been repealed. Along with removal of import quotas, tariff rates were also gradually reduced. The criterion for determining the speed and direction of the liberalization was to wait until an industry in question became efficient and internationally competitive enough to stand on its own feet.[4]

The decade of the 1960s was for Japan a period of accelerated growth, her economy expanding at an annual rate of some 10 percent. The actual growth outpaced Premier Ikeda's celebrated income-doubling plan that projected a doubling of national income in ten years starting from 1960 with an estimated annual growth rate of slightly above 7 percent. In fact, the economy expanded at 10 percent, and the income-doubling was completed in about seven years. Rapid growth continued until the oil crisis of 1973.

In the latter half of the 1960s Japan's balance of payments started to register a chronic and increasing export surplus, reversing the earlier trend. The time had arrived when the Japanese government could no longer afford the privilege of small-nation status, single-mindedly pursuing the goal of promoting growth of the domestic economy and more or less ignoring the impact of the Japanese economy on the rest of the world. Japan had become big and was continuing to grow. Her voluminous exports of manufactures were disrupting foreign markets. Trade frictions between Japan and the Western industrial countries became frequent and intense. MITI was now confronted with an added task of harmoniously integrating the Japanese economy with the world market.

Crisis and Change

This was also a period when the adverse effects of an extreme "production first" principle became visible in the nation. Air pollution, environmental destruction, the spread of pollution-caused diseases, the inadequacy of social infrastructure and housing, and consumerism were serious concerns of the day. Accordingly, the focus of the nation's industrial policy started to shift toward welfare measures and away from the objective of output maximization.

Since the oil crisis of 1973 the world has experienced the longest synchronized recession since the Great Depression of the 1930s. The growth rates of the major industrial economies as well as of the developing countries have slowed down considerably, with concomitant increases in unemployment and structural disloca- tion of domestic industries. Predictably, protectionism worldwide has been on the rise.

Caught by the global recession, the Japanese economy has shown its own strains, although its overall performance has been better than that of the advanced Western economies. After its recovery from the first oil shock, it managed to grow at 4–5 per- cent annually. While it withstood the second oil shock (1979) well, its annual growth rate has decelerated down to 3 percent in recent years. Unlike the U.S. and Western Europe, however, Japan thus far has not been plagued by that coexistence of high inflation and high unemployment known as "stagflation."

MITI's task is at present more difficult and complex than in the past. Internally, many industries (particularly energy-intensive ones) are severely depressed. When the economy is not growing fast, structural adjustment of industry is not an easy job to per- form. Legally and politically, MITI is no longer able to rely on in- duced export expansion as a means of offsetting deficient internal demand. Having caught up with the advanced West in technology and industrial productivity, Japan today does not possess the ad- vantage of being a chaser who can borrow technology and techni- cal know-how from more advanced countries. At the same time she is being chased by developing countries in more and more categories of manufactured goods. Besides, MITI's power position vis-à-vis private business has significantly weakened relative to the 1950s and the early 1960s. MITI cannot easily dictate or per- suade private business what to do in the name of the national in- terest because Japanese private industries—now big, advanced, and powerful—may or may not believe that what MITI thinks is good for the nation is also good for them.

Japan is a country smaller in size than California and devoid of natural resources. She is nearly totally (99.8 percent) import- dependent on oil, and half of the food her people consume is im- ported. Her imperative is to export enough of what she produces to pay for vital imports. Disintegration of the international economic order would quickly bring her industrial machinery to a grinding halt, provoking a national crisis. Economic security is a very serious issue for her.[5]

When Japan's economy was small and in the process of catching up, her national interest could best be served through the wholesale promotion of domestic industries in a context of internal competition combined with protection against advanced Western rivals. Now the infant industries have matured while the nation remains as resource-poor as ever. It is Japan who would be hardest hit by a spread of global protectionism; she can grow and prosper further only if world trade continues to grow. The new situation dictates that it is in Japan's interest to promote global free trade to the fullest extent.

Multilaterally and unilaterally, Japan has been reducing her tariff rates. While protectionism in agriculture and banking remains (a pattern not unique to Japan), her tariffs on manufactures today are in fact lower than those in the U.S. and Western European countries. Similarly, nontariff barriers ("buy national" laws, import quotas, discriminatory regulations, etc.) are comparable to their Western counterparts.

Character of Current Policy

National economies operate at different stages of development and are in a continuous process of structural transformation. A developing country learns to produce more advanced manufactures; combining its newly acquired technological capability with lower labor cost, it becomes able to compete with more developed countries in certain areas. Faced with this catching-up process, a developed country has two options: to raise import barriers to protect the domestic industries now threatened by competition from less-developed countries, or to phase out the depressed industries and shift resources toward technologically more advanced and higher value-added sectors. The former discourages the growth of free, multilateral trade; the latter promotes it. The current industrial policy of Japan is aimed at encouraging the international division of labor and preventing global protectionism.[6]

Industrial policy is a means to accomplish necessary changes in the nation's industrial structure as smoothly and quickly as possible. The Japanese approach is indicative, indirect, soft-handed, small-scale, and market-oriented. It fully recognizes the efficiency and effectiveness of the private market as the primary agent of economic activity; the state, at best, is merely to serve as a catalyst of industrial growth by supplementing or complementing (but not substituting for) the private sector. Unlike some Western countries (France and Great Britain), Japan has not nationalized major private industries in trouble and seldom directly intervenes with the management of private firms. The magnitude of state involvement in the private sector in Japan is much less and the type of involvement is less industry-related than is commonly perceived in the West.

Government's share of total R&D expenditures (excluding defense) is 28 percent in Japan, the smallest among the advanced countries. Comparable figures are 32 percent for Great Britain, 33 percent for the U.S., 41 percent for West Germany, and 47 percent for France.[7]

The Japan Development Bank is often cited as a powerful tool of government financing of industrial development in Japan. What is less known is that since 1976 about 90 percent of the bank's loans have been for environmental protection, energy conservation, improvement of infrastructure, urban development, and the like, and only about 10 percent for directly industry-related projects.

Beginning in the mid-1970s, most tax incentives for export promotion or those protecting particular industries have been curtailed. The bulk of the remaining tax incentives are for pollution control, development of alternative energy sources, economic cooperation with developing countries, and small businesses.

Since the first oil crisis many Japanese industries have been suffering from structural depression. Instead of protecting them so as to perpetuate their inefficiencies, MITI has pursued a positive adjustment policy by guiding the reduction of excess capacity, the reorganization of industry to gain scale effects, and R&D investments where the revitalization of a depressed sector is reasonably certain.

Governments of practically all major countries subsidize scientific research of all sorts (basic, experimental, strategic) through such various means as grants, preferential public loans, and cofinancing. While the size and specific content of public research assistance are conditioned by the particular needs and aspirations of each country, this common practice is based on the belief that scientific and technological progress is the prime engine of the dynamic growth of economic society, and that the absence of government assistance will hinder the prospect of such growth inasmuch as private firms (by definition) will hesitate to undertake those research projects that involve high risks, require large-scale expenditures, and do not appear profitable even though their long-term social (external) benefits are potentially great.

MITI's officials have argued that high technology should be the engine of recovery from the current global recession, and that in order to accelerate progress in high technology the advanced countries should cooperate with one another via joint research and sharing of information rather than attempting to monopolize individually the fruits of such technology. MITI has been initiating international dialogues with the U.S. and Western Europe through the recently organized joint committees on high technology.[8]

In the U.S., where the government heavily subsidizes defense-related R&D, private firms are allowed to make commercial application of the result of what was initially defense-oriented research; on the other hand, joint government-business financing of nondefense projects is generally considered illegitimate. Freed from this sort of ideological muddle, MITI has been participating in joint high-technology research with private producers in information electronics, an area that it envisions will be playing a strategic role in forthcoming years.

A case in point is Japan's joint-effort VLSI (very-large-scale integration) semiconductor project initiated in 1976, whose objective is to develop the state-of-the-art technology in logic and memory circuits. Of 72 billion yen budgeted for the project, 40 percent is government-funded.[9] Government participants come from MITI's Electronics Research Institute and Central Telecommunications Laboratory; corporate membership consists of Fujitsu, Hitachi, Mitsubishi, NEC, and Toshiba. The participating private producers will share the benefits of the newly generated technology, but they must compete independently in applying the technology to existing products and new systems.

One reason for government participation is the smallness of Japanese producers relative to American giants. In the mid-1970s

R&D funded by Fujitsu, Hitachi, and NEC combined was less than half of IBM's. Similarly, the combined semiconductor R&D expenditure of these Japanese companies was less than Texas Instruments' total.

The latest example of Japanese government-business cooperation is the so-called "fifth generation" or artificial intelligence supercomputer project (1982–91). Bold and dramatically futuristic, the project is headed up by a 100 billion yen government-industry consortium of eight leading producers, headquartered at ICOT (Institute for New Generation Computer Technology). Some believe that it will set a precedent for Japan by breaking away from the tradition of following U.S. computer technology. Not a few experts remain skeptical, however, and think that it may turn out to be another *Yamato,* the supersize battleship that was built but little used before being sunk during the Pacific War.

MITI's Fallibility

It is incorrect to think of Japan as a single-minded nation under the central command of its government and of MITI as a flawless, omnipotent, and omniscient force in its pursuit of industrial policy. The growth record of Japan's heavy and chemical industries in the 1960s seems to demonstrate MITI's might; yet the record has been less impressive in the areas of housing, infrastructure, and the cost of living. In addition, sluggishness continues to persist in textiles, pulp and paper, cement, bulk chemicals, aluminum, plywood, processed food, construction, and other industries.

MITI has made its share of mistakes and has experienced downward shifts of its power position vis-à-vis private business. Interministerial rivalry within the Japanese government is strong. Not infrequently MITI has had to cope with the more conservative policy stances of other ministries such as Agriculture and Forestry or Posts and Telecommunications. MITI's pro-merger, pro-cartel posture has often stirred severe resistance and criticism by the Fair Trade Commission.

In the early postwar years MITI opposed Sony's attempt at the commercial application of transistor technology, initially developed in the U.S., as unpromising.

In 1953 MITI advanced the idea of a "people's car." Through competitive bidding MITI was to pick one automobile company that would receive protection and subsidies as the officially designated maker of the people's car. The Japanese automobile producers reacted with little enthusiasm, and the idea had to be scrapped.

Indeed, the signs of MITI's declining power of persuasion became visible from the early 1960s on. Between 1962 and 1964 MITI tried to introduce the Law Concerning Temporary Measures for Promotion of Designated Industries (Tokushin Ho) as a legal means of industrial reorganization through mergers, rationalization cartels, and preferential credit arrangements free of the Fair Trade Commission's intervention. The plan, designed to prepare the designated industries for the impact of trade and capital liberalization, met with bitter opposition from the commission, politicians, and business and financial circles, and it never materialized.

In 1965–66 MITI administratively instructed Sumitomo Metals to reduce production, allegedly to prevent excessive competition. Having just completed a new, large-scale plant, Sumitomo refused to comply with the guidance. MITI retaliated by cutting down the coal import quota for the firm. Considerable tension arose between the two, although a compromise solution was later reached.

In the mid-1960s MITI attempted to reorganize the Japanese automobile industry—first by legislative means and later through administrative guidance—into three major groups, each specializing in a certain category of cars. The merger plan failed, the victim of concerted opposition from the industry, the Diet, and the Fair Trade Commission.

It is intriguing that in postwar Japan it has often been MITI that initiates a merger plan (typically to reduce excessive competition and gain alleged economies of scale), and then the private firms concerned resist it. By contrast, in the U.S. the sequence is usually reversed: private firms attempt a merger, and the antitrust division of the Justice Department reacts by opposing it. The Japanese pattern is presumably due to the force of company-level group orientation or the ethos of the corporate family, but this remains a hypothesis to be proved.

Lessons for the U.S.

What ought one to think of Japanese industrial policy, and what lessons, if any, does it offer for the U.S.? This is a question Japan-watchers in America have been asking. Some think we can learn a good deal from the Japanese experience (Vogel, Magaziner, Reich, Hout, Hadley);[10] others are skeptical about its usefulness to the U.S. (Tresize, Shapiro, Etzioni).[11] Not a few contend that the role of industrial policy in promoting the industrial growth of postwar Japan is grossly exaggerated.

To what extent has industrial policy really contributed to Japan's economic growth? In a way this is an unanswerable question—it is akin to asking who is responsible for Johnny's having grown to be a mature, productive person. Depending on one's perspective, the credit may be bestowed upon his parents, grandparents, sister or brother, friends, classmates, or that extraordinary teacher Johnny had in the fifth grade, and so on.

Likewise, there have been many favorable factors in Japan's growth: the abundance of inexpensive labor in the early postwar period, the availability of Western technology for Japan to borrow, global prosperity prior to the oil crisis, managerial competence, the geopolitical circumstance that permitted the country to bear only light arms, the undervaluation of yen in the late 1960s, etc. It is not possible, however, to pull out one factor and measure its precise contribution to the growth. Nor can we turn back the clock to 1945 and rerun the course of Japan's postwar history without industrial policy to see what differences its absence would have made.

Some observers fondly cite Sony, Matsushita, and Honda as instances of Japanese firms that have grown with little government help; presumably they are "proof" that managerial efficiency, an industrious work force, and market competition—not industrial policy—are responsible for the positive result.[12] But this observation is misguided. These companies grew because they were capable of growing on their own; it is not the business of industrial policy to help those who can help themselves.

A more answerable question might be: was the spectacular expansion of the heavy and chemical industries in the 1960s possible without MITI-sponsored structured competition with selective

protection for growth . . . and would the making of an industrial-
technological powerhouse in Japan have been feasible given a
total absence of MITI's pro-business scheme of socializing private
investment risks? It would take an incurable ideologue of the
Right to believe that a laissez-faire environment would have produced the same results.

Only Japan can live Japanese history, and her political, legal,
and economic institutions are reflections of her own tradition and
culture. Hence, nothing would be potentially more dangerous for
another country than the attempt to emulate Japanese industrial
policy. It is a particular situation that determines the rationality
and effectiveness of industrial policy; it is perfectly conceivable
that under a certain circumstance the best industrial policy is to
have none. Nonetheless, this is not to imply that we can learn little
from Japan; there are useful lessons—more often indirect and
subtle than direct and literal—for America.

The Japanese experience demonstrates that industrial policy
does not necessarily require enormous public funds and a large
number of bureaucrats. What matters is not the elaborateness of
the specific contents of a program but, rather, the competence of
the bureaucrats involved and the rigor of the analysis applied,
combined with a common recognition of the limits of the market
and an economic philosophy that transcends narrow self-interest.

Instead of directly intervening with the management of private
firms, MITI serves more as a catalyst or pump-primer of desired
economic activity. It makes continued efforts to build a consensus
between government and business on what is good for the country,
in an open forum participated in by diverse interest groups. The
Japanese experience suggests that so long as an atmosphere of
confrontation and mutual distrust prevails between the state and
private business, industrial policy will be inoperative.

The United States suffers from a peculiar allergy to state planning—peculiar because in the same country it is considered sane
and sensible for individuals to plan for their education, careers,
child-raising, and financial security rather than simply living day
to day. Even in the most conservative of private businesses, the
title of Executive Vice-President for Strategic Planning inspires
awe and respect, and not the suspicion that the person might be a
commissar sent by the state. Yet government planning is avoided

at any cost. Consequently, American economic policy is prone to be ad hoc and reactive and is subject to radical changes after each presidential election.

Japan offers an alternative version of economic planning. It is not of a dictatorial, coercive sort, but rather is meant to indicate or anticipate the forthcoming major developments that will affect the nation's economy and to help make necessary adjustments as soon and as smoothly as possible. Based on analysis of hard data, it adds an element of certainty, continuity, and consistency to the nation's economic policy. It is a case of programming for dynamic growth of a competitive economy; planning is thus an instrument of pragmatism devoid of socialist ideological content.

American postwar economic policy has been based on the so-called "neoclassical synthesis"—a doctrine that holds that a modern economy can be managed by a proper mix of monetary and fiscal policies generating sufficient aggregate demand for high employment without inflation, together with some government regulations to alleviate negative externalities of private production, and product-specific protectionism here and there as politically necessary. In this setting the private market mechanism, operating at the micro level, is assumed to be capable of achieving optimum allocation of resources.

The trouble with the doctrine is that the Keynesian monetary-fiscal policy mix is primarily meant to cope with the problems of short-run business fluctuations by adjusting the level of aggregate demand. It is not well equipped to promote economic growth, a long-term process that requires close attention to the supply side of the equation. The doctrine assumes, in effect, that a long run is but a succession of short runs, and that if we manage the economy satisfactorily in the short run it will grow on its own over the long haul. This assumption seemed to meet the empirical test up to the mid-1960s, but not thereafter.

Japanese industrial policy is in fact an instance of supply-side economics. Economic growth calls for an expanding supply capability of the economy, and involves the structural transformation of industry. While the market is efficient in allocating resources in the short run, it is not necessarily reliable in anticipating and solving long-term economic problems, especially those problems that have national (as against industry-specific) implications. Industrial policy is a supplement to the market, a way of accelerating industry's structural change necessary for economic growth.

In the U.S. the legitimacy of industrial policy in the sense of state-industrial cooperation thus far has been recognized only with respect to defense and other national security—related sectors. The Japanese experience suggests that industrial policy *can* be an explicit component of American economic policy, complementing the conventional macroeconomic policy tools.

Broader Historical Perspective

Historically, industrial policy has been closely connected with the economic nationalism of weak nations. The idea of infant industry protection was nurtured in the underdeveloped Germany of the nineteenth century, concerned as she was with the threat posed to her native industries by superior English manufactures. The thought of protecting fragile domestic industries against foreign competition was similarly strong then in France and the United States.

The industrial policy of late-nineteenth-century Japan was motivated by the fear of being colonized by Western powers. Since World War II its main objective has been to catch up with the advanced West through accelerated economic growth. Protectionism, an integral component of the policy in its early years, was justified as the right of a weak nation to attempt to raise its infants to a mature adulthood, a temporary measure to be dismantled once the mission was accomplished.

After some thirty years of sustained postwar growth, Japan has become a strong nation, producing 10 percent of the world's output. Still, she actively continues to pursue industrial policy, albeit of a professedly nonprotectionist sort. That a weak nation would have an industrial policy, aside from its success or failure, is understandable. But what is the industrial policy of a strong nation supposed to be like? This is an unresolved issue.

The character of industrial policy may be positive or negative. Positive industrial policy achieves industrial growth and efficiency, enabling the country to compete freely in the world market. Formulated and implemented incorrectly, however, it may exert a negative influence, protecting declining industries and prolonging their inefficiencies to the detriment of the country and the rest of the world.

As long as an international economic order is maintained under the hegemony of a powerful leader nation, the chance of the rise of negative industrial policy is limited. The true hegemon (England in the nineteenth century, the United States in the 1950s) has little need for negative industrial policy, while the type of policy pursued by the weak nations in the process of catching up tends to be positive. Once the hegemon's position starts to decline, however, the formerly strong is likely to have recourse to negative industrial policy. Great Britain after World War II and the United States today illustrate the point. Great Britain, having lost her industrial superiority, moved in the direction of nationalizing and heavily subsidizing her ailing industries after the war. Similarly, America, a champion of free trade in the 1950s, is currently witnessing a rise of protectionism, which is often considered synonymous with industrial policy.

The phenomenon is not difficult to comprehend. Overtaken by the once weak nation, the formerly strong nation feels frustrated. This provides an ideal breeding ground for short-sighted economic nationalism and negative industrial policy. The declining nation also has an older and more mature economy with many vested interests and pressure groups capable of bending the machinery of state to cater to their needs rather than letting it serve a healthy developmental role vis-à-vis embryonic industries that have less political clout.

The cohesion of postwar Pax Americana has waned, and the present-day distribution of economic power is conducive to the abuse of industrial policy. The world economy revolves around Western Europe, the U.S., and Japan, together producing more than 50 percent of the world's output. All three are strong but none uncontestably stronger than the rest. All have a similar industrial structure comprising steel, automobiles, computers, etc., which are exposed to competition from without. They also must reckon with catching-up forces from the developing countries.

This is a setting that helps ferment economic nationalism among the equally strong. Successful industrial policy in A begins to hurt B and C, who respond by invoking protectionist policy in self-defense, only to be retaliated against by A, and so on. Before long, industrial policy may unwittingly become a purveyor of international confrontation, aggravating rather than mitigating economic conflicts among nations.

While the degree of economic interdependence among nations has risen significantly since the war, there is still little substantive international harmonizing of macroeconomic and industrial policies. Japan's current industrial policy rests on the premise that her prosperity can continue only in the context of global prosperity. As Japan pursues industrial policy to further expand the frontier of her economy as a way of contributing to global prosperity, the very success of her policy will likely act as an irritant to the U.S. and Western Europe. It then becomes necessary for a strong Japan to practice restraint in the use of industrial policy by deliberately reducing its magnitude and the number of instruments employed. How well MITI will succeed in harmonizing Japan's industrial policy with those of other states, demonstrating that industrial policy can be a genuine catalyst of not only domestic but also international economic growth, remains to be seen.

4

MELVYN KRAUSS

"Europeanizing"
the U.S. Economy:
The Enduring Appeal of
the Corporatist State

The style of "industrial policy" advocated by Robert B. Reich, Lester Thurow, Felix Rohatyn, and other so-called "neoliberals" is frequently thought of as an updated form of socialism. Indeed, like socialism, it would essentially involve an increased politicization of U.S. economic life—where political elites rather than individuals in the marketplace make the important economic decisions. The neoliberals champion this politicization process not only because it allegedly will revitalize America's economic base, but also because of equity considerations. "The point," according to Reich, "is that any important economic choice is by nature political, but the political dimension is often systematically obscured. This submergence of politics results in economic policies whose burdens and benefits are allocated in ways that many people ultimately consider unfair."[1]

Yet if anything industrial policy as currently proposed is closest in structure not to socialism but to the state corporatism that Benito Mussolini brought to Italy in the 1930s—i.e., to fascism. In fact, current proposals to supplant the market economy by a process of political negotiations between big labor, big business, and big government—proposals, in short, for a "new industrial policy"—are little more than euphemisms for the corporate state.[2]

According to the original notion of the corporate state, workers and employers were to be collectivized into separate groups on the basis of exclusive representation in each industry. The union bosses and captains of industry were expected to bargain and reach agreement over such key economic variables as wages, prices, and hours of work, and then submit their agreement to the government for final approval. The corporate state, in other words, is a system where the political bosses make the big decisions and the little guys are expected to follow. How different is this fascist apparatus for economic decision-making from Reich's vision where "government, businesses and labor fashion explicit agreements to restructure American industry"? "Fashionable fascism" is an accurate term for this sort of neoliberal economic thought.

It is interesting to note that a similar politicization of economic life constituted the cornerstone of the New Deal of the 1930s. The National Industrial Recovery Act, which was said to be justified by the country's economic condition during the Great Depression, established "codes of conduct" for different industries. Along these lines, the proposed Reconstruction Finance Corporation (RFC) provides an explicit institutional parallel linking the neoliberal version of industrial policy with the New Deal and the Mussolini era. Though it is well known that the RFC is a Felix Rohatyn remake of the early Roosevelt version, it is less well known that the original RFC was inspired by Mussolini's Istituto per la Ricostruzione Industriale (IRI). The IRI was established in January 1933 to combat the severe Italian recession caused by

Mussolini's pegging the lira at too high a rate vis-à-vis other currencies (the so-called "quota 90" issue). The purpose of the IRI was to collect public and private funds for rescuing troubled Italian firms.

Originally set up to supply finance for Italian industry that private banks were either unable or unwilling to provide, the IRI's mandate was expanded under its first head Alberto Beneduce to encourage the reorganization and rationalization of the industries under its control—e.g., steel, machinery, shipping, electricity, and telephones. Though the mechanics of its operations were extremely intricate and novel because it was impossible to tell exactly where private enterprise ended and public enterprise began, its purpose was quite clear—to sustain several inefficient Italian industries that were relevant to "the interest of national defense, the policy of autarky, and the development of the Empire."[3] The economic historian Roland Sarti writes:

Every society that experienced the economic depression [of the 1930s] witnessed an increase in public regulation of business in the form of subsidies and price controls, but it was only in Italy that public and private initiative became intimately and permanently linked by means of institutional innovations. *IRI gave the government a control over the economy that was unequaled outside the Soviet Union.* The government tried to use that control in pursuit of its political objectives.[4] [Emphasis added.]

The lessons of the IRI should not be lost on the American people if an "Americanized" version of the IRI is presented as part of the Democratic economic program in 1984. Proposed by Felix Rohatyn, the RFC is strongly supported by the AFL–CIO, which sees a strong centrally directed industrial policy as an opportunity to increase its power in the marketplace. Says an anonymous Democratic congressional staff official quoted in *The Wall Street Journal:* "When power in the marketplace declines, people try to enhance their clout in the political process."[5] That indeed is one important reason why an "efficient" industrial policy is likely to be a contradiction in terms: only those who are losers in the marketplace are likely to be interested in developing the political clout to promote an industrial policy.

The Experience of Europe

The experience of Europe, as we shall see, strongly supports this suspicion. Europe's industrial policies have, if anything, proved to be heavily biased toward the losers in the marketplace who have political clout—industries that would perish without the life-support systems provided by government subsidies. European industrial policy in general has ended up supporting sunset rather than sunrise sectors of the economy.

Of all the countries in the West, Sweden is actually closest at present to the model that proponents of industrial policy have in mind for the United States. The Swedes are preeminent exponents of the consensus-style politicized economic life. They have a union-dominated "corporate state." Even Swedish industrialists share a disbelief in the free market. And Sweden's industrial policies are second to none in Western Europe. During the years 1977–79, for example, total industrial subsidies in Sweden were somewhat larger than the nation's total appropriations for national defense. The Swedes quite literally have put their industrial policy where their guns should be.

Swedish industrial subsidies rose from a modest 1.3 percent of GDP (gross domestic product) or 4.9 percent of value added in mining and manufacturing in 1970 to an extraordinary 3.6 percent of GDP or 16 percent of value added in mining and manufacturing in 1978. Virtually the entire increase can be attributed to a dramatic increase in firm-specific subsidies of a very selective kind; these grew from practically zero to a peak of 2.0 percent of GDP in 1978. Firm-specific subsidies amounted to one-half of the government's total corporate tax proceeds during the period 1970–79; they also amounted to one-half of the payroll tax paid by all industrial firms in that period.

Did these subsidies go to the bright and coming industries in Sweden, as Reich and other neoliberals would have us believe, or did they go to the "old men" of Swedish industry? According to the Swedish economist Bo Carlsson, three-fourths of the firm-specific subsidies in the late 1970s went to five industries, none of which could be considered "up and coming": shipyards, the steel industry, the forest-based industry, the mining industry, and the textile and apparel industry.

The shipyards alone received nearly half of these firm-specific subsidies. During the three-year period from 1977 through 1979, shipbuilding subsidies corresponded to 120 percent of the industry's total wage bill. During 1978 and 1979, the subsidies actually exceeded the value added in the shipbuilding industry; i.e., inputs in the production process were worth more when they arrived at the shipyards than when they left in the form of newly built ships. In the steel industry and the mining industry, the subsidies corresponded to 30 percent and 40 percent respectively of the total wage bill for the period 1977–79. Subsidies to the commercial steel industry were nearly as large as those to the shipyards, measured per employee. The subsidies to the forest-based industry went mainly to three firms, where they represented about 40 percent of the total wage bill for the period.

The pattern of Swedish subsidization is unambiguous. Rather than spark the new, Sweden's industrial policy has kept the old, outdated, and inefficient alive at great public expense.

This is a far cry from what, for example, Robert B. Reich represents the situation of European industrial policy to be. Reich writes:

Many of the tools that are used by [European] governments—subsidized loans, temporary tariffs or import quotas, targeted tax benefits—are similar to those used in America. But their purposes and effects are dramatically opposite: these nations are trying to guide their economies into higher-valued production.[6]

Sweden is not the only European country whose experience casts doubt upon the accurateness of Reich's assertions. The subsidy programs of five European nations—Great Britain, Italy, Norway, Sweden, and West Germany—are compared in table 1. Industrial policy proponents constantly make the assertion that the free market is a myth that prevents the establishment of an efficient industrial policy in this country—which is, they say, what we really need. In fact, European experience shows that the real myth is the notion of an efficient industrial policy in the first place.

As can be seen in table 1, the subsidy programs of the five countries vary substantially in magnitude, with Britain and West Germany at the low end of the spectrum (1.0 percent and 1.6 percent of GDP respectively), Sweden at the high end with 3.5 percent,

Table 1

Industrial Subsidies in Great Britain 1979–80, Italy 1978, Norway 1979, Sweden 1979, and West Germany 1980

	Great Britain 1979–80 mil. pounds	%	Italy 1978 bil. lire	%	Norway 1979 mil. Nkr.	%	Sweden 1979 mil. Skr	%	West Germany 1980 mil. DM	%
"General subsidies"										
Export subsidies	376	19.4	1,688	31.3	152[a]	3.2	1,507	9.8	1,750	8.0
R&D subsidies	267	13.8	75	1.4	614	12.8	1,643	10.7	4,450	20.3
General investment subsidies	2	.1	240	4.4	395	8.2	—	—	650	3.0
Employment subsidies to firms	209	10.8	—	—	125	2.6	396	2.6	—	—
Regional and small firm support	388	20.0	725	13.4	1,205	25.2	3,134	20.3	12,000	54.8
Subtotal	1,242	64.1	2,728	50.5	2,491	52.0	6,680	43.4	18,850	86.1
"Rescue operations":										
Sectoral subsidies	77	4.0	—	—	1,109	23.1	1,255	8.1	2,650	12.1
Specific firm subsidies	620	31.9	2,671	49.5	1,192	29.9	7,964	48.5	400	1.8
Subtotal	697	35.9	2,671	49.5	2,301	48.0	8,719	56.6	3,050	13.9
Total subsidies	1,939	100.0	5,399	100.0	4,792	100.0	15,399	100.0	21,900	100.0
Total as % of GDP		1.0		2.6		2.0		3.5		1.6
Total as % of value added		3.6		7.1		7.6		16.0		4.0[b]
"General subsidies" as % of value added in mining and manufacturing		2.3		3.6		4.0		6.9		3.4[b]
"Rescue operations" as % of value added in mining and manufacturing		1.3		3.5		3.6		9.1		0.6[b]

[a]The figure given represents only a minor fraction of total export subsidies.

[b]Estimated figure.

Source: Bo Carlsson, "Industrial Subsidies in Sweden: Macro-Economic Effects and International Comparison," *The Journal of Industrial Economics* 32, no. 1 (September 1983).

and Norway and Italy in between. Probably one-half of the industrial subsidies in Italy, Norway, and Sweden are of the general type—open to all comers who meet the requirements—while general subsidies account for significantly higher shares in the U.K. (64 percent) and West Germany (86 percent).

Regional and small firm support programs are the most important types of general subsidies and R&D subsidies the second most important type, with Germany leading in both categories. Export subsidies turn out to be the kind of general subsidy that varies the most in relative magnitude. However, since most export subsidies are given in the form of loans for which the actual subsidy element and the institutional arrangements vary a good deal, the large differences reported here probably reflect the poor quality or at least the poor compatibility of the data. General investment and employment subsidies seem to be relatively unimportant.

Subsidies are divided into two types: "rescue operations" to support ailing firms and industries, and "general subsidies." Rescue operations account for 35.9 percent of total subsidies in Great Britain, 49.5 percent in Italy, 48 percent in Norway, 56.6 percent in Sweden, and 13.9 percent in West Germany. Two-thirds of the rescue operations in Germany are directed toward the coal-mining industry, which also is a large recipient of subsidies in Britain, along with autos, shipbuilding, and steel. In Norway about one-half of the rescue operations involve the shipbuilding industry. And in Sweden, as detailed above, three-fourths of this type of selective measure is directed to the shipbuilding, steel, mining, forest, and textile industries.

Politicizing Economic Life

The reason for this dramatic growth of selective subsidies to inefficient firms and industries in Western Europe relates to the very politicization of economic life that neoliberal proponents of industrial policy favor. Workers in today's welfare states feel entitled not only to such political rights as freedom of speech, association, and assembly, but also to a job, in the profession of their choice, in the location of their choice, and at wages that allow the achievement of politically determined living standards.[7] This extension of political rights to the economic arena has been labeled the "revolution of rising entitlements" by the noted sociologist Daniel Bell. In particular, there has been a dramatic change in attitudes toward labor mobility in Europe's welfare states. During the 1950s and 1960s, political elites favored labor mobility on the ground that it would strengthen the economic base. Today, however, labor mobility is frowned upon because of its alleged deleterious social consequences. It is important to note that American proponents of industrial policy share this concern for securing workers such "economic rights."

To counter the winds of change, the politicization of economic life must, by necessity, take inefficient forms. No economy is an island. Forces of change that affect the domestic economy put particular pressure on its weak, noncompetitive sectors. It is the "rights" of workers in these threatened industries and firms that must be rescued by politics if they are to be secured. It thus is inevitable in societies that succumb to the notion of workers' "economic rights" that political elites subsidize inefficient firms and industries. Indeed, politicization of economic life is a sign of a responsive politics that results from the conflict between a changing world economy on the one hand, and social commitments that cannot be met in a world of change on the other.

What this means is that there exists in welfare economies an inherent incompatibility between free trade and an efficient industrial policy. Once again, Sweden provides a case in point. Bo Carlsson writes:

The Swedish subsidy program in 1979 was substantially larger than that of any other country in the comparison. This is true for both general subsidy schemes and rescue operations but particularly for the latter. . . . Could it be that Sweden, traditionally a proponent of free trade, faced greater difficulties during the 1970s than the other countries and, having disarmed itself of other protective measures, had to resort to subsidies as a remedy?[8]

Proponents of a new industrial policy in this country propose to combine free trade with "efficient" subsidization. But the two are inherently in conflict.

Elsewhere I have argued that the substitution of domestic industrial policies for explicit tariffs and quantitative restrictions in welfare economies amounts to a "new protectionism."[9] This new protectionism is more difficult to combat than the old one for at least three reasons. First, it is more difficult to identify and measure the precise extent to which various commodities are subsidized by the new protectionism. Hidden protectionism is more difficult to combat than the more explicit kind. Second, offending countries consider their industrial subsidies to be purely internal matters even though these subsidies can have substantial effects on international trade. As a result, nations are less likely to submit their domestic subsidies to international negotiations to reduce them. Finally, industrial policies do not have the same social stigma as overt protectionism. The bitter aftertaste from the "beggar-my-neighbor" protectionist policies of the 1930s continues to linger among contemporary policymakers committed to currently fashionable notions of international cooperation. Being more respectable, industrial subsidies are more likely to appeal to modern-day politicians who want the benefit of tariff protection but not the cost of its social stigma.

Indeed this conflict between the free-trade posture of politicians on the one hand and their underlying protectionist desires on the other is the major reason why international trade policy reeks with hypocrisy and doublethink. Measures such as "trade adjustment assistance," for example, which are clearly designed to thwart imports, are publicly defended on the ground that they are necessary to promote them. Goran Ohlin, for example, writes in his introduction to an OECD study on European industrial policies that

adjustment assistance seems in practice often designed to bolster the defenses against imports rather than clear the ground for them. . . . No industrialized countries have so far pursued adjustment assistance policies specifically designed to promote imports although a few attempts have been made to accelerate the contraction of industrial sectors. More often, however, public policy has sought to delay the transfer of resources.[10]

Protectionism in the name of free trade is what industrial policy is all about.

Regional Policy

Prevailing hostile attitudes toward labor mobility in Western Europe explain not only the increased incidence of "rescue opera-

Table 2
Sundry Regional Subsidies for Several Western Countries, 1975

	Non-discretionary regional investment and other incentives (differences from national)			
	Depreciation	Investment grants	Other	Remarks
UK	—	RDGs (20% for mining, manufacturing, and construction)	REP — (1972/73 expenditure £101m)	1. RDGs — 22% in special development areas 2. RDGs — (1973/74 expenditure £225m)
France	Accelerated (50% first year)	—	—	—
West Germany	Accelerated depreciation in zonal border area only: 50% (moveables), 30% (immoveables) freely in first five years, in addition to normal depreciation	10% but reduced to 7.5% for cyclical reasons (expenditure £50m)	A small amount of assistance with transport costs in zonal border area (at £5 million pa)	1. Special measures for West Berlin 2. Grants only available on certain carefully specified criteria, the most important of which is that sales should be primarily outside the region
Italy	—	—	1. 10-year tax holiday 2. Reduction in transport costs 3. Reductions in social security contributions	
Sweden	Depreciation loans for buildings and machinery	Location grants of max of 35% or 50% depending on area of total investment costs. Investment grants and loans may not exceed ⅔ of total investment costs	Transport subsidy equal to 15%−35% freight discount. Assistance towards training of employees. Govt. guarantees loans for operating capital	Employment premiums in inner development area if firms abide by collective wage agreements
USA	—	—	—	1. Main regional measure is infrastructure support 2. There are taxation and other differences between States, but these are thought not to be very great
Japan	Special depreciation	—	Cheap (but not very cheap) loans; some preferential tax treatment	Assistance is automatic provided that criteria as to investment and employment are met

		Discretional regional assistance		
	Forms and rates of industrial assistance	Provisions to limit investment in congested areas	Other measures	Remarks
UK	Industry act offers great flexibility (1973–74 estimate £35m)	IDC System	LEA aids: Advance factories Training grants (Estimated 1973–74 cost £55m)	Assistance to ship-building (£32m in 1972–73) is mainly on regional grounds
France	Tax concessions, four rates 12–25% depending on region	Taxes in Paris area, Permis de Construire, like the IDC's	Funds made available from FDES, IDI and FIAT through the Societes de development regionale. Also direct persuasion of large firms	—
West Germany	1. GA funds (90m per annum) up to 10%–25% (reduced to 9%–22½%) depending on location, but investment grant if taken is deducted from these limits. 2. Some Lander aids (£15m pa) 3. Some cheap ERP loans	—	—	1. Five categories of growth centres for GA funds. 2. Upper limit to amount of support and cost per job limit, in addition to specific appraisal criteria
Italy	Grants or cheap loans for up to 50% of capital expenditure depending on size of enterprise and area of Mezzogiorno	Fines for job-creating investment in certain congested areas. Power of CIPE to veto investment projects	Support to State enterprises in return for obligation to make 80% of new investment (and 70% of total) in the South	1. Growth centre policy 2. Numerous smaller incentives also available, e.g., exemption from stamp duty
Sweden	—	—	Special releases from IF funds	
USA	No significant direct assistance	—	Some support for training and through public procurement	
Japan	—	Legal control on industrial building in certain metropolitan areas, but no proper dispersal systems	—	

Source: Alan Whiting, "Overseas Experience in the Use of Industrial Subsidies," *The Economics of Industrial Subsidies,* ed. Alan Whiting (London: Her Majesty's Stationery Office, 1976).

tions" subsidies, but also the important role played by regional development in Europe's industrial policies. Twenty percent of Great Britain's, 13.4 percent of Italy's, 25.2 percent of Norway's, 20.3 percent of Sweden's, and 54.8 percent of Germany's general subsidies go for regional support. Table 2 contains a detailed list of current regional subsidies for various European countries. Quite clearly, regional policy is a big business in Europe, and not a very productive one at that.

In its simplest terms, the purpose of regional policy is to bring work to the workers rather than have workers go to the work. That regional policy adversely affects the overall efficiency of the domestic economy is clear, since it subsidizes labor in low-productivity uses; without it, labor would be forced to move into areas of higher productivity. Regional policy thus is the opposite of what Robert Reich means by a new, "efficient" industrial policy. Yet Reich advocates changes in the U.S. tax code to encourage companies to stay in communities when, from a purely economic point of view, it would be better for them to leave. Moreover, he argues that

the federal government might establish regional development banks to provide low-interest, long-term loans to industries that agree to restructure themselves to become more competitive. The banks would also supply cities and towns in the region with low-interest financing for maintaining and developing infrastructure such as roads and sewage-treatment plants.[11]

This vision of an infrastructure-led regional policy for the U.S. clearly is based on the European model. According to Alan Whiting:

The great bulk of [European] federal development appropriations for regional development goes in grants-in-aid to State and Local government for improving the infrastructure (education, road building, hospitals, etc.) to make the problem areas more attractive to industry.[12]

In Italy, for example, there is an obligation imposed on the Mussolini-created IRI to place a high proportion of its new (80 percent) and total (60 percent) investments into the South (the Mezzogiorno). Whiting writes:

There has been a tendency for development in the South to be rather capital-intensive, and improvements in transportation have subjected some local industries to strong competition from firms outside the Mezzogiorno with the result that many smaller firms have found themselves in difficulty.[13]

But while the economy of the Mezzogiorno has become increasingly diversified, it is difficult to resist the conclusion that a good deal of the South-to-North labor migration in Italy has been due to the fact that the IRI has brought the wrong types of projects to the Mezzogiorno. Labor-intensive, not capital-intensive, infrastructure would correctly match the Mezzogiorno's condition of labor abundance and employment needs. Could it be the "cooperation" between the IRI and the construction companies that build the roads that accounts for the infrastructure bias of Italy's regional policy?

Whatever this particular case may be, infrastructure-led regional policy is a waste of valuable resources for more conventional economic reasons than graft. This strategy of infrastructure-led development is essentially "cart before the horse" economics.[14] Infrastructure is the cart and private industry the horse of economic development—not the other way around. The lack of infrastructure may be a bottleneck in economies already experiencing strong growth, in which case the rate of return from investment in infrastructure can be expected to be high. But in poor nations (and regions) the absence of infrastructure is more a sign of economic stagnation than a reason for it. The rate of return from public investment in these cases has proved to be extremely low. The usual result of infrastructure projects meant to spur economic growth both in developed and less-developed countries is empty roads, schools that graduate people who cannot find jobs in the local area, and so on. The spark may be there, but development in the region seldom catches fire.

Research and Development

A final component of Europe's industrial policy that warrants investigation is subsidization of research and development. Industrial policy advocates are enthusiastic about R&D because they view the upgrading of labor skills or human capital as the key to economic prosperity. "Financial capital formation is becoming a less important determinant of a nation's well-being than human-

Table 3
Sundry R&D Subsidies for Several Western Countries, 1975

	Support to cooperative research	State research for industry	Favorable tax treatment	Project support	Other	Remarks
			Support for R & D			
UK	Grant to RAs	IREs	—	Mainly for advanced-technology NRDC	—	Cost 1973–4: AT £174m, other £23m
France	'Enveloppe recherche,' i.e., grants to laboratories out of the budget	—	50% first year depreciation	Development aid through direct govt. financing of firms	Tax exemption of profits from licenses. Special programmes such as the 'Plan Calcul'	—
West Germany	Grants	—	Accelerated depreciation (see table)	AT support	10% (now 7.5%) grant for investment qualifying for accelerated depreciation	Also some aids from Lander
Italy	State participation in research societies (e.g., marine technology, housing technology) of which currently 4	Experimental laboratories mainly for traditional sectors	—	Cheap loans from IMI fund, repayable if success. Little AT support	—	IMI Fund c. £100m and is to be raised $^{2/3}$
Sweden	Financial support to industrial research associations	—	—	Support to technical R & D grants for technical research. Also interest-bearing loans	—	—
USA	Some support from National Science Foundation	Federal installations and laboratories	Capital expenditure may be written off in first year	AT industries	—	Increasing emphasis on civilian rather than military technologies
Japan	Selected projects financed by govt. Joint research endeavour — National Research and Development Programme	15 Institutes and laboratories concentrate on basic research	95% first year depreciation, and discretionary accelerated depreciation for investment making use of research results	Little AT support. Cheap loans to finance new technologies (£12m per annum)	Tax deferment of three years or 3–6% of current sales revenues for investment in qualifying pollution control equipment	—

Selective intervention — advanced technology industries

	Aircraft	Space	Nuclear	Computers	Remarks
UK	Concord development & production Rolls Royce RB211, etc. Other R & D support ***	National satellite programme; FSRO ****	Reactor R&D by AEA; loans to British Nuclear Fuels ****	Support to ICL for new range, and assistance through procurement policy ***	KEY: Subsidy-output ratios: *— 0–5% **— 5–10% ***—10–25% ****—25–100% *****—over 100%
France	***	****	****	**	—
West Germany	Launching aid; credit guarantees for production finance; aid with sales finance ***	ELDO, ESRO, and a national programme ****	Grants mainly to industry, and assistance to electricity supply industry for demonstration plants *****	R & D support	Also grants (on small scale) for advanced electronics R&D
Italy	No special measures ***	ELDO and ERSO ****	No significant industry	No support	—
Sweden	*	No significant industry	***	Unsubsidized	—
USA	*	****	**	**	—
Japan	Loans for R&D and to airlines for purchase of new and domestic aircraft *	Scientific and Applications Satellite Programmes ****	Preferential tax treatment, cheap loans, and some payments for R&D work ****	Grants for R&D and soft loans **	Cheap loans are from Japan Development Bank. Also assistance for some electronics projects (grants for R&D, cheap loans, and special depreciation)

Source: Alan Whiting, "Overseas Experience in the Use of Industrial Subsidies," *The Economics of Industrial Subsidies*, ed. Alan Whiting (London: Her Majesty's Stationery Office, 1976).

capital formation," says Reich. "The skills, knowledge and capacity to work together within America's labor force will determine our collective standard of living."[15]

There are two points to be made concerning Europe's experience with R&D subsidies. The first is that from a quantitative point of view, subsidies for R&D have been less important in Europe's industrial policies than many people in this country would have us believe. Only 14.4 percent of Great Britain's, 1.4 percent of Italy's, 12.8 percent of Norway's, 10.7 percent of Sweden's, and 20.3 percent of Germany's general subsidies go to R&D. Table 3 contains a list of specific measures that various European governments have implemented to support R&D in the mid-1970s.

The second point is that despite enthusiasm for R&D support by industrial policy proponents in this country, Europeans are far more skeptical of their economic value. For example, Alan Whiting writes that "the strongest argument against the support of R&D is that it does not stimulate economic growth. There is ample evidence to show that the performance of UK high technology industries receiving government support for R&D has not been any better than such industries not receiving this support."[16] Echoing this conclusion is R&D expert Professor K. Pavitt:

> There is no reason to believe that a reduced government commitment in high technology will harm Britain's long-term economic performance, or the strength of its industrial technology. The experience of other industrialised countries shows no correlation between the scales of commitment to high technology and any measures of economic performance or technological quality. . . . In addition, as Eads and Nelson, Jewkes and others have argued, the concentration of government resources on commercial development activities has not, on the whole, led to commercially successful innovations or to noteworthy external benefits.
>
> Why have the high technologies consistently succeeded in pre-empting such a high proportion of government funds for industry related R&D, not only in the UK, but also in other Western European countries, and in spite of severe and authoritative criticisms of such programs? . . . With their links to defence, to certain basic industrial requirements, and to exciting technical challenges, could it be—as Jewkes has suggested—that high technology is the last refuge of the enthusiastic nationalist?[17]

West Germany has been cited by industrial policy proponents as a model where national "consensus" allegedly guides the economy into higher-valued production. It is, of course, true that Germany has become a prototype of the union-dominated corporate state — it has worker codetermination on corporate boards. And Germany does give important subsidies to its high-tech industries. But the result has not been a happy one for a country that after World War II experienced an "economic miracle" under a policy of government nonintervention. William Safire writes:

Only yesterday, West Germany was the embodiment of industriousness and resolve; today it is a nation with a raging case of intellectual anomie, entrepreneurial timidity, and diplomatic desperation. A Western bulwark is turning into a Western headache.[18]

It is quite evident, for example, that Germany has lost ground in such fields as optics, consumer electronics, and computers. "Things have improved in the automobile and chemical industries," says Herbert Wolf, the chief economist at Commerzbank AG in Frankfurt. "But the electrical and electronic industries have fallen behind Japan, making no real progress over the past five years."[19]

Government economic planners talk openly of West Germany's lack of entrepreneurial zeal and dwindling access to venture capital — factors essential to the development of high-tech growth industries. "It is no surprise that according to expert opinion," says Rudolf Sprung, an official of the Economics Ministry, "we lag far behind the development of other countries, particularly the U.S. Some talk of being 20 years behind."

West German Chancellor Helmut Kohl is reported to have taken a personal interest in the high-tech advances in California's Silicon Valley and is said to bemoan privately the fact that no such region exists in West Germany. It is ironic that while the German chancellor longs for an American-style Silicon Valley in Germany, some Americans are yearning for German-style industrial policy in the U.S.

In the final analysis, of course, the ultimate test of European industrial policy must be the economic performance of European economies. Table 4 indicates the average annual growth rates of real gross domestic production for selected industrial countries during the periods 1960–70 and 1970–80. Interestingly, though industrial policy proponents never tire of criticizing U.S. economic performance relative to Japan and West Germany, the decrease in growth from the 1960s to the 1970s was less in the U.S. (−30.2

Table 4

Average Annual Growth Rates of
Real Gross Domestic Product,
Selected Industrial Countries

	1960–70	1970–80
United States	4.3%	3.0%
United Kingdom	2.9	1.9
Japan	10.9	5.0
France	5.5	3.5
West Germany	4.4	2.6
Sweden	4.4	1.7

Source: World Development Report, 1982, World Bank.

percent) than in either Japan (–54.1 percent) or West Germany (–40 percent). And recently (1980–82) this trend has become even more pronounced. Thus the call for a new industrial policy in the U.S. amounts to a call to catch up with the losers.

Value of the Marketplace

It may be useful to conclude this chapter by listing some reasons why a scaling down—not up—of the economic power of politicians is currently warranted.

First, there are important political reasons why individual citizens rather than a political elite should guide the allocation of resources and distribution of income in the economy. As Charlotte Twight notes:

Economic activity can serve either of two fundamentally incompatible purposes. It can work to satisfy consumers' actual demands for goods and services, or it can be used to accomplish the social goals of designated political leaders with only perfunctory regard for consumers' wishes. The former economic approach makes the consumer's choice sovereign; the latter empowers a political elite to control the goods and services available to consumers.[20]

Note that this political elite may or may not be democratically elected; it matters little to the individual citizens whose preferences are thwarted by the consensus. Also note that the conflict between individual citizens and the political elite affects in-

dividuals not merely in their role as consumers; it extends to individuals in the workplace as well.

In fact, it was precisely the conflict between individuals in their
roles as employers and workers, and the political elite, that
resulted in the U.S. Supreme Court's declaring the National Industrial Recovery Act (NIRA)—the New Deal's legal linchpin—
unconstitutional in 1935.

The NIRA set standards for wages and hours worked in several
industries, including the poultry business. The Schechter Brothers
were chicken slaughterers and hired workers on terms (longer
hours, lower wages) that violated the industry codes. They were
brought up on charges of violating the NIRA and found guilty in
the lower courts. Upon appeal to the Supreme Court, however,
their guilty verdict was overturned and the NIRA declared unconstitutional. In what has to be considered a truly magnificent
victory in this country for the individual over the political elite,
four brothers from Brooklyn in the poultry business were able to
bring down Roosevelt's corporate state because it violated their
constitutional rights.

But did the Schechter Brothers case kill the goose that laid the
golden eggs in the process of defending individual freedom, as
many Roosevelt supporters claimed at the time? Not very likely.
As this essay attempts to document, the record shows political
elites to be less able to make correct economic decisions than individuals freely interacting in the marketplace. And this is true
regardless of whether, on the Soviet model, these decisions were
imposed by a single dictator or, on the "corporate state" model
favored by many neoliberals, were the outcome of negotiations
between the captains of industry, union leaders, and government
officials.

Theoretically, the most important reason for this outcome relates to the question of knowledge. The interactions of buyers and
sellers "automatically" clear competitive markets where prices
and quantities are free to adjust. Gluts eliminate themselves by
reducing prices. Shortages disappear by causing prices to increase.
The question is where the political elites get the "superhuman"
knowledge to avoid setting "glut prices" or "shortage prices"—
that is, how they choose prices precisely at the point where quantity demanded is equated with quantity supplied. Despite the fact

that we live in a high-tech computer age, there still is no way around this fundamental knowledge problem, which was pointed out by Nobel Laureate Friedrich A. Hayek in his early attacks on socialism.

Neoliberals like Reich and Lester Thurow place great faith in "engineered" comparative advantage. They trust politicians to pick the industries that, with a little help from their friends, can become winners in big-time competitive markets. "Engineered" comparative advantage can best be explained by a simple example. Consider a midget who wants to play professional basketball. There are only two ways the midget can possibly compete. The first is for someone to tie the feet or the arms of the big guys; the other is to give the midget a pair of stilts. Both involve subsidies to the midget. The first is an indirect subsidy analogous to protection by a tariff, for example. The neoliberals are against this politicization as unproductive. The second is a direct subsidy— and the neoliberals consider this politicization to be enlightened. Though both come to the same thing, they are in favor of one but against the other.

Will the midget ever grow up and be able to compete without subsidization? That is what the engineers of comparative advantage are betting on. But how do the policy elites who give the subsidies know which recipients will make it on the international competitive market and which not? The overwhelming experience with industrial subsidies is that losers in the marketplace with political clout get subsidized and stay that way—that is, losing and subsidized. The winners do not need such help.

5

EUGENE BARDACH

Implementing Industrial Policy

While one may believe, even believe very strongly, that "industrial policy" will not make us any wealthier or happier or freer or friendlier to one another, it is impossible to be sure. After all, industrial policy has not yet been tried in this country, so who has good evidence? But, say the critics, many elements of industrial policy have indeed been tried, and have often disappointed. Yes, concede the proponents, but from now on things will be different; having learned from past mistakes, we will design future policy so as to avoid them. Is this not conceivable? Yes, it is conceivable, even possible. But it is not likely.

Policies begin with hope and aspiration and, if they survive the legislative process, end up as agencies and committees and negotiating relationships and operating routines. (This, at any rate, is true of policies that contemplate ongoing activities rather than the achievement of a one-time effect.) That is to say, no policy is complete without being embodied in the institutional

91

forms and processes of government. Policy hopes and aspirations
float in the realm of pure spirit, and if they do not get taken up in
some more corporeal form they might as well not exist. Yet once
they do, they are in every way transformed. The joining of spirit
and flesh, of idea and institution, creates a genuinely new and separate entity, an entity with a life and dynamism of its own. To put
it a little differently, policy instruments, or implements, are not
neutral and inert; they lead lives of their own. Unfortunately, the
recorded natural history of many species of policy implements is
spotted with failures and a number of highly destructive episodes.

Therefore, if we want to explore the prospects for industrial
policy, we must make some assumptions about the character of
the implements that will be fashioned to give it effect. If these implements look familiar enough, furthermore, we may be able to
offer reasonable predictions, based on experience, about the success or failure of the policy ideas behind them. Thus, while
acknowledging the impossibility of saying much with certainty
about industrial policy, which is admittedly new and unproven, we
are on much firmer ground if we prognosticate about the performance of the implements to be used in executing it, a subject about
which at least some theory and evidence are available. From what
I have seen, the proponents of industrial policy have not offered
very specific blueprints describing the means of implementation.
However, a major objective behind industrial policy is to "coordinate" the various elements of tariff policy, export policy, labor adjustment policy, and so on, which advocates claim are presently
disconnected and "incoherent." More specifically, these are:

- Protectionist measures against imports, including both tariff
  and nontariff measures.

- Subsidies or other forms of assistance to exports.

- Adjustment assistance to workers and communities affected by
  irreversible economic decline.

- Subsidies to, and stimulation of, research and development.

- Measures to upgrade the technical skills of the U.S. workforce.

- Antitrust policy, in regard to its effect on industry structure.

- Assistance in the development (or maintenance) of physical in-

frastructure needed for industrial development (or maintenance).

- Risk-sharing with industry in the form of direct loans and loan
guarantees.

- Tax policy to stimulate investment.

- Government procurement policy.

Nothing but a very large and very independent agency, ap-
proaching or even achieving Department status, could serve to
"coordinate" these policies. Let us call it the Agency for Industrial
Policy (AIP). The Agency would bundle together a large number of
the bureaus and offices and agencies and programs and commissions currently dotting the governmental landscape and playing
some role in implementing any of the ten functions listed above.

Of the new elements—those that had not existed prior to adoption of the new industrial policy—that would probably appear in
the AIP, only one is worth discussing, but it is very important indeed. It is the organization that would channel credit through
direct loans, loan guarantees, and subsidized loans to worthy industries, sectors, and firms. Felix Rohatyn, the most vocal advocate of such an entity, has called it a "modern Reconstruction Finance Corporation."[1] Let us call it, generically, the "Bank." Proponents of industrial policy are by no means united on the
desirability of a large-scale Bank. However, even more than "coordination," it is the most original and eye-catching feature of "industrial policy" as that phrase is currently used. Vice-President
Walter Mondale has endorsed a version of the Bank called the
"Bank for Industrial Competitiveness," proposed in a House bill
introduced by Rep. John LaFalce.[2]

The Bank and the AIP, then, are the two implements of industrial policy that we will examine in this chapter. While there
are certainly many others, such as grants-in-aid to education and
subsidies to university-based researchers and tax breaks for U.S.
exporters, these are not *new* implements or policies, and each of
these would be more appropriately treated in a volume devoted to
education policy or tax policy or science policy. In the next section
we consider the prognosis for the Bank; and following that we
return to the AIP, of which the Bank is likely to be a part.

Prospects for the Bank

An implementation analysis of the Bank must recognize that the
"implement" in question, the Bank, will evolve over time and that
its evolution will be greatly affected by—and will in turn affect—
perceptions of its ongoing performance and dilemmas. Basic
parameters, however, would be set by its initial legal as well as political mandate. This mandate is likely to be many-faceted, internally contradictory, and deliberately ambiguous, for it will reflect
the multiplicity of interests that will be built into its founding
coalition.

Some constituencies will want a Bank to promote growth at
home and competitiveness abroad. Others will see the Bank as a
way to channel funds into declining industries, particularly those
with employees who vote in their own districts. Still others will
want the Bank to play a lead role in helping to coordinate and
bring coherence to the other elements of industrial policy within
the AIP. They will see the leverage of the Bank as important in
playing this "lead agency" role. Still others—very few others—
will want to see the Bank as the first step on the road to "economic
planning," or at least as pointing the way to a larger role for
government in the allocation of capital in the economy, mainly
because they distrust government less than they distrust "Wall
Street" and other symbols of finance capitalism. Still others will
see in the Bank an opportunity—a vehicle—to test, nay, to prove,
their faith in "cooperation" among business, labor, and governmental elites as a way of accomplishing great social projects.

Many of the constituencies described above distrust one
another, and some might fail to support the Bank concept if they
believed that others would dominate. There are, after all, built-in
conflicts among all these objectives. However, most of these constituencies would obtain at least symbolic satisfaction. The Bank's
mandate would contain words, and operational authority, that
gave hope to as wide a range of constituencies as possible. The
founders of the Bank would reason, correctly, that a task as large
as "reindustrializing America" or "restoring national productivity" would need to transcend narrow interests, that it would
need support over the long haul, and that it would need to mobilize
a broad political consensus.

At the same time, everyone would agree that the Bank should in no way be "politicized." The legislative mandate will contain language to this effect, as will the legislative history. The legal form of the Bank will probably be some sort of independent government corporation like the Synfuels Corporation or the TVA, which were also intended to be proof against "politicization." A Board of Directors will be assembled that will be explicitly bipartisan or nonpartisan and will draw its membership from business, labor, and government. The idea will be to protect the Bank against politics not by sanitizing it but by neutralizing and diluting its immediate political environment. As with the Synfuels Corporation, multiyear funding will be assured by Congress, at least during the Bank's first phase of life.

All these measures and no doubt others will help the Bank protect itself against the crudest expressions of vote-pandering in the Congress. However, an entity that is financed at least in part by taxes and that owes its existence and authority to government ultimately needs to develop a source of political support *somewhere.* If key congressional elites will not be its support, another source must be found. The presidency, for instance. Or the national Democratic party. Or a coalition of Republican financiers, laborite Democrats, and the liberal media elite. In the long run, the Bank's lending policies will have to win favor from enough well-situated constituencies to permit it to continue with its work.

First, let us consider how the Bank will carry out its mandate to promote American economic growth and productivity. A central argument by industrial policy advocates is that there are economies of scale in the cumulation of high-skills activities and industries and sectors, and that because these tend not to be realized in the profits of individual firms, they do not enter the calculations of managers and investors. It is worth quoting one theorist at some length on this point, because in the abstract the theory sounds compelling:

Comparative advantage is a dynamic and multidimensional phenomenon. This means that policy measures can change comparative advantage—development of a skilled labor force, achievement of economic scales of production, linkages between different types of symbiotic industries, and so on—and are in some sense the result of dynamic evolution, one in which policy has in the past played an important role in some countries. Policies based on a dynamic view of comparative advantage lie behind Japanese IP [industrial policy] and appear to have been one of the important factors in the recent success stories of economic growth in the Southeast Asian countries.[3]

The important question is whether government officials working for the Bank and/or the AIP will in fact be able to create the so-called "linkages between different types of symbiotic industries" better than the natural dynamics of the marketplace. The answer is that if they do so their success will have been produced entirely by good luck, for at present there are simply no proven intellectual and analytical tools with which to decide what dynamic combinations are worth stimulating or how to go about it. Here is the testimony of Charles L. Schultze, chairman of the Council of Economic Advisers from 1977 to 1980 and presently a senior fellow at the Brookings Institution, who is relying on the research of Assar Lindbeck of the University of Stockholm:

What a country will specialize in is determined by a combination of historical coincidence and momentum. Individual entrepreneurs search for a niche in the market. Once one or more firms in a country successfully establish a foothold in the market for some special product, forces come into play that can heighten, at least for a while, that country's comparative advantage in the manufacture of that product. A growing market leads to economies of scale for the original producers. Ancillary firms spring up to supply the new industry's special needs. Workers and managers acquire skills and know-how. Success tends to breed success.

In short, the winners emerge from a very individualistic search process, only loosely governed by broad national advantages in relative labor, capital, or natural resource costs. The competence, knowledge, and specific attributes that go with successful entrepreneurship and export capability are so narrowly defined and so fine-grained that they cannot be assigned to any particular nation. The "winners" come from a highly decentralized search process, the results of which cannot be identified on the basis of abstract criteria. As Lindbeck points out, there is nothing in Swedish natural resources or national character that would have foreordained that Sweden would be preeminent in the production of ball bearings, safety matches, cream separators, and automatic lighthouses. Nor, it might be added, is there a basis in observable national characteristics to have predicted Japanese dominance in the motorcycle industry or the American success in pharmaceuticals and the export of construction management and design.[4]

Unfortunately, the analysts and directors who develop the Bank's lending strategies are likely to have quite different views.

They will imagine that they are able to fathom the secrets of successful economic development. They will be guided by nothing more than fashion, however, or more correctly a combination of fashions, those they themselves fancy and those that politically influential figures in their environment also fancy.

For instance, it is a certainty that the Bank will tend disproportionately to favor projects with a touch of technological glamor. Robert Reich's paean to the products Japan has favored— "precision castings, specialty steel, special chemicals, . . . sensor devices, . . . fiber-optic cable, fine ceramics, lasers, large-scale integrated circuits, and advanced aircraft engines"—leaves no doubt that in his view we are well advised to do the same.[5] Whatever might be the merits of expanding, say, the gypsum wallboard industry (and indeed I have no idea what they are), such dull and graceless products will definitely not attract the attention of the Bank's loan officials and directors.

While certain subtle strategies to promote the diffusion of one or another technical innovation might be warranted,[6] governmental loans or credit guarantees to particular firms or industries, however high-tech, are not one of them. There is no *a priori* reason to think that private capital and credit markets significantly undernourish the high-technology sector or particular firms within it. Nor is there reason to believe that government decision-making in this area would be any better than that of private lenders and investors. Indeed, it is likely to be a lot worse; because government officials would in effect be spending taxpayer funds, they would be more likely to support excessively risky and imprudent ventures (unless, of course, the officials were so eager to avoid such accusations that they did the opposite).

On the other hand, the advocates of government support for high-tech industries may be less concerned with possible imperfections in the capital market than with those in the labor market. The main difficulty here is that the education and training of the country's labor force depends in large measure not on the market but on public-sector management of the system of schooling. Surely this system should be improved, and the investment in technical training courses should probably be enhanced, but neither the quality nor the scope of our educational system would be better dealt with if we called them issues of "industrial policy."

Besides technological glamor, what other fads might attract the Bank's attention and capital? National prestige, for one. In pursuit of prestige the British and French built the Concorde, the United States escaped by a hair's breadth from creating its own supersonic white elephant, and France invested heavily in a failed effort to create its own national computer industry. (Of course, since among the Western developed countries national prestige almost always involves items of technological glamor, there is considerable overlap between prestige-mongering and technology-mongering.) Energy conservation might be another attractive fad. Could anything be more natural than for the Bank to sponsor a high-tech "industrial park" in the desert powered entirely by the latest technology in solar collectors or photovoltaic cells? The motifs of conservation, planning, new technology, and "demonstration effects" merge irresistibly. Inasmuch as industrial policy advocates argue that private enterprise is too conservative, a third fad could be "boldness" for its own sake. The Bank would support large-scale and highly visible projects like the planned Westway development in New York City or the San Francisco Bay Area Rapid Transit system, both of which show highly negative benefit-cost relationships.[7] Lured by "boldness," the Bank could well expand its desert-based solar-powered high-tech industrial park into an "integrated, balanced planned community," thereby adding "planning" to the motifs to which it pays homage.

It is important to note that faddish ideas are not necessarily crackpot ideas. It will not be possible to screen out the winners and the losers on the basis of initial plausibility or the lack thereof. As Lindbeck and Schultze remind us, development is truly evolutionary, full of surprises. The advantage of private industry relative to government, however, is that the market runs a swifter and rather more effective process for scrutinizing the results of the millions of experiments being tried out in any year in the economy; the half-life of an unsuccessful experiment is probably measured in months. Mistakes in government can persist much longer, perhaps forever. Leaders are loathe to admit to them, and powerful constituencies grow up that benefit from their continuation.[8]

That the Bank will channel credit to firms, industries, and sectors in distress is certain. This will be, if not the most important, then the second most important mandate the Bank will receive.

Yet the originators of the mandate, and the Bank directors, will not intend that the Bank should bail out every failing concern in the country. They will bridle at the thought that the Bank's rescue efforts might be promiscuous rather than decorously selective. Yet it is hard to see how promiscuity can be prevented. Hundreds of thousands of businesses, and even more plants and parts of plants, fail in any given year. Even if the Bank is strictly defined as a lender of last resort, the pool of potential applicants is huge. Hence, allocational criteria will have to be found. The number of affected employees will be the most important criterion, so big businesses will be favored. This will lead to a second criterion. Once a "big business bias" is observed (or predicted), "small business" will be elevated as an explicit criterion, and a "set-aside" program will probably be created. This will only continue a widespread and possibly self-defeating practice already prevalent in government procurement practices.[9] A third allocational criterion will probably be the potential for "turnaround." But do not all faltering-but-not-yet-dead enterprises have this potential? It is unlikely that adequacy of collateral will serve as an allocative criterion either. The Small Business Administration's 7(a) loan program requires the borrower to put up collateral, but the SBA is not always too fussy about its adequacy or recoverability in the event of default, and losses have been substantial.[10]

Some arguments for the Bank have been predicated on its replacing an admittedly vulnerable Congress as the governmental institution that absorbs demands for bailout assistance of the Chrysler and Lockheed variety. According to Charles Walker and Mark A. Bloomfield, for instance, it would be run by "a hardnosed, take-charge financial type accustomed to driving hard bargains and making them stick."[11] It is very difficult to say just how much pressure such an institution would be able to withstand. It is easy, on the other hand, to reason that it would be less successful than the Congress and the President. True, it might have more *will* than these explicitly political organs to ignore the pleas of petitioners, though bureaucratic incentives to maintain and enhance the Bank's function are a force to be reckoned with. Yet will is not the only thing that counts. The legislative process is time-consuming, unpredictable, and accessible principally to interests capable of spending large sums of money on lobbying activities and able to mobilize large numbers of voters. The reefs and shoals of the legislative process discourage most would-be claimants from even attempting to navigate its waters, and bring low the great majority of those with the temerity to make the attempt. These hazards originate in the disproportionate power of minorities in the Congress. While it is concentrated minorities in the electorate that can mobilize Congress to "bail out" particular industries or firms, it is also a set of concentrated minorities— many Republicans and conservative Democrats, and representatives from districts not likely to enjoy federal largesse for distressed industries or firms—that are positioned to frustrate and delay and block the efforts of the rescuing party. The relatively more orderly and routinized workings of even a tough, businesslike Bank would make the federal Treasury much more accessible to smaller interests with less money and with fewer voters behind them.

The case of the old Reconstruction Finance Corporation (RFC) is instructive here. The RFC began its life in a useful sort of way. Created in 1932 by Herbert Hoover, it blossomed under Roosevelt and acquired the important function in the Depression of salvaging the nation's banks. Here was a clear-cut mission that public but not private capital could perform. The banks were threatened because depositors lacked confidence in each other not to start runs. No market can work at all unless the participants have reason to believe their transactions will be completed as anticipated, and capital markets are more vulnerable than most to insecurities on this score. The RFC was able to infuse enough new capital into the private banking system to rebuild depositor confidence; and, as a public agency ultimately backed by taxpayer dollars, it did not itself have to rely on the good will and confidence of private lenders.[12]

The RFC did not, however, end its career when this and some other useful sectoral rescue missions were accomplished. In the postwar period, the RFC became transformed from an emergency financial institution into a national investment bank. In 1940, the agency had made 1,125 business loans totaling $68,803,000. In 1947 the number of loans was up ninefold and their value mounted to $393,000,000. For fiscal 1950, loans totaled over half a billion dollars. The Truman administration, deeply fearing another depression, urged the RFC to "lend more, lend faster, and lend to the right ones. So its loan policy was not a policy but a blank check."[13] One result was a large number of loans to very weak businesses. Almost half the 103 loans sampled by a congressional investigating committee showed the RFC funds being used to refinance debts to banks, insurance companies, and other private lenders who wanted to escape the risks associated with their clients' businesses.[14] Another result was the allocation of credit to businesses of doubtful importance to the public interest, such as casinos and rattlesnake farms. Loans were made to a host of businesses and individuals whose merits consisted solely of their political significance to the Truman administration and the Democratic National Committee. Finally, bribery and other forms of corruption infected the top echelons of the RFC; and this more than anything else was the cause of the agency's demise.

Naturally, a contemporary RFC-type Bank would attempt to prevent the scandals and improprieties of the old RFC. Snake farms and mob-supported hotels and casinos would be taboo. In addition, because the catalogue of public vices has grown enormously since the early 1940s, the Bank would ideally like also to avoid lending to firms that ostentatiously foul the environment, that follow racist or otherwise discriminatory policies in hiring and promoting employees, and that tolerate large numbers of employee injuries. Unfortunately, in the normal course of things a certain percentage of the Bank's loans will find their way into the hands of firms and individuals with reputations for one or another vice, whether deservedly or not. In order to prevent these mistakes from happening too often, and more importantly, to protect itself from criticism when they do happen, the Bank could require applicants to certify that they are in compliance with a host of statutes and regulations, as is now the case for major contractors and grant recipients. In many cases, would-be borrowers would face a genuine compliance problem, not necessarily because they are wrongdoers but because the rules to which they must adhere are themselves overinclusive and unreasonably stringent.[15]

In all cases, much paperwork would be required. This would come on top of the already considerable paperwork caused by most applicants' marginal creditworthiness and the Bank's consequent need to check collateral and personal characteristics especially

closely. A survey of banks participating in the SBA's loan
guarantee program, for example, found that 91 percent claimed
that SBA documents were more complex than those associated
with regular commercial loans. Fully twice as many nonparticipat-
ing banks (72 percent) complained about the excessive paperwork
as did the participating banks (35 percent), thereby suggesting
that the paperwork burden was a significant deterrent to bank
participation. The paperwork and the associated clearance procedures also contributed to lengthy delays. Forty-two percent of
the participating banks complained about these. The average
turnaround time from the borrower's first contact with the bank
to the receipt of funds (in cases where the loan was approved) was
114 days, and of course a good many cases must show delays much
longer than this.[16]

So far we have been discussing the evolution of the Bank as it
attempts to win friends and supporters. But an equally important
survival requirement is to placate and neutralize critics. One fear
voiced by critics of the Bank proposal I believe may be discounted
—namely, the prospect that the Bank will lead the country down
the road to national planning if not "socialism." It is not that some
Bank advocates would not desire this, but they are few and
relatively powerless. Power aside, the Bank could of course lead
the country down this collectivist road by drift, inadvertence,
stupidity, and bad luck. Too many forces are posed, however, to
allow movement very far in this direction. The Bank directors will
remember the fate of Franklin Roosevelt's National Resources
Planning Board, which was summarily abolished by a suspicious
Congress. While tolerance for the rhetoric of "planning" and
centralized management may have grown slightly since the early
1940s, the deep reservoirs of populistic conservatism in the mass
electorate guarantee that the Bank will not turn us into either a
socialist paradise or a nightmare.

The most passionate critics of the Bank will be the competitors
of those firms that have successfully secured loans. They will
question the wisdom of a system that seems, to them, arbitrarily to
favor one commercial rival over another. They may attempt to
block the making of such loans in the event that they have timely
warning of a competitor's pending coup. Or, crying for fairness,
they might queue up behind their competitor seeking loans for

themselves as well. In any event, an environment swarming with jealous competitors is a threat to be neutralized, and the Bank will look for ways to do so. One strategy is to make sure that all the jealous competitors are foreigners, who normally have little political power. The implication is to favor our export industries and firms. (A similar implication, buttressed also by the desire to protect jobs from foreign competition, is to do nothing to help domestic importers.) A second strategy is to make loans to *all* the firms in a given sector or industry. An ideal candidate for this strategy is an industry with relatively few, but large, firms— large, because administrative inconvenience is reduced and the political visibility of the loans is increased—that are also battling foreign imports.[17] Steel and autos come quickly to mind.

In the current political debate, the alarm of unfair competition is less likely to be raised by angry business firms than by aggrieved regions and states, which will in effect speak for adversely affected employee interests. Geographical interests can also throw more weight around, since congressional representatives and senators, dependent as they are on geographically defined constituencies, are more responsive to "Sun Belt/Frost Belt" sorts of pressures than to pressures from several firms or even the better part of an industry (which pressures are not always easy to organize in any case). The Bank's strategy for dealing with this will probably be to adopt a set of internal (and confidential) "guidelines" for use by loan officers that identify geographical "problem areas" where "less than adequate attention has been paid."

All these things will happen not because the Bank wants to be narrowly "political" or opportunistic, but because it must, like any other governmental institution in our society aiming to survive over the long run, embody or at least pay tribute to notions of democratic virtue. It must be at least minimally popular, accountable, prudent with taxpayer funds, environmentally sensitive, racially unbiased, fair to commercial competitors, and "equitable" to domestic regional interests. Given that there is considerable latitude anyway in the Bank's mandate to go forth and do economic good, it is conceivable that democratic virtue could be accommodated by productive virtue: loan proposals essentially "tied" on the latter grounds could be secondarily ranked on the former grounds. It is hard to imagine, though, how the world could sort itself out that nicely. Trade-offs between the two virtues would seem inevitable. Democratic virtue will almost surely substitute for productive virtue in fair measure. Whether one evaluates the Bank positively or negatively in the last analysis will depend on where one believes the optimal mix of productive virtue and democratic virtue is located. For those who have no patience at all with the latter, the conclusion is clear from the outset. Those who believe in some admixture of democratic virtue in the productive economy will have to decide how much is too much and whether the Bank is likely to furnish too much.

The Quest for "Coherence"

Recall the ten functions of industrial policy that might plausibly be regrouped in whole or in part under a new Agency for Industrial Policy. Critics as well as advocates of industrial policy are united in believing that these functions are now relatively uncoordinated and that such coordination as there is appears to be ad hoc. The critics of industrial policy choose either not to see in this lack of explicit coordination a problem, or else to remain silent about it. Proponents of industrial policy, on the other hand, believe that we are sacrificing "coherence." We cannot, say the proponents, now choose *not* to have an industrial policy, since most of the elements are in place already and are having their effects on the economy, albeit unintentionally. We can only choose, they claim, between following an unconscious and uncoordinated policy and bringing together the various pieces into a more self-conscious and "coherent" whole.[18]

I do not find in the writings of industrial policy advocates a clear statement about the meaning or purpose of "coherence." Its character and beneficence are simply assumed. This assumption requires examination, however, and for us to do so requires a stipulation as to what the quest for coherence probably aims to achieve. I would posit the two goals of (1) substituting more beneficial (less costly) policy elements for less beneficial (more costly) elements, and (2) achieving a synergy among the several constituent elements of industrial policy, or at least preventing the occurrence of its opposite, mutual cancellation and frustration. We consider the effect of coherence on these two objectives in turn.

Proponents of industrial policy are generally agreed that protectionist measures are undesirable, and these are high on their list of noxious elements to be displaced by invoking a more coherent industrial policy. Certainly protectionism is costly to consumers and economically wasteful. Tariffs and kindred measures introduce rigidities into the composition of employment, in that workers (and other resources) remain too long in high-cost domestic industries rather than switching to more competitive industries. Yet tariffs and other types of import barriers are aggressively sought by workers and firms threatened by foreign manufacturers. These interests are often aided, moreover, by firms and by workers in other industries who fear that their profits and jobs will be threatened in the foreseeable future too. Support from businesses and from state and local governments indirectly affected by private-sector job loss enters the combination as well. The result is intense pressure on the Congress and the President to furnish protection of one kind or another: tariffs, import quotas, negotiated "orderly market agreements" and other such "voluntary" restraints on imports, discriminatory regulatory treatment of imported products, "domestic content" requirements on items (notably autos) produced at home with some foreign-made component, and "Buy-American" practices (whether explicit or implicit).

There is at least some possibility that industrial policy could somehow contain or reverse the protectionist tide by offering a superior substitute to the affected interests, that is, a substitute that would prevent damage to jobs and capital assets while not introducing all the indirect economic losses associated with tariffs. The Trade Adjustment Assistance provisions of the Trade Act of 1974 represented just such a strategy. Under this program workers who lost employment due to import competition have been able to receive extended unemployment benefits (up to a year rather than twenty-six weeks), retraining, and relocation assistance. (The Trade Adjustment Assistance Program has now been effectively displaced by the Job Training Partnership Act of 1982, which supplies over $200 million annually to the states to assist displaced workers.) Moreover, one could imagine that, under the rubric of industrial policy, agreement by the government to invest in research and development benefiting the threatened industry could be exchanged for agreement by firms and by workers in the industry to forego tariff and nontariff protection. Or the assistance might be linked to the implementation of an industry "plan" to adjust in some way, which might be allowed under our antitrust laws, say, provided the AIP approved it.

The objection to such reasoning is that putative *alternatives* to protectionism would almost assuredly become *adjuncts* to it. Trade adjustment assistance under the 1974 act has been heavily utilized by automobile workers, but this fact has not stopped the UAW from lobbying vigorously for domestic content legislation. Large subsidies of all kinds, from monies for R&D to loans for individual vessels to a policy of buying breaded fish sticks for the school lunch program, have flowed to the American fishing industry, but the industry has still done all that it could to exclude foreign fishing vessels from American waters.[19] In fact, the very existence of nonprotectionist assistance to an industry in order to deal with the problems of foreign competition is *prima facie* acknowledgment of the legitimacy of helping the industry with protectionist measures as well. After all, if the industry did not "need" protection, why is it getting all those other forms of aid? Indeed, in some contexts one could imagine that protectionism would recommend itself politically as a *more* attractive way to help industry than would subsidies, for the latter are often financed out of the government budget whereas the erection of import barriers is financed indirectly through higher product prices. As for protectionism's high cost in the systematic misallocation of resources, these may be unnoticed altogether. Most importantly, in the absence of import protection the government's subsidy costs go up!

Another problem with the alleged substitution theory is that, even if it worked, the result might still be detrimental. This is true in the case of R&D, for example. Since we may assume that the total sum of government resources to support R&D is finite, it is not necessarily a wise investment to direct them disproportionately to import-threatened industries when other industries might in fact furnish much more productive opportunities.

Let us turn now to the objective of increasing synergy (or, at a minimum, decreasing self-defeating conflict and entropy). Synergy entails combining things in such a way as to get something more out of the whole than simply the sum of the parts. A possible example would be using the threat of countervailing tariffs in negotiating import restrictions or bargaining for fewer restrictions on our own exports. However, I believe that the quest for coherence, and the synergy that might follow from it, aims at grander effects. I would imagine that the ideal-typical synergistic intervention by the AIP would involve utilizing the Bank to guarantee a loan:

- to a firm that was on the verge of achieving a dramatic technical breakthrough in reducing the costs of production but would not have done so without government assistance. And,

- the breakthrough was such that it could be readily diffused among all firms in the industry once it had been demonstrated in one firm or plant. And,

- the industry in question was rescued from a deluge of West German and Japanese imports. And,

- the main plants in the industry employed large numbers of workers and were located in the Frost Belt. And,

- the product being supported was widely used in American industry and the reduced cost of supplying it to industry would reduce American product prices in a variety of areas (what Magaziner and Reich call a "linkage" industry).[20] And,

- the new markets thus created signaled an opportunity for America to upgrade the skills and technical practices of its work force.

I leave aside whether such remarkable investment opportunities, or even close approximations to them, exist and can be better identified by government agencies than by the private sector. What would the AIP do if it could find one? Could it exploit the opportunity effectively? It is exceedingly unlikely.

Government agencies do not have a very good record of accomplishing even medium-scale efforts at development assistance, much less very complex ones. Jeffrey Pressman and Aaron Wildavsky have described, for instance, the four-year-long failure of the Economic Development Administration to help World Airways build a new hangar, which was conditioned on World's promise to provide jobs for the long-term unemployed in Oakland, California.[21]

More recently, Margaret Dewar has provided a lengthy account
of failed efforts by the federal government to bail out the New
England fishing industry. Two failures are particularly instructive. One was the "Seafreeze Atlantic" project, a $3 million sub-
sidy to American Stern Trawlers to build a relatively high-tech
"factory ship" of the type then (1966) coming into use by the fishing fleets of other nations. Alas, the project was battered by the
human elements. American Stern Trawlers offered low wages and
few fishermen applied for jobs; many of those hired had never
been to sea on a fishing vessel before; those who had were not used
to spending three months traveling to and working in far-off fishing grounds but were accustomed to the 7–10 day voyages of the
traditional New England fleet; the crew's inexperience hindered
them in sorting out the problems encountered with the fancy new
trawling gear aboard; and German officers directed the fishing
while "most of the fishermen were immigrants who could not understand the officers' instructions." Each time the ship put into
port, nearly all the crew resigned, and on one such occasion the
crew virtually mutinied and "went on a rampage of vandalizing
the boat."[22]

The second instructive failure comes from the project of the
Bureau of Commercial Fisheries to increase consumer demand by
raising the quality of the fish landed by New England Boats. In
1957 the Bureau publicized voluntary guidelines for sanitation
and product inspection, visited processing plants, and accompanied the fishermen on their voyages to demonstrate improved
methods of handling fish. However, once the Bureau's experts had
departed the scene the fishermen and processors stopped observing the new guidelines, and the industry was left only with the
"minimal requirements enforced by the Food and Drug Administration and the state inspectors in shore plants."[23] These two
cases illustrate one of the main lessons learned by the students of
policy implementation in recent years. Successful implementation
requires the harmonization of complex and multiple resources
widely dispersed among private firms and workers and a variety
of public agencies in different levels of government. Government
project managers work very hard at fashioning and delivering the
resources they can in fact control but are then reduced merely to
hoping for the best with regard to the availability and suitability

of the ones they can't. Because the interests that control these other resources normally do not see things quite the way the government project managers do, their vision being affected by their own situations and prospects, the required cooperation is only infrequently forthcoming.[24]

In some degree, this problem is well understood by the current generation of policymakers and their advisers, and undoubtedly the designers of the AIP will attempt to mitigate the problem. *Faute de mieux,* they will look mainly to organizational and procedural solutions. For instance, they will try to capture as many disparate bureaucratic entities as possible for the AIP in the hopes of "improving coordination." Very likely even the Bank would, for many purposes, be included as an administrative subunit of the AIP, though it would be given much policy and budgetary autonomy.

This first large problem that AIP designers will face will be the reluctance of most existing bureaucratic entities to be transferred, since in most cases they would face a decline in power and status. Some will probably be able to resist successfully. Perhaps chunks from the Department of Commerce will be the easiest to pry loose, inasmuch as most of the functions of the AIP will be close to those of Commerce and the Commerce Department bureaus and agencies would reason that they could dominate the new organization. It is perhaps indicative that President Reagan's proposal for a new Department of International Trade and Industry (DITI) would be based on Commerce's International Trade Administration, other Commerce Department offices, and the Office of the U.S. Trade Representative.[25] But what would the dominance of Commerce entail for the office in the Labor Department that administers trade adjustment assistance and that also might be moved? Or the State Department's Bureau of Economic and Business Affairs? They would almost certainly not wish to leave their present environment for a territory controlled either by a traditional rival (Commerce, for the Labor people) or by a lower-status group of functionaries (Commerce, to the State Department).

Of course, certain administrative entities will not be brought into the new Agency under any conceivable scenario. The procurement functions of the Defense Department and of the General Services Administration will remain where they are. The R&D

functions of the Energy Department and the Defense Department will stay put. Clearly the Treasury Department will not yield its authority over many important tax issues. Entities like these are simply too important to too many policies besides industrial policy to relocate them in the AIP.

A time-proven proposition from the public administration literature on the effects of reorganization is that reorganization does not usually alter much the propensity of subunits to coordinate their work. If the units did not work well together before the amalgamation, it is unlikely their relations will improve by much afterwards. Quite properly, each bureau or office that legitimately claims, or is given, "a piece of the action" must look to perform its own specialized function competently and accountably. The bureau in charge of promoting R&D, for instance, will not look kindly on attempts by the bureau in charge of retraining and relocating displaced workers to give the latter's clients preferred access, let us say, to jobs with one of its own contract recipients. Nor will the division responsible for making subsidized loans to communities seeking to develop the infrastructure for industrial parks appreciate being told by the division in charge of loan guarantees for high-tech small businesses that their geographical ordering of priorities is all wrong and should be altered to conform to the latter's ordering. In our system of government, conflicts such as these are legitimate, endemic, and almost never resolved by hierarchical decision. Hierarchical decisions by the top management of the AIP may, over time, shift the balance of forces in a given direction; but because they are always vulnerable to changes in political forces and to turnover in personnel, "decisions" are never permanent and the conflict among subordinates is never fully resolved.

How will the Agency manage the residual (but not small) level of internal conflict and mutual disdain? Various procedural solutions will be installed. Constituent bureaus and offices will be linked by coordinating committees. Multiple copies of applications for loans, grants, contracts, adjustment assistance, subsidies, tariffs, antitrust exemption advice, etc., will routinely be submitted to all of the offices and bureaus, both within and outside the AIP, that might somehow be pertinent to the proposal. Project groups and task forces will come and go with the needs of the moment. But the likely efficacy of all these devices is very limited. In fact, there is a substantial probability that all these formal and informal attempts, by creating new bureaucratic stakes to argue over and multiplying the number of frictional contacts, will make matters worse.[26]

Congress is another source of disorder and "incoherence." Even if the AIP is able to effect a certain amount of useful reordering among bureaus internally, it is exceedingly unlikely that Congress, with its maze of committees and subcommittees and its deeply institutionalized reluctance to rationalize and reallocate committee powers, will move rapidly to reorganize its oversight functions so as to conform neatly to the new order of administration. Because the oversight function is combined, albeit sometimes indirectly, with budgetary influence, congressional committees and subcommittees can and do exercise a great deal of effective power over agencies. An unreorganized Congress, therefore, can potentially cancel whatever benefit executive-branch reorganization might achieve.

Undoubtedly, the prospects for greater coordination and coherence would be improved if the AIP, in its day-to-day work, could rely on a clear-cut, detailed, and intellectually defensible economic and political doctrine. It is hard to see what it might be, however. Phrases like "competitiveness abroad," or "transition to higher value-added industries," or "assistance to troubled producers" do not imply very much about how to act in specific cases. And there is certainly no formula for finding the optimum balance between allocating resources to helping prospective winners versus assisting possible losers. Instead of coherence and coordination, therefore, the main achievement of an AIP may be to bring most of the chaos together in one place where it can more easily be mocked and deplored by media pundits and academics.

Industrial Policy as Upside-Down Energy Policy

Not everything about industrial policy is bad for our economic and political health. The advocates of industrial policy are almost certainly correct in saying that we need to spend more money, and spend it more wisely, on research and development. Antitrust policy needs to be adjusted so as to permit more joint research and

development efforts, as well as more collaborative efforts to promote exports by competitor firms. Substantial improvements are
needed in our education system, from kindergarten through graduate school. Improving strategies and tactics for opening foreign
markets to freer trade is always a worthwhile item for the foreign
policy agenda. More effective measures to assist workers in ac-
quiring new skills and to relocate their homes and families are in
order. And surely there is no substitute for a successful (and
lucky) macroeconomic policy. However, none of this requires an
RFC-type Bank to allocate capital, or a central Agency for Industrial Policy (called by whatever name) to "coordinate" these
and other policies into a "coherent" whole.

It is these last two measures that appear to me to constitute the
core of the "industrial policy" concept currently being debated.
Thus understood, industrial policy is an insubstantial phantom at
best or a destructive poltergeist at worst. There is no good reason
to invite it into the halls of government.

But the invitation is being issued anyhow. The Democrats obviously like industrial policy because its bread-and-butter promises appeal to many of their constituents threatened by foreign imports, because they have little else of constructive import to offer
the electorate, and because they do not need to discuss the
specifics in order to seem plausible. It is their answer to the Republicans' supply-side economics.

For partisan competitive reasons, even the Reagan administration, which one hopes must surely know better, has countered
with its own proposal for a Department of International Trade and
Industry.

It is harder to understand the sources of support for "industrial
policy" in the business community, such as they are. To be sure,
many U.S. businessmen are adversely affected by foreign imports,
and a good many others are frustrated at their inability to export
more goods, either because the strong dollar undermines their
price-competitiveness or because they run into various national
trade barriers. But there appears to be a fascination in the business community with industrial policy that goes beyond calculations of self-interest. In a special issue entitled "The Reindustrialization of America," published in June 1980, *Business
Week* trumpeted this message:

U.S. industry has lost its competitiveness in world markets, and even business shares some blame for this decline. . . . A new social contract may be needed, along with a national policy for industry and for stimulating investment and exports. . . . The lesson of other nations, particularly Japan and Germany, is that it will [work]—if the U.S. can create a new consensus on goals.[27]

And it has not escaped notice that two of the leading partisans of industrial policy are Irving Shapiro, recently retired chairman of DuPont, and Felix Rohatyn, a prominent New York investment banker. As much as any other business and financial figures in America, these two men are regarded as business "statesmen" who aim to articulate a vision and goals for business institutions in the larger social and political environment.

No doubt it is the urge to be a statesman and, to boot, a worldly diplomat shuttling back and forth among labor, industry, and government building a policy consensus, that moves business figures such as Rohatyn and Shapiro. Their world view is of a piece with that of the self-proclaimed business statesmen of the Progressive era who favored cooperation among businessmen, clean government, and scientific public administration, and who made common cause with publicists and reformist politicians, though admittedly never with the representatives of labor.[28] Indeed, the adversarial culture that pits business against labor, special interests against the public interest, ethnic groups against each other, and everyone against the government has injured the economy, the society, and the polity. If the consensus-seeking spirit of industrial policy can improve on this culture, that will be a valuable contribution of the new Progressivism.

We can do without its rationalism, however—i.e., the mistaken belief that with the tools of reason we can define broad economic and social goals and chart in detail how to achieve them. Yet the appeal of such rationalism is deep. It promises to bring order out of chaos; it means the beginnings of mastery, the end of drift. Such too was the promise behind the idea of a "national energy policy" in the mid-1970s. As the Ford Foundation study on "America's Energy Future" put it, this was "a time to choose." Surely, said the report, "drift is . . . the worst of the alternatives before us."[29] Common solutions link national energy policy and industrial policy too: consensus, choice, governmental policy, and execution. Substitute

the word "industrial" for "energy" in the following text of the Ford
Foundation report, and almost nothing is lost in the translation:

It is our judgment that while real, workable choices exist, none of them is
easy or automatic. An energy future based on the pattern of the past will
require at least as much positive action by lawmakers, administrators,
industry leaders and citizens as one that rests upon a more conservative
energy growth rate. To manage rapid growth today without disruptive
shortages demands, among many other things, skill (and luck) in jug-
gling foreign policy entanglements, grave damage to the environment,
and soaring costs. Government must inevitably participate in making
and carrying out these hard choices.[30]

Today, ten years after the Ford report, it is easy to see that national energy policy is no longer with us. Today's market prices induce both conservation and additional supply; federal and state
environmental laws deal (alas, ineffectively and expensively) with
pollution and environmental spoilage whether energy-related or
not; and the Defense Department (aided a little by the Energy
Department's strategic petroleum reserve) is supposed to guarantee the availability of oil from the Persian Gulf. The end of national energy policy was brought about by the deregulation of oil
prices. Its one remaining vestige, the regulation of natural gas, is
scheduled to disappear very shortly, though there may be some
unfortunate delays. In retrospect, all the problems bundled
together for rhetorical purposes as "national energy policy" issues
have been better addressed separately.

The same sorts of Progressively minded intellectuals, business
leaders, and political liberals who a decade ago made much of the
alleged need for a national energy policy today assert the need for
an industrial policy. The main difference is that ten years ago
these theoreticians followed the gods of no-growth, whereas today
they have transferred fealty to the gods of high-growth. When the
gods of high-growth too lose their charm, there will be only one set
of growth gods left, those of sideways growth. I predict that in
1994 it will be observed (once again) that people live in all the
wrong places and need to be redistributed geographically. We will
then be obliged earnestly to debate issues of "residential policy."

III

Current Problems

6

MURRAY L. WEIDENBAUM and MICHAEL J. ATHEY

What Is the Rust Belt's Problem?

Are America's basic industries, pressured by overwhelming import competition, becoming an anachronistic "Rust Belt"? Must government step in to assure the survival of older, heavy industries, especially in the Midwest? Are we becoming a service economy focusing on information, hamburgers, and dress shops?

The facts available to answer these questions are undramatic, not supportive of any extreme position, and thus uncompetitive in the marketplace for public policy viewpoints. The truth of the matter is that some of this nation's heavy industry is no longer competitive and is in the process of shrinking in size and importance; steel and automobile companies have reported the most dramatic cutbacks. Yet, on balance, the answer to each of the questions is a clear "no." If there is a "Rust Belt," it is far more a question of perception than reality.

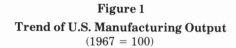

Figure 1
Trend of U.S. Manufacturing Output
(1967 = 100)

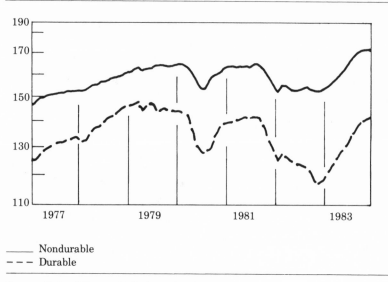

_____ Nondurable
– – – Durable

Source: *Federal Reserve Bulletin,* various issues.

Analytical Traps

By and large, American manufacturing companies—hard goods
and soft goods producers alike—are holding their own while adjusting to the business cycle. As can be seen in figure 1, both durable and nondurable manufacturing sectors in the United States
have recovered from the 1981–82 recession. By December 1983,
total industrial production had attained an all-time peak.

In view of these facts, how do we account for the gloom-and-
doom talk about the sad prospects for U.S. manufacturing industries? First of all, the casual observer tends to generalize from a
few highly publicized instances of true distress. Moreover, the
positive side of economic events is rarely considered newsworthy
and thus escapes widespread public attention.

But, perhaps most important, the authors of the new gospel of industrial policy—as well as other "megatrend" thinkers—have fallen into one of the oldest analytical traps. They have drawn heroic and long-term conclusions from the most recent data that they have seen. Many of the gloom-and-doom soothsayers were doing their writing in 1981 or 1982 when the economy was declining and, in a simpleminded fashion, they merely extrapolated that decline into the future. Such action is on a par with reacting to the spring rains by rebuilding Noah's ark.

However, to react with euphoria to news of the upturn is, of course, as silly as treating the downside of a business cycle as a fundamental and lasting new development. It is intriguing to note that some observers at the conservative end of the political spectrum are beginning to do just that. To write about the runaway boom of the 1980s is also misleading because it sets up unattainable expectations.

It is useful to examine the trend of output in key sectors of the American economy. As shown in table 1, total durable goods production dropped 11 percent from 1981 to 1982. Smaller declines occurred in the broader aggregates, such as all manufacturing and total industrial production. All three aggregate measures, however, remained substantially above the levels of the 1970s. The point is not to underestimate the severity of the recent recession. Rather, it is to perceive the underlying strength of the American economy.

When we examine individual industry groups, we find a more diverse pattern. For example, primary metals (including steel) took a bad tumble, declining by 31 percent between 1981 and 1982. In contrast, transportation equipment (which covers both automotive and aerospace production) was down by 9 percent and instrument producers (a heavily defense-oriented sector) reported a 5 percent drop.

Of greater interest is the nature of the snapback in 1983. Two industry groups exceeded their 1981 highs: electrical machinery and transportation equipment. At the other end of the spectrum of performance, the 1983 recovery in primary metals (up 15 percent) did not bring that industry back to its 1975 level of output. Nevertheless, taking full account of the variations among industries, it seems clear that the decline in heavy manufacturing in-

Table 1

Production in Selected Durable Goods,

Manufacturing Industries

(1967 = 100)

Industry group	1970	1975	1980	1981	1982	1983	Dec. 1983
Primary metals	107	96	102	108	75	86	91
Fabricated metal products	102	110	134	136	115	120	130
Electrical machinery	108	117	173	178	169	186	204
Nonelectrical machinery	104	125	163	171	149	151	163
Transportation equipment	90	97	117	116	105	118	128
Instruments	112	132	171	170	162	159	167
Total durable goods	102	109	137	141	125	135	145
All manufacturing	106	116	147	150	138	148	158
Total industrial production	108	118	147	151	139	148	157

Source: *Federal Reserve Bulletin*, various issues.

dustries that was so noticeable in 1982 did not represent a new and durable long-term trend. Rather, the decline was primarily the result of a severe but short-term cyclical contraction.

This report focuses on output as the prime indicator of the economic performance of business firms. Yet there is a great amount of interest in employment. It is the high levels of unemployment that exacerbate pressures for restricting imports and for providing federal bailouts of domestic corporations. However, public discussions rarely acknowledge the relationship between production, job creation, and productivity. That is, in an economy with rising productivity (technically, output per worker hour), we would expect that employment rises more slowly than does output. In fact, instances of slowly growing or stable output might be accompanied by declining employment. That is, declining employment does not automatically and inevitably imply declining production. And the health of an industry is determined not by its demand for inputs (labor, capital, etc.) but by its supply of output—by its contribution of goods and services to the society's standard of living.

It can be seen in table 2 that total manufacturing employment in the United States has fluctuated in the range of 18 to 20 million since 1970; 1982's performance, although low, was merely at the bottom end of the range. The decline that year was followed by an expansion in 1983 that extended to every major hard goods sector. These statistics clearly do not support a counsel of despair.

Statistical Analysis of U.S. Manufacturing, 1970–82

The burst of concern about the decline of U.S. manufacturing has focused on the older, low-tech industries often referred to collectively as the "Rust Belt." Let us see what the facts are. We divide the industries into two groups: high-tech and low-tech.[1] We do this by ranking manufacturing industries by the ratio of their R&D expenditures to sales. The high-tech industries are those whose ratio exceeds the average for all manufacturing in 1980. The low-tech sectors are those with R&D-to-sales ratios below this average.[2]

We now turn to the question "Is there a Rust Belt that is in decline?" To answer this, we examine the most comprehensive body of data available, the statistics on income produced by two-

Table 2
Employment in Selected Durable Goods, Manufacturing Industries
(In thousands)

Industry group	1970	1975	1980	1981	Dec. 1982	Dec. 1983[a]
Primary metals	1,260	1,139	1,142	1,121	816	881
Fabricated metal products	1,560	1,458	1,613	1,592	1,359	1,448
Electrical machinery	1,871	1,702	2,091	2,092	1,957	2,146
Nonelectrical machinery	1,984	2,057	1,494	2,507	2,066	2,169
Transportation equipment	1,853	1,715	1,900	1,893	1,696	1,873
Instruments	527	550	711	727	695	705
Total durable goods	11,208	10,688	12,187	12,117	10,559	11,394
All manufacturing	19,367	18,323	20,285	20,173	18,193	19,271

[a]Preliminary.

Source: U.S. Bureau of Labor Statistics, various statistical releases.

digit manufacturing industry, as reported in the national income and product accounts for the period 1970–82.[3] On the basis of econometric analysis, we group each industry into one of the following three categories: (1) those that showed a rising trend in output over the period, (2) those that showed a stable trend, and (3) those that showed a declining trend. Results for the period are presented in table 3.[4]

As can be seen, there is no statistical support for the claim that the low-tech industries are declining or, as a group, even reaching a period of stagnation or stability. Why, then, do so many commentators contend that low-tech industries are declining? We suggest three possibilities: (1) they draw long-term conclusions from the data for the last few years, (2) they equate trends in employment in an industry with its overall health, or (3) they implicitly define "declining" as growing more slowly than the rest of the economy.

Table 3
Trend in Real Income Produced
by Industry, 1970–82

Trend in output	High-tech industries	Low-tech industries
Growth	Machinery, except electrical Electric and electronic equipment Other transportation equipment Instruments and related products Chemicals and allied products	Lumber and wood products Furniture and fixtures Stone, clay, and glass products Fabricated metal products Miscellaneous manufacturing Food and kindred products Tobacco manufacturing Textile mill products Apparel and other textile products Paper and allied products Printing and publishing Petroleum and coal products Rubber and miscellaneous plastic products
Stability	Motor vehicles and equipment	Leather and leather products Primary metal industries
Decline	None	None

Source: Murray L. Weidenbaum and Michael J. Athey, "The 'Decline' of U.S. Manufacturing: Empirical Evidence and Policy Implications" (St. Louis: Center for the Study of American Business, Working Paper no. 87, 1984).

The business cycle rediscovered. The period from 1970 to 1982 was a time of major economic disruptions. With supply shocks from the rapid rise in food exports and an oil embargo followed by a dramatic rise in oil prices, the U.S. economy was subjected to wide swings and deep recessions in 1973–75, 1980, and 1981–82.

The majority of two-digit manufacturing industries followed this same pattern. In the 1950s and 1960s, they showed a relatively stable upward trend, taking in stride the recessions that occurred during this time. This, however, was not the case in the 1970s and early 1980s. In the face of severe recessions, the manufacturing industries experienced much deeper and longer declines than in the earlier period. This is the environment from which the proponents of an industrial policy have developed their arguments.

Focusing our attention on the period 1981–82, we see all the industries suffering what appears to be a significant decline. But, on reflection, when the economy goes through a recession it is not surprising to see the manufacturing industries decline more than proportionately. The other side of the coin, however, is that in 1983 these same industries recovered from the recession more rapidly than the rest of the economy. Thus, historical data do not support the conclusion that the low-tech industries are declining.

Is employment the problem? To many people, an upward trend in employment is a sign of a healthy and growing industry. All but two of the high-tech industries experienced growth in employment over the period 1970 to 1982 (see table 4).[5] Thus, there is some logic in taking the trend in job creation in those industries as a rough approximation of general growth.

When the same analysis is made for the low-tech industries, we obtain more mixed results. Six of the fifteen low-tech industries show declining trends in employment, while only four industries demonstrate signs of growth.

The question that must be addressed, however, is whether or not it is necessarily true that an industry that is reducing its labor force is truly a declining industry. This proposition—which underlies so much of the popular writing on industrial policy—does not necessarily hold. Surely an industry whose output is declining

Table 4

Trend in Employment by Industry, 1970–82

Trend in employment	High-tech industries	Low-tech industries

Growth	Machinery, except electrical
	Electric and electronic
	  equipment
	Instruments and related
	  products
	Chemicals and allied products
		Furniture and fixtures
		Printing and publishing
		Petroleum and coal products
		Rubber and miscellaneous
		  plastic products

Stability	Motor vehicles and equipment Other transportation equipment	Stone, clay, and glass products Fabricated metal products Food and kindred products Paper and allied products Lumber and wood products
Decline	None	Primary metal industries Miscellaneous manufacturing Tobacco manufacturing Textile mill products Apparel and other textile products Leather and leather products

Source: Murray L. Weidenbaum and Michael J. Athey, "The 'Decline' of U.S. Manufacturing: Empirical Evidence and Policy Implications" (St. Louis: Center for the Study of American Business, Working Paper no. 87, 1984).

is also likely to be reducing employment. Yet there are other reasons why employment may be decreasing. Referring back to table 3, we recall that most of the industries have been growing in terms of output, and the three exceptions are holding their own. This means that most of those industries that are declining in terms of employment are at the same time increasing their productivity.

More aggregate analyses show that, in each of the past six recoveries, a higher level of manufacturing output has been attained with fewer workers working fewer hours. This is primarily a result of the long-term trend in productivity growth, combined with the cyclical effects of overhead reduction and the closing of the least efficient production facilities.[6]

The relevant point is that employment problems may arise when a healthy industry is merely adjusting to changes in its environment. That is, many of the industries classified here as low-tech are becoming more automated in order to compete and survive in the marketplace. In many specific instances, company investments in new productive equipment have increased the productivity of individual workers and thus reduced the demand for total employment. For example, in the textile industry, lasers inspect 10,000 yards of cloth an hour—fifteen times faster than a human once could. In the steel industry, lasers and innovative sensing devices perform inspections and even check refractory lining wear in steel-making furnaces.[7] Economizing on labor costs, of course, can be a key to maintaining an industry's competitiveness.

The manufacturing sector relative to the economy. Some of those who worry that low-tech industries are declining do not focus on decreases in output in an absolute sense. They consider an industry's performance to be unsatisfactory if it is not growing at least as rapidly as the economy as a whole. Hence, if the low-tech industries are declining according to this definition, we should observe over the period 1970 to 1982 a significant negative trend in the ratio of industry income to national income.

To test this hypothesis, we use a statistical methodology similar to that developed for table 3.[8] In table 5, we see that high-tech industries have been growing at least as fast as the economy, two at a faster rate. That should come as no surprise. What about the low-tech industries? According to the proposition being examined, we should expect that these industries would demonstrate slower growth than the national average, or even a decline. This is true of some but not all. Five of the fifteen industries are growing less rapidly than the economy as a whole. However, such industries as tobacco manufacturing and petroleum and coal products have been growing faster than the economy. Hence, any tendency for low-tech industries to grow more slowly than the economy is by no means universal.

In short, the data on national income by industry, when viewed in real terms during the period from 1970 to 1982, do not support the claim that the old-time industries located in America's "Rust Belt" are going the way of the dinosaur.[9] All of the industries, both high-tech and low-tech, show at least stability over this period, with no examples of industries with absolute long-term declines in levels of output.

Table 5

**Industry Growth Patterns Compared
to the National Average,
1970–82**

Trend	High-tech industries	Low-tech industries
Growing faster than national income	Machinery, except electrical Instruments and related products	Tobacco manufacturing Petroleum and coal products
Growing at about the same rate	Electric and electronic equipment Other transportation equipment Motor vehicles and equipment Chemicals and allied products	Lumber and wood products Stone, clay, and glass products Primary metal industries Fabricated metal products Food and kindred products Paper and allied products Printing and publishing Rubber and miscellaneous plastic products
Growing more slowly or declining	None	Furniture and fixtures Miscellaneous manufacturing Textile mill products Apparel and other textile products Leather and leather products

Source: Murray L. Weidenbaum and Michael J. Athey, "The 'Decline' of U.S. Manufacturing: Empirical Evidence and Policy Implications" (St. Louis: Center for the Study of American Business, Working Paper no. 87, 1984).

Shortcomings of Existing Industrial Policy

In the debate on industrial policy proposals, it is important to note that many existing government policies affect industry in important ways and often have contributed to the difficulties faced by the manufacturing sector. These negative impacts of government action are, in the main, side effects of laws designed for other purposes: providing a more equitable tax structure, redistributing income and wealth, enhancing the quality of life, improving the physical environment, and so forth.

Intentionally or not, many of these policies have weakened the manufacturing sector of the economy, either by increasing its costs or by reducing the amount of capital available for expansion

and for new product development. This influence on the fundamental structure of American industry can be seen as manufacturing companies shift portions of their work force away from the
creative and productive areas of business such as R&D, manufacturing, and marketing. The result has been an increase in overhead functions such as legal activities, accounting and finance,
public affairs, and government relations.[10] For the individual firm,
changes in the corporate work force may be essential to respond to
pressures from government agencies and self-styled public interest groups. But the effect of these shifts on national productivity and competitiveness is negative. Poorer industrial performance, in turn, leads to calls for an industrial policy.

If we overlook these structural responses to existing governmental policy, all that is visible are pleas for bailouts, subsidies,
and other special assistance. But, on reflection, the willingness of
government to bail out a Lockheed or a Chrysler is not surprising.
It is the price that Congress pays to avoid dealing with the underlying industrial problems that arise from the present pattern
of governmental intervention in the economy.

A focal point for the current advocates of industrial policy is the
proposed reestablishment of the Reconstruction Finance Corporation (RFC), sometimes under a more euphonious name such as a
"national development bank." Attention is usually focused on the
contributions that the RFC made during the Great Depression of
the 1930s and World War II. Yet, most of its loans to business were
made in the postwar boom period of the late 1940s and early
1950s.

There is much to learn from the operations of the RFC. Its history shows that government subsidy of business encourages a
misallocation of resources and provides opportunity for political
favoritism. The RFC experience also demonstrates that government programs develop a life of their own and persist long after
the problems for which they were created have been solved.[11]

Variations on the negative theme of propping up the economy's
"losers" are not limited to the notion of bringing back the RFC.
Some would attempt to stop economic change by dealing with the
so-called "runaway plant problem"; their response is to make it extremely difficult and costly to move or close down an industrial
facility. This "King Canute" approach ignores the reasons why

companies are forced to take such actions in the first place. Frequently, in fact, those plants have lost their competitiveness due in large part to the government policies advocated by the same groups that now support legislation against runaway plants. Proposals also overlook the negative signals that would be sent to any company considering building a new plant in a region that had adopted restrictive legislation (and a few states already have done so).

Close cousins of this negative approach are proposals to "protect" various industries and markets from foreign competition and to inhibit American investments overseas. None of these approaches would lead to a more productive or more competitive economy. They often would shelter companies and localities from their own mistakes.

The simple-minded dichotomy that sees only expanding high-tech and declining low-tech industries needs to be examined more carefully than has been done by the widely publicized prognosticators of the demise of traditional industry. If industrial giants of the past such as Andrew Carnegie and Harvey Firestone were to visit their old companies, they would be pleasantly surprised by the array of high technology now in use: industrial robots, sophisticated process control, laser inspection, flexible manufacturing systems (FMS), automated material handling, and CAD/CAM (computer-aided design along with computer-aided manufacturing).[12]

Deere & Company's sprawling tractor works provides a good example. The facility includes four FMS installations and sixteen machining centers—groups of totally automated machines and conveyors linked to a computer. In addition, visitors can see robotic welding and robotic spray painting with computers providing total integration of conveyors, towlines, monorails, cranes, and automated storage and retrieval systems. There is hardly a conventional forklift truck in sight.

Many companies have adopted "flexible manufacturing," a high-tech marriage of robots and computers. Deere's plant can turn out tractors in more than 5,000 configurations. General Electric now makes 2,000 versions of its basic electric meter at a single small plant.[13] In a new facility, General Motors has installed a robot system that paints its cars. The man-machine interface is being redefined. Manual operations using gears, pulleys, and belts have often been replaced by microprocessors, keyboards, electronic switches, and cathode ray tubes.

It is ironic that, just when the promoters of industrial policy in the United States are bemoaning the effects of reliance on free markets, writers in the USSR are blaming that nation's poor economic performance on the centralized nature of the Soviet state. Here are some of the "outdated . . . peculiarities of the system of state economic management" that Soviet economists bemoan:

- "a very high degree of centralization in economic decision-making"

- "the inhibition of market forces"

- "a centralized system of allocation of materials and supplies to all enterprises"

- "the centralized regulation of all forms of material incentives for workers"

- "overlapping authority and resulting confusion among ministries and agencies"

- "the limited economic authority and, as a result, the limited economic liability of enterprises for the results of their economic performance"[14]

It is intriguing to read the Soviets' own description of how individuals attempt to adjust to this "most rigid regimentation of economic behavior":

The population always enjoys a certain amount of freedom to respond to the limitations imposed by the state. . . . When established rules and regulation . . . affect the vital interests of certain categories of people, they look for ways to circumvent the constraints and satisfy their requirements. Then the state introduces still harsher measures to block undesirable forms of activity, in response to which the population comes up with more refined methods that make it possible to meet their interests under the new conditions.[15]

All this, however, need not lead to a do-nothing approach to the serious economic questions that face the United States. There is a growth strategy that involves no expansion in government power or federal spending. Its elements are basic: tax simplification, regulatory relief, lower deficit financing, and curtailed government lending. In each of these areas, much can be done.

The 1981 tax reductions were surely helpful. But the sad fact of the matter is that the tax code is far more complicated today than it was just a few years ago. To anyone who has ever tried to fill out the tax forms for a small company, it is clear that simplification is not just a pleasant thought, but rather a vitally important need.

Similarly, the regulatory relief effort has accomplished much in reducing the burden of new rules. But fundamental improvement can come only from revising existing statutes that mandate unreasonable burdens of compliance, such as the "zero discharge" goal of the Clean Water Act and the "zero risk" provision of the Delaney Amendment to the Food, Drug, and Cosmetic Act.

Furthermore, it is ironic to contemplate the numerous industrial policy proposals for funneling federal funds to "worthy" private investment areas at a time when the federal government is running budget deficits in the neighborhood of $200 billion a year. The most effective way to increase private capital formation is just the reverse of the RFC approach—to reduce the federal drain on private saving represented by massive deficit financing. Finally, federal lending programs are a classic example of robbing Peter to pay—or lend to—Paul. They do nothing to increase the pool of private saving. But they do reduce the amount available in the private market.

The most effective strategy for encouraging economic growth is no secret: it is to reduce government barriers and achieve a better-functioning market economy. However, this approach is not accompanied by any guarantee. In a truly dynamic, competitive economy, we do not know in advance where the new product breakthroughs will occur. And the benefits will not be evenly distributed. But we do know that society as a whole will be better off, since it is likely that most—though not all—industrial workers and employers will enjoy higher real incomes and improved living standards.

Surely positive public policy should enhance productivity, capital formation, and international competitiveness. The negative approaches embodied in most industrial policy suggestions, which extend further the role of government in the economy, are all adverse to these key economic goals. Given the gap between the ideal embodied in most policy proposals and the shortcomings of actual practice, a cynic would perhaps conclude that the optimum amount of change in government actions directed toward the industrial economy is zero.

7

REGIS McKENNA

Sustaining the Innovation Process in America

In the current debate about industrial policy, much is being said and written about the importance of research and development.[1] It is argued that our ability to remain the world leader in industrial innovation depends upon the number of dollars annually expended upon R&D.[2] It has been noted that while other nations have increased the proportion of their GNP spent on research and development, American R&D expenditures have been on the decline.[3] If indeed a new era of industrialization is upon us, it is further argued, then without constant efforts to keep on the cutting edge of advanced-technology industries, the United States may lose its position as the world's technological leader.[4] This loss in turn would mean a competitive decline in industrial growth sectors with ramifications for our economic strength for years to come. Because research and development is essential to innovation, our future industrial health seems to depend heavily on the support our nation gives to a strong R&D base.

But there are many factors not taken into account in this argument. The internal structure of research and development in the U.S. is much more complex than is generally assumed, complicating the simple goal of increased R&D funding. In this chapter we will attempt to break down the prevailing monolithic conception of the R&D process, analyzing the several stages and the different groups and differing purposes involved in product creation.

Phases of Product Creation

One important factor omitted from the "increase R&D" argument is the relationship of the structure of product creation to an industry's manufacturing and marketing abilities. It is erroneous to presume that better research will produce stronger industries; the relation between product creation and marketing ability is neither direct nor simple. For instance, structural features that give an industry innovative superiority may actually harm that industry in mature markets. An understanding of the ways in which the structure of product creation affects the structure of manufacturing and marketing within an industry does much to elucidate the R&D argument within the industrial policy debate.

Product creation in high-technology industries will be discussed as a relationship of three processes. In one process, the actual creation of a new product goes through the stages of basic research, applied research, product development, and manufacturing/marketing. A tangible product exists after product development, but it is not a purchasable commodity until it has been manufactured and brought to market.

The process of originating a new product can also be viewed as a series of institutional relations among the government, universities, and small, medium, and large companies. In this process, we see the government sponsoring, and the universities performing, basic research; a mixture of government, industries, and universities involved in applied research; the small, start-up companies as the primary performers of product development; and large companies showing different marketing strengths at the stage of manufacturing. Product creation and the participation of the product creators in the process will be discussed together.

The third process entails the financing of each stage of product creation and the recovery of investment during the marketing stage. Since the ostensible purpose for marketing new products is to achieve a profit, willingness to invest in various phases of product creation is determined by the potential return on investment a new product can offer. The product life cycle acts upon the potential for investment returns. In this cycle, market placement and learning curve economies affect the competitiveness of various types of firms. Here we will discuss the financial dimension of the product creation cycle both within the objective phases of product creation and as a separate section on finance.

After analyzing in general terms the various dimensions of the product creation cycle, we will go on to examine two industries to see what this cycle looks like in reality. In examining product creation, high-technology industries are a logical focus, both because of their higher rate of R&D expenditures and because of their importance to the future direction of the American economy. Semiconductors and biotechnology are both young, rapidly growing, advanced-technology industries. Each fits the general pattern of product creation outlined here, and yet there is an important difference betweeen them: the rate of innovation in semiconductors is among the fastest of any of the so-called "future" industries, while each new innovation in biotechnology still proceeds through a laboriously long R&D process. In semiconductors, product changes are occurring so rapidly that it is nearly impossible to separate incremental improvements from product innovations, while each new product in biotechnology has the added delay of the slow federal approval process before it can become a marketed commodity. Since the rate of innovation in an industry is one of the primary links in connecting the process of product creation to marketing strength, an analysis of these different industries helps to show the range of possibilities in innovation's relation to marketing.

Basic Research: Science-Oriented Investment

The structure of the American educational system and the priorities of the United States government do much to shape and drive scientific research in this country. This is the stage of the innovative process most directly influenced by social concerns.

Academic freedom encourages more invention but makes its results more difficult to hold on to. Likewise, the priorities of the federal government shape the awarding of funding for research, so that, for instance, recent years have seen the expansion of the Department of Defense's R&D budget and the constriction of the Department of Health and Human Services' research concerns.[5] Current public concern about military defense or about heart disease affects the potential emergence of semiconductor products or biotechnology goods a decade or two from now. The social values and objectives that direct the pursuit of basic research also provide the foundation from which product creation progresses.

Basic research, as an industrial investment, is something that few companies have the resources or motivation to pursue. Twenty- to thirty-year periods of product development are more the norm than the exception.[6] Smaller firms do not have the resources to make that kind of investment. Large company labs and universities are the primary sites for this research,[7] and industry as a whole has shown a decreasing willingness over the last two decades to fund the research taking place at universities.[8] Basic research, as the initial stage in the product creation process, is the most distant not only from a saleable commodity but also from the return on investment that sales create. Thus despite industry's dependence upon scientific inquiry for ideas from which to develop products, there is little financial incentive for all but the largest companies to perform, or to fund, basic research.

The alternative to corporate funding for universities' basic research activities is government funding. The federal government currently contributes more to basic research in this country than all other sources combined.[9] Most of this money goes to universities, and the rest is distributed among industry, private nonprofit research centers, and the government's own research facilities. However, to say that large amounts of public funds are spent on basic research does not indicate how much of this money benefits product creation. There has been a dramatic shift in recent years toward more defense-related research and development, to the point that the DOD is now the primary source of federal R&D expenditures.[10] While it is unclear how much of this R&D investment has civilian industry-related benefits, it is significant that there has been a recent shift of defense-related R&D

expenditures away from basic research and toward more development funding. As a recent Congressional Budget Office report states:

Of all the major government agencies which fund significant amounts of R&D, DOD spends by far the smallest proportion on basic research and on overall research (i.e., basic and applied). Moreover, the predominance of development within the DOD R&D budget has been increasing. . . . The greatest boosts in [DOD's R&D] spending have been in the development of strategic weaponry and advanced technologies. The smallest increase has been in the category of "technology base," which has the greatest relevance for civilian industrial activities.[11]

America's strength in product innovation is rooted in a spirit of free inquiry in its universities that has been remarkably productive of scientific discovery. Yet while academic freedom facilitates successful research, it also increases the rate at which research results diffuse to other nations. U.S. universities attract many talented foreign students and exchange scholars whose abilities contribute to the resources of our university system. One result, however, is that these academics may carry the research knowledge they have gained back to their home countries. And although openness helps to inspire innovation, other countries seem more adept than the U.S. at exploiting such benefits for national advantage. This difference between the U.S. and other nations is most apparent in licensing procedures and patent structures; the inadequacies of these protective measures in the U.S. exemplify our relative lack of concern for shielding scientific and innovative advances from foreign access.[12] On the whole, Western Europe and Japan are far more effective at protecting nationally developed technological advances.[13] So the openness of our educational system and research structure is both an inspiration towards creative work and an impetus for the diffusion of its results.

Applied Research: Industry-Oriented Investment

Once scientific endeavors become directed toward particular industrial results, the research is termed "applied." There is a common definitional problem in pinpointing the role of applied research in product creation. Those who speak of basic and applied research and those who discuss research and development are often using the same distinctions between the phases of creation. But, unlike development, applied research does not result in a specific product design. And unlike basic research, the results of which can be valued for their intrinsic worth, applied research is successful to the degree that it brings industries closer to new commodities or better manufacturing processes. Being neither the starting point where knowledge is produced, nor the point of realization where knowledge results in a product, applied research suffers the woes of a middle child: ambiguity and neglect.

There is no natural champion for applied research, no institution whose primary function or interest is this stage of product creation. Universities, whose focus is to expand scientific knowledge, have little interest in directing their efforts toward specific applications unless they receive specific funding to do so. Small companies lack the resources to utilize research that has not already passed through the applied stage. Besides industry and universities, the third major actor in the business of research— the federal government—is less concerned with applied research than with basic research and development. Indeed, its neglect of this stage of R&D has grown worse in recent years.[14]

Since applied research neither happens wholly under the auspices of the government or universities, as is primarily true with basic research, nor is performed almost entirely by industry, as is the case with product development, an ambiguity exists as to the sponsorship and control of this stage of product research. Applied research is picked up by both those doing basic research and those doing research and manufacturing, as a means of compensating as necessary for a company's or university's primary R&D functions. Large industry labs, such as Bell Labs and Xerox's PARC labs, do applied research as a means of bringing forward their basic research; that is, to bring it closer to product development.[15] Recently formed industry associations, such as the Semiconductor Industry Association (SIA) and the Microelectronics and Computer Technology Corporation (MCC), move backward from development to fund basic and applied research, with the intent of creating an information foundation from which products can be designed.[16] The federal government encourages integration by universities in order to support applied research.[17]

The structure of applied research thus determines important aspects of the relationship between universities and companies, and among universities, industry, and the federal government. It requires that the secondary concerns of all participants be flexible enough to muster the primary effort necessary to complete the job.

Development: Product-Oriented Investment

Product development is the final stage in the research and development process. The completion of this phase of product creation coincides with the emergence of a new product ready to be brought to market. This is the most directed phase of product creation; unlike basic and applied research where there is less concern with short-run profit, the success of development depends on the marketing viability of the end product. The drive that fuels successful new product innovations (as they are embodied in product development) is a financial one; it is the desire for economic returns that brings forth a product from scientific discovery.

The principle performers of product development are small start-up firms. These are the innovators. Inspired by venture capital to take the greater—but more potentially rewarding—risks, these leading-edge firms are generally very competitive, efficient users of capital. Unlike the corporate giants, who must invest a substantial proportion of their resources in their bureaucratic structure, small development firms direct all their efforts toward one end—developing a new product to be brought to market. And since a new start-up company's existence depends on the success of its first development project, necessity presses it to innovate a product for market. Thus, necessity and ability make the small venture-sponsored firms the champions of product development in high-technology industries.

Small venture firms possess organizational advantages that help to make them superior product innovators. Start-up companies lack both the bureaucratic baggage and the capital leeway that make for less focused efforts by larger corporations. For instance, a giant such as Xerox has supplied major quantities of important research, but internal bickering over priorities and the slippage of research results to other firms through departed personnel have kept it from effectively developing many of its breakthroughs.[18] Small firms have a far greater clarity of purpose, and the resulting efficacy in product innovation has been noted internationally. Small companies like Apple, Intel, and Genentech are viewed by many as the greatest strength of American high technology.[19] Indeed, industries in Europe and Japan are now seeking to replicate the American model of venture-sponsored development firms.[20]

Unfortunately, the very circumstances that drive small start-ups to be the best developers are also a source of potential weakness. To reiterate, the success and viability of the start-up firm initially depends on the success of a single development project. Before that project is completed, however, all efforts are investments; not until there is a product to be brought to market can returns be made. This tends to make small venture firms capital-starved and financially vulnerable—conditions that have led them to be the greatest source of technology licensing to the Japanese.[21] Increasing this tendency is another source of potential weakness, located at the manufacturing and marketing stage. Low start-up costs and an abundance of venture capital make market entrance relatively easy and the competition among small firms quite high. On the other hand, the potential of that market is mostly unknown, so the element of risk is tremendous. This factor exacerbates the financial vulnerability of these leading-edge firms so important to the industry as a whole.

Product development represents not only a stage in product creation, but also the point of realization in the product life cycle. When development is completed, there is a new product ready to be brought to market and become a commodity. Being the first developer and marketer of a product is a competitive advantage because of the lead it gives a company in markets. How long this advantage can be sustained, however, depends on the speed with which the technology becomes diffused and at which the product life cycle advances. As an industry matures and advances along the product life cycle, ability in manufacturing and marketing becomes more essential to a company's competitive position. The advantage of innovative strength, of being a good developer, depends on the rate at which the industry matures—or in other words, the rate at which innovation declines. In industries that are perpetually marketing new products, a small innovative company will retain a strong competitive position longer than in an industry where new products emerge infrequently. Thus, the role that product development plays in the competitive strengths of different firms in an industry depends on the maturity of that industry and the rate of innovation within it.

Manufacturing and Marketing: Recovering the Costs of Product Creation

Before a product comes to market and is sold, the entire progression through basic research to product development represents investment costs. The investment in a single product may represent years of time and effort, starting with government-funded experiments in a university laboratory and ending many years later with a new silicon chip produced by a small semiconductor company. The United States spends $75 billion annually (approximately 2.4 percent of GNP) on research and development.[22] Much of this represents a social investment, since government research funding is a major source of support for higher education.

The subsequent industrial investment that results in the creation of a commercial good also represents a substantial cost that must be recovered before a product can be profitable. This is the driving necessity for new products and new industries: to produce a return on investment that recoups the costs of product creation. Without such a return, the investment is a loss, and has generated no new capital to fund the next generation of product innovations.

The necessity to secure a return on investment creates a push for short-term profits in U.S. industries. Much has been written recently about the short-sighted perspective of American business relative to that of other countries.[23] Indeed, the advantage that makes American high-technology industries leading innovators may in turn be the basis for their disadvantages in manufacturing and marketing. Much attention is given to product innovation rather than to process innovation. The speed and fluidity that bring American technologies onto the market first may eventually represent a weakness in those markets that require depth and patience in order to retain an established niche. These differences are demonstrated by the small start-up, which brings forth new ventures, versus the established giant, which standardizes the product and perpetuates its market.

The costs of manufacturing change over time, as volume expands and companies learn to produce a commodity more efficiently. As volume rises, learning curve advantages reduce the cost of each unit produced. This cost savings can be used either to lower a commodity's price or as a return on investment to be used for other purposes. Firms with heavy debt loads from development costs have few options, since their need to recoup the costs of investment is acute. Companies with greater financial resources can use learning curve advantages to lower their prices and expand their market shares. Yet learning curve advantages are product-specific, and a high rate of innovation in an industry can nullify many of those gains: as a new product emerges, the old becomes obsolete, and its market vanishes.

Another factor capable of obscuring the cost advantages of the learning curve is foreign competition. Differences in financial structures among countries are responsible for differences in determinants of the cost of capital and of the terms by which debt must be repaid. Japan's financial structure has made it possible for the Japanese to compete effectively against U.S. firms for market share. Japanese firms have lower capital costs and lack immediate financial pressure to repay investments, so they can enter a market with a unit price that undercuts that of American firms and hinders their sales.[24] The potential for foreign companies to thus block the returns on investment for new American products is one of the greatest threats to our nation's high-technology industries.

Investment returns can serve several functions. They can be used for process development, for incremental improvements, or for innovating a new product. Both process development and incremental improvements are crucial to product standardization and the long-term market dominance that standardization makes possible. Yet this is not the path most often chosen by small American firms. In the last decade or so, returns on investment have been used by these firms as the primary source of funding for new rounds of innovation, rather than for process technology.[25] Thus early blockage of investment returns can mean long-term difficulties for American advanced-technology industries, not only by preventing market dominance but also by hindering the formation of capital for the next round of innovation.

Finance

Understanding the phases of product creation in high-technology industries requires a familiarity with the financing process that motivates and makes possible the creation and marketing of a new product. The cycle of research, development, manufacturing, and successful marketing is also a cycle of investments and an eventual return on those investments. The investment begins as a public expense with government funding to universities for basic research. The source of funding for applied research is more ambiguous: there is a multiplicity of sponsors, each providing inadequate funding. That ambiguity evolves into clarity by the stage of product development, where the investment is directed and the capital efficiently utilized. Once a product has been manufactured and brought to market, the financial flow changes direction and previous expenditures begin to find replenishment.

There are several means of obtaining funding for a high-technology company. For the most part, industrial funding sources can be categorized as debt, equity, or profits. Established companies can use profits as a means of funding product creation only when previously created products have been successfully marketed and produce an adequate return on investment. But for new companies that have no other products to achieve profits yet, profit-funding is not even a possibility. Start-up firms depend primarily upon equity financing. Debt costs are shaped mainly by the prevailing interest rates. The cost of equity is difficult to derive, because it depends upon the particular capital market utilized, unlike the cost of debt, which can be taken more straightforwardly from the interest rates.[26] Unquestionably, the cost of equity exceeds the cost of debt across all U.S. capital markets. Yet some equity sources are less clear than others.

Debt financing, though less expensive than equity, is employed only one-third as often as equity sources.[27] This underutilization of debt is caused by both stringency on the part of banks and an unwillingness to be constrained on the part of companies. A major criticism of American lending institutions is the low level of risk

they are willing to accept, meaning that the potentially most profitable (and riskier) industrial projects cannot secure debt financing.[28] Nor is there much patience within the banking community,
whose concern for shorter-term, steady repayments further
restricts the type of loans they are willing to make. On the industrial side, a general sense of unwillingness to abide constraints
and reduce a company's freedom of financial action diminishes
the proclivity to turn to debt as a source of funding. Inflexible
banks and unwilling companies combine to make debt an under-
utilized funding source.

Equity's importance comes from both its greater overall importance as a source of finance and its role as venture capital, which
is the most productive source of funding to high-technology start-
up companies.[29] Among capital markets, venture capital is a more
abundant, less expensive source of finance. It has been argued
that this reflects an overall redistribution away from traditional
markets, such as the New York Stock Exchange, that fund the
more mature (and currently less competitive) industries.[30] This
realization is critical since current arguments that the high cost of
capital has slowed the growth of the U.S. economy are based on
the high cost of equity, which the analysts have determined only
from traditional capital markets.[31] Without considering the venture market, it is not possible to understand how finance is working successfully to fuel new industrial sectors.

The venture capital market went through a major resurgence in
the late 1970s, due to important changes in Securities and Exchange Commission regulations and to the substantial decreases
in the capital gains tax (the Steiger amendment) that occurred in
1978.[32] Between 1977 and 1981, the size of the venture capital pool
doubled from $2.5 billion to $5.0 billion.[33] The development of the
venture capital market and of high-technology industries has
been complementary, for the growth in venture capital investment firms has reflected the expansion in attractive investment
opportunities as well as an increased incentive to invest. The suppliers of venture capital are the professional risk-takers in a financial structure that does little to inspire long-term risk investments. Most venture capital investments go to small firms introducing new technical innovations. These firms have high productivity increases and spend the larger proportions of their

resources on development.[34] In short, venture money goes to high technology.

Biotechnology

In many ways, the 1980 Supreme Court decision that man-made organisms are patentable marked the birth of the biotechnology industry.[35] This was a signal to investors that the commercial potentials emerging from recombinant DNA research were clear for development. Although the discovery of the molecular structure of DNA occurred in 1953, it has been unclear until recently what the government's response would be to the existence of genetic engineering projects made possible by the scientific breakthrough.[36] The court decision, along with the capital gains tax cut of 1978 (which inspired an expansion of the venture capital market), caused a huge outpouring of investment into the biotechnology industry. Hundreds of millions of dollars have been laid out in the belief that biotechnology is an industry of the future.[37]

Each industry is unique in its product creation structure, and biotechnology's is different from that of the other advanced-technology industries. The product creation process in biotechnology is more integrated than in most industries, because of the prominence of the knowledge producers (the basic research scientists) in product development. Like most new industries, biotechnology is presently dominated by small, innovative firms. These firms depend upon the scientists' developing commercial products from science, and their inexperience in the requisites of marketing and business is a major source of difficulty for the industry. Because of the governmental regulatory procedures affecting biotechnology, bringing a product to market is a long, expensive process. This adds strength to the efforts of large drug and chemical companies to capitalize on the financial vulnerability of the small development companies, who are forced to share their new product designs for the sake of financial support. Thus, although venture capital plays a significant role in funding the start-up firms in biotechnology, as it does in all high-technology industries, venture funding is insufficient. There is a greater need for large corporate funding, and a greater tendency toward backwards integration by large firms, at an earlier stage in this industry's development. Thus emerges the story of biotechnology's particular product creation process, which will be drawn out in this section.

Biotechnology is a unique industry insofar as it is the most direct marketer of scientific discoveries. In contrast to the semiconductor industry, there is a clear connection between new ideas emerging in fields such as microbiology and biochemistry, and the products being developed in biotechnology. While the course of product creation in biotechnology creates a closer affinity between stages of basic research and product development, greater distance arises between the stage of product development and manufacturing/marketing. Most biotechnical products need to be reviewed by government agencies (in particular, the FDA) before being certified as safe for manufacturing, and must follow federal regulations for the production and distribution of each new product. The development process itself is quite long and, unlike in other high-technology industries that bring developed products quickly to market, in biotechnology the wait between developing and marketing can be quite time-consuming as well. This makes it highly expensive to invest in developing a new biotechnical product until it is ready for market. Dow Chemical has estimated that the cost of developing a new pharmaceutical biotechnical product is $30 to $35 million and seven to ten years' time.[38]

The time and expense that go into each new biotechnical product intensify the importance of patents to this industry. The effectiveness of patents in lengthening the period for which an innovation remains unduplicated, and in increasing the expense of duplication, is much greater in biotechnology than in other industries.[39] Without patent protection, the investment in developing a product may be for naught; the length of the FDA approval process prevents a firm from quickly bringing a new product to market as a means of exploiting an innovative lead. In November 1982, after Stanford failed to receive a second, reinforcing patent on plasmid use, speculation began about the security of investments in Stanford's original patented process, which had already brought in $1.4 million in royalties.[40] Thus the lag between development and marketing in biotechnology means that patents are regarded as essential evidence of an innovation's security.

A survey report by the National Science Foundation that was

released in March 1983 examined a grouping of 1,116 U.S. biotechnical patents.[41] The results of the NSF analysis indicate much about the strength and stability of different sectors of the American biotechnical industry. The greatest holders of patents were the large, mostly pharmaceutical firms (such as Marck, Eli Lilly, Upjohn, and Miles Labs), each of which had more than twenty patents apiece.[42] American universities had obtained a large share with seventy-six patents, while the small new genetic engineering firms carried only twelve patents.[43] Though it might initially seem surprising, this information fits well with a larger understanding of the biotechnology industry.

Time and financial resources are the key variables of this patent-holding pattern. Large companies have both on their sides. Larger firms have greater resources to wait out the patent approval process, since their economic viability does not depend upon a single new product's being successfully marketed. It is for this reason that many small development firms in biotechnology are forced to turn to the larger chemical and pharmaceutical companies for financial backing while they wade through the patent and FDA approval process. For example, Genentech, a small biotechnology company that first developed human insulin, has found it useful and even necessary to form an agreement with the giant drug firm Eli Lilly, which will bring this new product to market.[44] Through the joint venture process, smaller companies that are not careful may lose the patents covering products they have developed. Indeed, many small companies, being unable to survive the competitive environment that has arisen in this new field, are forced to succumb entirely and become absorbed by larger firms. Several analysts have suggested that the nearly 200 new biotechnology firms founded before 1983 are beginning to dwindle, with several start-ups being bought out by larger drug and chemical companies.[45] One thing the patent-holding pattern suggests, then, is that longer-term marketing strength and economic stability lie with the larger companies.

The financial pressure caused by the long process of product development and approval, which has given an advantage to larger companies with greater resources, has also begun to change the pattern of research in biotechnology. There appears to have been a gap between the priorities of research scientists and those

of the investment capitalists willing to back this rising new industry based upon the financial returns it seemed to promise. Now
that gap is closing, as the financiers are becoming aware of the
necessary development/marketing lag of biotechnology projects,
and as biotechnologists become conscious of the speed with which
they must create a financial return.[46]

The compromise on the industrial side is exemplified by an increased emphasis on short-term profits on the part of small firms.
For example, small companies such as Speywood Lab (which initially isolated Factor VIII, used in treating hemophiliacs, in 1982)
are cutting their long-term research projects in favor of shorter-
term, more immediately profitable ones.[47] The one long-term project that Speywood is still pursuing involves a method for processing Factor VIII from pig's blood, which is being done jointly with
Genentech.[48] This project manages to defray the major costs of
research through its partnership with another company, and still
works to guarantee future returns on the original Factor VIII
discovery.

Both for the universities and for the biotechnology companies
involved, the relationship between firms and faculties has been
problematic. Scientists' and academics' efforts to manage small
biotechnology firms have caused several conflicts between the interest in promoting good research and the desire for successful
marketing. Issues that have caused clashes have been time (short-
term pressure to market versus long-term desire to investigate);
expense (seeking to minimize investment costs versus maximizing
project resources); and direction (creating the most saleable commodity versus achieving the greatest scientific advance).[49] Besides the difficulties that arise from the business end of biotechnology's scientists/industry connection, there is a series of ethical
questions being asked on the university end about the depth of
this association. In 1982, the congressional subcommittee study-
ing this issue recommended that faculty members not be allowed
to hold interest in companies whose projects use their research.[50]
Before that, Harvard University decided not to pursue some
aspects of DNA research for which the school would be answerable to the industrial sponsors.[51] The questions raised by these in-
cidents concern how the purpose and premises of the university
might be altered by a subjective, nonneutral involvement in the
biotechnical industry's development.

On the financial side, the financiers willing to invest in new biotechnology companies are those able to pursue long-term, high-risk investments. These are the venture capitalists. The high start-up costs for a small lab and the decline in government funding for basic research make venture capital funds essential to the small innovative companies that presently populate the field.[52] The question that might follow, however, is why financiers choose to support the development of new products in small start-up firms rather than within the confines of better equipped, large companies. In answer, large companies themselves understand that the motivating factor of scarce resources and the lack of bureaucratic density are advantages for quick, efficient product development, and small venture capital subsidiaries are regarded as "the best vehicle for exposure to revolutionary changes in the marketplace."[53] Yet to compensate for the tremendous amount of risk involved in funding a small biotechnology company, venture capitalists normally work closely with their investments.[54]

What this section has outlined is how the rate of innovation, the presence of venture capital, the youth of this new industry, and the roles of small companies, large companies, and universities affect product creation in biotechnology. Innovation happens quite slowly, and the length of this process is artificially increased by the government approval and patenting process. This increases the distance between the phases of development and marketing. The presence of so many academics in the industry causes conflicts between the needs of doing research and the requisites of successful marketing. The difficulties of bringing a new product to market weaken the position of small, innovative firms, which are then more dependent upon joint ventures and large corporation funding for their survival. Venture capital, both from independent investment firms and from large drug and chemical companies, also has a more controlling presence among biotechnical start-up companies that are particularly long-term, high-risk investments. Yet these small firms play a crucial role here, and in other high-technology industries, as highly efficient and effective product innovators. This industry is still extremely young, meaning that the number of start-up companies and the presence of competitiveness among them is quite high. Maturity is beginning to change this, as many biotechnology ventures are bought out by large drug and chemical companies, and the importance of manufacturing and marketing increases.

Semiconductors

Unlike the biotechnology industry, the semiconductor industry has been marked by rapid innovations since its inception in the 1950s.[55] Constant advances in technology over the last quarter of a century have helped the industry to defy the traditional maturation process that has been a source of great difficulty for other American industrial sectors. In semiconductors, there have been several periods when major innovations have caused a new wave of small start-up firms, interspersed with periods when industry moved to standardize and mass-produce the new innovations after their emergence on the market. During these latter periods, medium- and large-sized companies held a competitive edge over smaller firms because of their greater marketing expertise. In the last three rounds of the innovation-standardization cycle, the availability of venture capital has played a critical role. From 1966 to 1972 the industry was highly innovative, and many new merchant firms (or small start-ups) were born, inspired by the thriving venture capital market. During the mid-1970s, when venture capital was scarce, innovation was slower and few start-up firms emerged again until the late 1970s, when venture capital again became abundant. The rate of innovation, the youth/ maturity characteristics of the industry, the roles of small and larger companies, and the presence of venture capital have all helped determine the structure of product creation in the semiconductor industry.

While innovation has always been a persistent factor in semiconductors, it has been major innovations that have changed the structure of the industry. For instance, in twelve of the fifteen years between 1961 and 1976, new types of integrated circuit product families were introduced in the industry, but the truly major innovations of this period were two: metal oxide on silicon (MOS, created in the mid-1960s), and the microprocessor (invented at the start of the 1970s).[56] These two technical advances were jointly responsible for the wave of some thirty start-up companies formed during this period.[57] Yet the smaller, constant changes in circuit design throughout the 1960s and 1970s also gave a level of dynamism to this industry, pushing prices down and competition up. Indeed, the continual evolution of semiconductor technology has made it difficult to distinguish between incremental advances and product innovations. Innovation and change have been prominent characteristics of the semiconductor industry during its two-and-a-half-decade history.

Part of this dynamism can be understood by placing semiconductors in the larger context of high-technology electronics-based industries. Consumer electronics, computers, telecommunications —all of these have depended upon advances in integrated circuit technology. Each time a more efficient and less costly semiconductor chip emerged, there were consequences for the computer industry. The first company to employ the new technology would have a competitive edge over other firms; in turn, this would increase pressure within the semiconductor industry to produce new innovations, so as to win new customers in the computer market. This sort of "industrial synergism" among advanced-technology industries has done much to promote vibrant rates of innovation and a competitive environment.[58]

However, to focus simply on innovation would be an incomplete way of representing the history of semiconductors. During the middle 1970s, semiconductors exhibited more of the characteristics of a mature industry in which standardization, learning curve economies, and marketing strategies play critical roles. Advances based upon MOS technology continued to be made, increasing integrated circuit storage capacities, but these changes were of a more incremental nature.[59] Instead of new start-up companies, what emerged were "captive" enterprises, i.e., producers within the larger electronics system houses. Also, several semiconductor merchant firms expanded into the consumer market with calculators and digital watch divisions.[60] These were signs of a stabilizing industry populated by large, more bureaucratically dense firms that were more diversified and hence less vulnerable to market fluctuations.

The late 1970s marked the beginning of a new phase in the semiconductor industry based upon the introduction of very-large-scale integration (VLSI) technology and the potential for customized and semicustomized circuits. The growth in new start-up companies has been outstanding, and there are some one hundred companies that have been "lured into the field" of gate array (semicustom) technology in search of the potentially *billion*-dollar market that this innovation offers.[61] But alongside this resurgence in small merchant companies, the competition over random access memory (RAM) technology among the large, established firms continues. Indeed, what is unique about the current period of the semiconductor industry is its dual nature: it contains characteristics of a mature, stable industry and of a young, innovative industry at the same time.

The ambiguity of the current integrated circuits industry is indicative of the different intrinsic natures of RAM technology and custom design technology. Changes in RAM technology are singular and straightforward: they involve an increase in the density and capacity of a single chip.[62] This technology paves the way for custom technology, whose implications are much more complex: as chips become increasingly more dense they take on more of the characteristics of an entire electronics system.[63] It is the straightforward, nearly incremental nature of RAM innovations that makes them more appropriate to large companies with a capacity for product standardization. But custom innovations more befit the skills of small venturing firms, which are rich in the enterprising talents of an inventor and poor in the production skills of a seasoned manufacturer. Custom technology is the key to the presence of small firms in today's semiconductor industry: "A number of new merchant U.S. start-up firms and captive producers are rapidly pursuing new custom opportunities, belying the view that the era of small firm primacy is history."[64] So the dual nature of the technological advances now occurring in the semiconductor industry also represents a dual industry structure in small/innovative and large/stable companies.

Another approach to understanding the incidence of product creation in integrated circuits is by examining the financial cycles that have paralleled the innovation cycles in semiconductors. Between 1967 and 1972, thirty start-up companies were established to exploit the new MOS technology.[65] These firms were all funded by venture capital, either directly by the private venture capital market, or through funds funneled from larger firms.[66] In the equivalent time period that followed—1972 to 1978—only twelve new firms were established, partly because of a lack of available investment funding for start-ups. The 1969 legal change that brought the capital gains tax up to 49 percent effectively halted the growth of the venture capital pool, which was slowly drained through the early 1970s.[67] The stagnation of product innovation among semiconductor firms in the middle 1970s corresponded to the stagnation of new investments among venture capitalists. In 1978, the Steiger amendment chopped the capital gains tax back to 25 percent, and the immediate result was a new swelling of the venture capital market. In the semiconductor industry there has been a similar expansion, with at least twenty new venture-backed firms appearing since 1978. Availability of venture funding has been a necessary prerequisite for the emergence of small start-ups, and as such has been intimately tied to the rate of innovation in this industry.

A comparison of the semiconductor and biotechnology industries shows both similarities and differences in the product creation process. In both industries, major new innovations and product development have been accomplished by small start-up firms, while larger companies are the champions of volume manufacturing and marketing of standardized products. Yet smaller firms have played a stronger role in the semiconductor industry than in biotechnology, where the sluggish rate of innovation makes small firms more vulnerable and dependent upon the resources of large corporations. Each industry has found venture capital essential to the formation of new companies, but biotechnology has found venture capital insufficient to cover its typically costly, prolonged product development process. Thus, new biotechnology firms are more involved in joint ventures and other forms of intraindustry cooperation to bring new products to market. Both industries show signs of youth, with many small start-up companies and a highly competitive environment. But the semiconductor industry simultaneously shows signs of maturity; there are many large companies manufacturing standardized products in secure markets. Both industries show a unique pattern of product creation, yet each confirms the basic cycle of product creation stages laid out in the first part of this paper.

Innovation and Maturity

In the current discussion about the problems of American industry, much attention has been given to the need for a strong "R&D
base." America's traditional role as the world's leading industrial
innovator may be foredoomed as other nations gain strength in
high-technology industries and threaten to replace the U.S. at the
forefront of industrial advance. Mature industries, such as steel
and autos, already appear to have been eclipsed in the international marketplace by other leading industrialized nations and to
be threatened by the newly industrializing countries. What is the
cause of this decline? It would appear that complacency bears
much of the blame; security provided a sense of safe markets
and predictable competition, so that manufacturing strategies
revolved around such things as product standardization and incremental cosmetic changes rather than product innovations. The industries where America's competitive position seems more secure
are those for which a high rate of innovation is almost assumed;
the advanced-technology industries place the United States at the
leading edge of the current technological revolution. Since R&D is
clearly essential to innovation, it is logical to conclude that it is in-
exorably linked to American competitive strength.

The simplicity of the R&D argument faults the conclusions
drawn from it. The connection between R&D and successful
marketing is obscured rather than elucidated when product creation is treated in such blunt, undifferentiated terms. R&D itself is
a misnomer; far more appropriate is the term "product creation,"
which encompasses the several stages involved in moving from
scientific advances to product manufacturing that bring a new
commodity successfully to market. The product creation process is
a complex interweaving of universities, the government, and companies of various sizes involved in sponsoring and performing
basic research, applied research, product development, and
manufacturing/marketing. There is no monolithic R&D process,
no single actor to give birth to each new product as it advances
from the lab to the market. It is the interaction of many institutions, combined with the financial process of investments and
returns, that drives industrial change and creates a new product.

Perceiving the process and the stages involved in product creation is a necessary prerequisite to understanding how innovation and industry maturity shape industrial competition. Our innovative strength has derived from the role of small start-up firms that develop new products for market. Risky innovations in advanced-technology industries owe their existence to small venture firms, which have been the most efficient and effective product developers. Internationally, this is our greatest competitive strength in high technology, but as a strength it is not necessarily sufficient to maintain a competitive advantage. It has been argued in this presentation that while small, venture-backed firms are the prime source of innovation in an industry, more mature industries rely on different skills—ones befitting large corporations— to maintain a competitive position.

Maturity, however, is an ambiguous term—it does not simply refer to an industry's age. More specifically, maturity is tied to the progression through the product life cycle. In industries further along in their product life cycles, manufacturing and marketing skills are critical; at earlier points in the cycle, it is innovative efficiency that determines competitive position. Ironically, an industry can show features of age and youth simultaneously, as is currently the case for semiconductors. Since each separate product has its own life cycle, it is the cumulation of cycles within an industry that gives a general tenor of youth or maturity to that industry. Older industries with a constant high rate of innovation show signs of youth, while younger industrial sectors in which innovation happens quite slowly are likely to demonstrate maturity features at a much earlier stage. This has been approximately the case with semiconductors and biotechnology, respectively.

Maturity, or a slow rate of innovation, is not an intrinsic competitive disadvantage. Rather, mature markets are those that give advantages to our Japanese competitors *because* of the latter's greater skills in, and attention to, marketing and manufacturing. Product standardization, process innovation, high-quality production, and incremental improvements are all Japanese strengths. Other nations, including the Japanese, have yet to demonstrate the innovative ability shown by Americans. The test of our competitive future will be the ability of American industry to improve some manufacturing and marketing skills without forfeiting those abilities that make us the leading product innovators and developers.

IV

Government Policies and Reforms

8

BRUCE BARTLETT

Trade Policy and the Dangers of Protectionism

About five years ago Washington policymakers suddenly discovered that U.S. competitiveness in world trade had begun to erode. It is hard to say what precisely led to this sudden concern about competitiveness. In part it was a reaction to continuing trade deficits after 1977 (see table 1). But it was also a belated effort on the part of Democrats to respond to charges of economic mismanagement being made by Republicans. Not wishing to believe that their own policies of excessive government spending, excessive taxation, and inflationary money growth were responsible for declining productivity, declining standards of living, and rising unemployment, the Democrats searched furiously for another explanation.

The Department of Labor undertook a massive investigation of U.S. competitiveness in 1979 that was published the following year. Two major points were developed: First was the need to concentrate more resources on the development of high technology,

Table 1

U.S. Merchandise Trade Balance, 1970–1982

(billions of dollars)

Year	Exports	Imports	Balance
1970	42.5	−39.9	2.6
1971	43.3	−45.6	−2.3
1972	49.4	−55.8	−6.4
1973	71.4	−70.5	0.9
1974	98.3	−103.8	−5.5
1975	107.1	−98.2	8.9
1976	114.7	−124.2	−9.5
1977	120.8	−151.9	−31.1
1978	142.1	−176.0	−34.0
1979	184.5	−212.0	−27.6
1980	224.2	−249.8	−25.5
1981	237.0	−265.1	−28.1
1982	211.2	−247.6	−36.4

Source: Department of Commerce, Bureau of Economic Analysis.

an area where the U.S. excelled. Second was a preoccupation with the alleged unfair trade practices of our competitors, especially the Japanese.[1]

The important thing to note about these conclusions is that they easily lent themselves to direct governmental action and are microeconomic rather than macroeconomic in their focus. For example, if the explanation for declining productivity is a decline in research and development expenditures, then the obvious answer is simply more government funding for R&D. Similarly, if the trade deficit is the result of unfair trade practices by our trade partners, then the answer is intensified negotiations to reduce their trade barriers and U.S. retaliation. In neither case, therefore, would an alteration of domestic macroeconomic policy be necessary. Thus, Democrats have been able to respond to the challenge posed by Republicans promoting supply-side tax cuts without admitting that their domestic macroeconomic policy is at fault.

The current debate over industrial policy still falls along the same lines. Those who support industrial policy believe that U.S. economic problems are essentially microeconomic and treatable with direct government intervention, and those who oppose industrial policy believe that the problem is macroeconomic, requiring tax, budget, and monetary reform rather than government planning.

Industrial "Targeting"

Although it is downplayed by industrial policy advocates, trade protectionism is a major element of their program. This protectionism sentiment mainly takes the form of a preoccupation with industrial targeting. On the one hand, industrial policy advocates are very concerned that targeting by our foreign competitors is an unfair trade practice, but on the other they hope to emulate the alleged success of our competitors by targeting U.S. industry as well.

In its most basic form the argument for trade restrictions as a component of a national industrial policy has been well expressed by the late Lloyd McBride, president of the United Steelworkers of America, in a speech to the National Press Club on July 5, 1983. "The ability of foreign governments to flood the United States with below-cost products," he said, "is the result of a practice known as 'targeting.'" Targeting, McBride said, works as follows:

A government makes a conscious decision to promote a chosen industry by giving it preferred treatment. This often means government ownership (as in the case of British Steel), tax breaks, favorable loans, outright grants, import protection, and subsidies not available to other industries.

With this kind of government nourishment, the targeted industry develops rapidly and soon has a capability to produce far more goods than its domestic market demands. It is at this point that the subsidized industry looks for opportunities to dump its excess production on foreign markets.

Because of our high consumption and generous trade laws, the United States is the obvious dumping ground. We are a sitting duck.

McBride then goes on to chronicle a laundry list of woes, ranging from unemployment to rising trade deficits, which are the result of foreign industrial targeting and the failure of the U.S. to respond in kind.

Backing up McBride's claims with analysis are numerous studies, largely prepared by law firms in support of import relief for particular businesses and industries. Three studies especially worth mentioning are: *The Effect of Government Targeting on World Semiconductor Competition: A Case History of Japanese Industrial Strategy and Its Costs for America,* produced by the law firm of Verner, Liipfert, Bernhard and McPherson for the Semiconductor Industry Association; *International Trade, Industrial Policies, and the Future of American Industry,* produced by the same law firm for the Labor-Industry Coalition for International Trade, an ad hoc organization of businesses and unions suffering from international competition;[2] and the petition of the National Machine Tool Builders' Association to the U.S. Department of Commerce asking for import relief under section 232 of the Trade Expansion Act of 1962, produced by the Washington law firm of Covington & Burling and the economic consulting firm of Data Resources, Inc.

It is important to contrast the arguments made in studies such as these from those made by industrial policy advocates such as Robert Reich, who continue to advocate free trade.[3] Although Reich may write books that are praised by Democrats like presidential candidate Walter Mondale, in reality industrial policy has no political value without an element of trade protectionism. It is precisely the fact that import relief is a major component of industrial policy, as it is understood in the political sphere, that allows its proponents to promise they can save jobs and revitalize basic industry without resorting to government spending programs, which are difficult to promise at a time of $200 billion budget deficits. An examination of statements made by the Democratic presidential candidates shows that only Reuben Askew stands foresquare against trade restrictions—no doubt the result of his having served as President Carter's special U.S. trade representative. All of the others, to varying degrees, support some form of protectionism and industrial policy.[4]

Arguments for Protectionism

When one thoroughly examines the protectionist argument one finds that two arguments seem to repeat themselves. First is a variation of the infant industry argument. Second is a variation of the predatory pricing argument. Unfortunately, neither stands up to analysis.

The infant industry argument is one of the oldest in international trade theory. It goes as follows:

1. Some newly established activities are initially high-cost relative to established foreign enterprises and require time to become competitive.

2. It does not pay any individual entrepreneur to enter an infant industry at free-trade prices; but

3. The industry, if developed, would permit an economic return after the initial losses; and therefore

4. The industry requires a temporary period of protection or assistance during which its costs will fall enough to permit it to survive international competition without assistance.

Supposedly, this is what Japan has been doing for its "infant" industries, like semiconductors, and the reason why Japanese firms have been so successful. U.S. firms are, in effect, saying they want the same thing: a temporary period of protection during which they can gear up to meet the Japanese challenge.

In fact, this points out the fundamental problem with the infant industry argument: namely, that it ends up being a "home industry" argument. This fact becomes obvious when one sees the expansion of targeted industries to include steel, aerospace, telecommunications, and other well-established industries. In other words, targeting is merely a new justification for old-fashioned protection.

In any case there is precious little data to show that infant industry protection works. Indeed, if Japan's targeting actually accomplishes what its critics say it does, it is the first time that infant industry protection has succeeded. Recent empirical work by Anne Krueger of the World Bank, for example, has failed to turn up any evidence that protection elicited any growth in output per unit of input in infant industries.[5]

Nor is there evidence to show that declining industries ever restructure themselves during a period of protection so as to allow for the eventual elimination of such protection. What tends to happen is that industries that should decline, because they have lost their comparative advantage in international trade, end up declining anyway, only at substantially higher cost to the economy.[6]

The predatory pricing argument tends to run as follows: A nation subsidizes its exports to the U.S.; the domestic industry dies out, leaving consumers vulnerable to foreign price-gouging. Thus, protecting the domestic industry, even at a cost to consumers in terms of higher prices, actually protects them from paying even higher prices later on.

Predatory pricing has long been a staple of antitrust theory, and the arguments for it and against it are equally true in the international trade arena as well. Conventional wisdom suggests that firms have achieved monopoly status, or at least could in principle achieve it, reaping monopoly profits from predatory pricing, but diligent efforts to find any case in which this has ever occurred have proved futile. At least in the domestic sphere it seems that achieving monopoly profits through predatory pricing is impossible.[7]

At a more basic level, however, support for a U.S. industrial policy seems to boil down to the idea that since others do it we should, too; otherwise we would be allowing foreign countries to dictate the structure of U.S. industry. As the Labor-Industry Coalition for International Trade put it:

The concept that the United States must reduce production in any section—such as steel, automobiles or semiconductors—as a result of decisions taken by foreign governments, is tantamount to resigning ourselves to having our economy shaped by the policies of others rather than by the impersonal operations of the marketplace. Our adherence to a "laissez-faire" philosophy under these conditions would mean that the structure of American industry would be determined, not by market forces, but by the industrial policies of other governments.[8]

The problem with this line of argument is that two wrongs do not make a right. Although foreign industrial targeting may have negative effects on the U.S. economy, adoption of an equivalent American policy may only make matters worse. Also, we tend to forget that foreign targeting, or subsidies for that matter, may serve to increase U.S. welfare rather than reduce it. If nations subsidize exports to the United States at the expense of their own taxpayers, providing us with commodities or products we could not or would not produce in any case, then the U.S. is unambiguously better off for it. Even if foreign countries subsidize products we do produce, it is not clear even in the short run that we are in any way worse off.[9]

The Failure of "Targeting"

It should also be pointed out that persistent efforts to prove that Japan or any other country's success is attributable to targeting or industrial policy have failed to do so. A recent report by the U.S. International Trade Commission, for example, stated:

> Evidence to support the claim that industrial targeting benefits the targeting country has been inconclusive. Such evidence generally consists of a selection of successful industries in successful countries, assertions that their success is due to targeting, and conclusions that the country's success is due to the targeting of those industries. . . . Where rigorous attempts have been made to make these kinds of comparisons, they have failed to demonstrate any overall benefit from targeting. That is, although it is known that targeting can change the mix of industries within a country, no one has clearly demonstrated that targeting adds to the general economic welfare of a country.[10]

The Commission added that "it is problematic whether such targeting will have any effect on aggregate employment in the United States, particularly in the longer run, because exchange-rate adjustments will tend to prevent targeting of specific industries from affecting the overall U.S. trade balances."[11]

Similar conclusions were reached in a major study of the electronics industry by the Office of Technology Assessment of the U.S. Congress:

> Can . . . industrial policies create comparative advantage? The answer is clearly no. Competitive success in electronics, here and abroad, depends on many factors, of which government actions are only one. Taken alone, public policies are seldom as important as the capabilities of a nation's private companies: human resources and their utilization, including the quality of management; costs and availability of capital; technological ability in electronics and the complementary infrastructure; overall market conditions—these are more central to international competition. Public policies can add or subtract from them, but the ability of governments to compensate for weaknesses—or to reverse declines in competitiveness—is circumscribed. Although they can either help or hinder industrial development, *public policies alone do not determine—directly or indirectly—the competitive standing of electronics industries in any nation.* [Emphasis in original.][12]

Paul Krugman also makes the point that even if we could show
theoretically that targeting or subsidizing exports would be a net
plus for the economy, it is highly unlikely that hard-nosed economic analysis would be the basis for such a decision.

In practice, an industrial policy aimed at meeting foreign competition
would probably lead to government encouragement of investment precisely where the returns to investment are depressed by the targeting of
other governments. . . . In meeting foreign policies, the U.S. would thus be
targeting an industry where the market returns are bound to be low. . . .
In general, meeting foreign industrial policy seems to be almost a recipe
for picking sectors where there is excess capacity and low returns.[13]

In fact, the evidence showing declining competitiveness is highly selective.[14] Although the U.S. merchandise trade deficit has
widened over the years, it is not because of faltering American exports. Indeed, U.S. exports as a share of world exports have risen
from 15.3 percent in 1977 to 17.3 percent in 1982, despite a strong
dollar, which makes exports more expensive. The deficit has come
largely from rising imports, especially oil. If one excluded oil imports from the calculation the U.S. would have a healthy trade
surplus. (See table 2.)

Table 2
U.S. Petroleum Imports, 1970–1982
(billions of dollars)

Year	Imports
1970	2.8
1971	3.3
1972	4.3
1973	7.6
1974	24.3
1975	24.8
1976	31.8
1977	41.5
1978	39.1
1979	56.0
1980	73.8
1981	75.6
1982	59.4

Source: Department of Commerce, Bureau of Economic Analysis.

Robert Z. Lawrence of the Brookings Institution also points out that trade is not the only factor causing structural change in the U.S. economy. He points to five additional factors:

- The share of manufactured products in consumer spending has declined because of changing patterns of demand associated with rising income levels.

- Some of the long-term decline in manufacturing employment reflects higher productivity in that sector.

- Because the demand for manufactured goods is highly sensitive to the overall rate of GNP growth, the decline in manufacturing output is to a large extent simply a function of slower U.S. economic growth since the early 1970s.

- The U.S. comparative advantage in international trade has shifted away from basic manufacturing toward other sectors of the economy.

- Short-run changes in U.S. competitiveness may be due to changes in exchange rates and cyclical conditions both at home and abroad.[15]

Concern about the trade deficit seems to be largely camouflage for those eager to get import relief by conjuring up nonexistent problems. In point of fact, the trade deficit is really a meaningless concept. Whether the United States runs a surplus or a deficit with Japan means no more than whether New York runs a deficit with California. There is no evidence that the trade deficit has had any real impact on the U.S. economy.[16] If anything, it should have led to a deterioration of the currency, but in fact the U.S. dollar has risen against virtually every other country in the world even as the trade deficit has risen.[17]

Macro vs. Micro Policies

Although industrial policy advocates pay lip service to the need for a proper macroeconomic policy, they are in fact avoiding the issue—and with good reason. Most advocates of industrial policy know too well that our industrial decline—to the extent there has been decline—is attributable to bad macroeconomic policy. But

they don't wish to address this point because it would force them
to come up with a better alternative, which would require them to
make hard choices about taxes, spending cuts, and monetary
policy. They can avoid making such choices by confining themselves to microeconomic issues.

There is, to be sure, a legitimate case to be made for better
microeconomic policy. But no one—not even industrial policy advocates—argues that better microeconomic policy alone will do
very much to encourage investment in the face of current high
real interest rates, to encourage trade in the face of a strong dollar, or to reduce unemployment, without some corresponding
macroeconomic policies. In short, the big issues, the ones most
people are concerned about—unemployment, deficits, high interest rates—are largely immune to microeconomic solutions.

The fact is that the microeconomic problems our nation is
suffering from are largely the result of bad macroeconomic policy.
We have had three recessions in the last ten years. We have seen
interest rates rise to unprecedented levels. We have had double-
digit inflation and double-digit unemployment. These are simply
not microeconomic problems. However, they do have microeconomic implications. This is the point to which industrial policy
advocates ought to be addressing themselves.

The fact is that all macroeconomic policies have microeconomic
implications. That is to say, macroeconomic policies affect
different industries differently. Inflation, for example, hurts
capital-intensive industries more than labor-intensive industries
because it distorts depreciation allowances, causing the effective
tax burden on capital-intensive firms to rise. This is because
depreciation allowances are still based on historical, rather than
replacement, cost. Until depreciation is indexed, as we have indexed personal income tax rates, this problem will remain.

Inflation also reduces the ability of firms to raise capital,
because it adds an inflation premium to interest rates, encouraging flight from financial assets to real assets, and because taxes
must be paid on nominal, rather than real, capital gains.

Business cycles also have microeconomic impacts. Much of this
has to do with the fact that many provisions of the tax code
designed to aid capital formation are really pro-cyclical. For example, the investment tax credit allows firms to deduct 10 percent

of the cost of an investment in capital equipment from their tax liability. But if a firm has no profits, then it has no tax liability from which to deduct the credit. Firms may also have excess deductions from depreciation that similarly have no value in the absence of profits. Interestingly, an effort to make the tax code more neutral by allowing firms with excess deductions, in effect, to sell them to firms that could use them—the infamous tax-leasing provision of the 1981 tax bill—was almost immediately rescinded by those same people now pushing industrial policy.

The elimination of business cycles—which Keynesian economists told us were obsolete just a few years ago—the permanent elimination of inflation, and the elimination of tax preferences with differential impacts on different industries in favor of outright abolition of the corporate income tax would do far more to aid basic industry than protectionism, a new Reconstruction Finance Corporation, or a national economic planning agency.

Of course it would also be desirable to reduce government's take of currently available capital by cutting government spending. But this would require industrial policy advocates to confront those currently receiving government aid. It would also be desirable to encourage the creation of more capital by stimulating saving. But this would require giving tax breaks to the people with the most money to save, namely the rich. And it would also be desirable to have less government regulation and control of business investment. But industrial policy advocates seem to have little taste for deregulation, favoring instead new regulations in the area of trade restrictions, plant-closing laws, and requirements that business investment be more "socially responsible."

It would also force industrial policy advocates to admit that many of the organizations supporting them are doing so only because of their own self-interest. Among these hidden agendas, import relief seems to be a primary motivation.

Rationale for Free Trade

In the end, the arguments for free trade are as true today as they were in the time of Adam Smith. The goal of industrial policy and protectionism is today the same as it was in Smith's time: to subordinate the welfare of the consumer to that of the producer. But, as Smith reminds us:

Consumption is the sole end and purpose of all production; and the interest of the producer ought to be attended to, only so far as it may be
necessary for promoting that of the consumer. The maxim is so perfectly
self-evident, that it would be absurd to attempt to prove it. But in the
mercantile system, the interest of the consumer is constantly sacrificed
to that of the producer; and it seems to consider production, and not consumption, as the ultimate end and object to all industry and commerce.[18]

When policies are seen from the point of view of the consumer,
therefore, it becomes readily apparent how harmful many of the
current arguments for industrial aid are. The proposal to require
foreign auto makers to comply with domestic content rules, for example, "may be viewed as a tax on the consumption of vehicles,
with the difference that what would be tax revenue, were there an
explicit tax, is now embodied in the excess costs of domestic production."[19] The Congressional Budget Office estimated that the
domestic content bill currently before Congress would cause car
prices to rise by nearly $500 by 1990, cause GNP to be 0.1 percent
lower, and cost 67,000 jobs.[20] Another recent estimate put the cost
of all trade restrictions to U.S. consumers at $71 billion in 1983.[21]

Even proposals to restrict foreign "dumping"—i.e., selling a
product in a foreign market for less than it sells in the domestic
market—are implicitly protectionist when viewed from the point
of view of the consumer.[22] If foreigners want to, in effect, tax their
own citizens to give a gift to U.S. consumers, why should we com-
plain? Why should we refuse, as Milton Friedman put it, "reverse
foreign aid?"[23]

The reason is that, in trade policy as in the budget, the views of
special interests often outweigh the public good. This is because
special interests have a powerful motivation to get protection or
subsidies, while the cost of such measures is spread out over the
mass of consumers.[24] Even the total mentioned above of a $71
billion cost of all trade restrictions to consumers comes to only
$300 per person. Thus the cost of any particular trade restriction
is likely to be negligible for individuals. For example, according to
one estimate, the limit on Japanese auto imports that has been in
effect since early 1981 works out to be just $8 per person per year.
But it saved some 20,000 jobs, even if the cost was $60,000 per
job.[25]

Reagan Administration Policy

The Reagan administration has generally fought efforts to undermine free trade and opposes, at least officially, establishment of
an industrial policy. Nevertheless, there are disturbing signs that
the administration is moving along an increasingly protectionist
path and may even be succumbing to the lure of industrial policy
as well.

Although the Reagan administration's record on this score—
i.e., granting protectionist relief to various industries, subsidizing
exports through the Export-Import Bank and other mechanisms,
and restricting exports for various national security and other
foreign policy reasons—is probably no worse than other recent
administrations, one is inclined to agree with Milton Friedman's
assessment:

Recent protectionist measures by the Reagan administration have
severely disappointed those of us who expected this administration to display a higher threshold than earlier administrations before it sacrificed
principle on the altar of short-term political expediency. In foreign trade,
it seems that we were clearly wrong.[26]

It is also disturbing that the administration seems to be becoming more protectionist, rather than less so. A recent decision to
grant import relief to the textile industry, for example, was made
at a time when the industry is in a substantial recovery and
against the recommendation of the Cabinet Council on Trade.
Especially disturbing is the role played by commerce secretary
Malcolm Baldrige, who appears to be the leading protectionist in
the administration.[27] It is disturbing because of the administration's proposal to combine the Commerce Department and the Office of the U.S. Trade Representative into a new "Department of
Trade" which, presumably, would be headed by Baldrige.

The Department of Trade idea has been a staple of industrial
policy proposals for a long time. It is seen as a way of imitating the
success of Japan's Ministry of International Trade and Industry
(MITI).[28] However, free trade advocates have been highly skeptical of the idea, fearing that bureaucratic pressure will cause the
new trade department to be more protectionist than the U.S.
Trade Representative has been.[29]

It is harder to document the administration's drift toward in-

dustrial policy, since on numerous occasions its prominent spokes-
men have denounced the idea.[30] However, there is evidence that
the administration has fallen into the same trap the Carter administration fell into of believing that U.S. industrial competitiveness has sharply deteriorated and, by inference, that government
intervention is required to rectify the situation. Toward this end
President Reagan has appointed a National Commission on Industrial Competitiveness, headed by Hewlett-Packard president
John A. Young.[31] Although this commission has not yet issued a
report, it has been widely seen as the first step in development of a
Republican version of industrial policy.[32]

It is tempting to believe that governments can solve their economic problems by targeting industries and selectively using
trade protection to enhance export competitiveness, and there are
some very sophisticated arguments for why this might work.[33]
But they are far outweighed by the historical record. The leading
scholar on the subject of industrial innovation, Professor Richard
Nelson of Yale, for example, recently concluded after a long investigation that the net effect of government efforts to "pick winners" in industrial competition was "unequivocally negative."[34]
The economic arguments against protection are equally well
grounded in experience. Thus one is forced to conclude that efforts
to implement some sort of industrial policy, to target industries, or
to impose protectionism as a means of accomplishing such goals
are counterproductive and doomed to failure.

9

WALTER E. HOADLEY

Banking and Finance: The Cost of Capital in Japan and the United States

Financial markets and institutions are seldom free of government influence, if not direct intervention, in all countries including the United States and Japan. The practical day-to-day functioning of the financial system is so universally accepted as vital to public well-being that government guidance and oversight could hardly be absent.

Industrial policy has vastly different meaning for U.S. and Japanese financial institutions and managements. In the United States the issue is most often seen narrowly either as foreshadowing more government interference or merely as a new title for

173

ongoing relations with regulatory authorities; in Japan it is accepted, albeit with diminishing enthusiasm, much more as a practical way of economic life. This is because banking and finance are
recognized more as *means* to achieve national strategy than
largely as ends themselves, as in the United States.

The banking and financial systems of the U.S. and Japan
necessarily have many technical operations in common. Moreover, they compete and function in the same general global economic and financial market environment.

Many clear-cut differences are apparent, however, in both
domestic and international activities, in regulatory policies, and in
practices. Most striking are the contrasts between the largely uncoordinated banking and financial policies and regulations in the
U.S. and the more directed policies and guidance procedures in
Japan designed to further national objectives.

The principal characteristics of the American and Japanese
banking and financial systems will be seen more clearly in a
review of (1) the impact of structural changes, (2) the factors
determining the cost of capital, (3) the direction of new policies,
and (4) the question of future global leadership responsibility.

Impact of Structural Change on Financial Markets

In many respects the basic challenge confronting U.S. banking
and finance is structural change. Much the same holds for Japan
and other major industrial nations.

Many new and powerful forces are operating throughout banking and finance with worldwide repercussions. They include increased international interdependence, substantial domestic budget deficits, persistent doubt that inflation can be brought and
kept under control, rising concerns about economic instability and
volatile financial markets, accelerating technology altering competitive costs, mounting availability of financial and related information, new financial control and service delivery systems, large-
scale sovereign debt restructuring, persistent flight of capital,
chronic currency misalignments, more competition for funds by
public and private borrowers, and deregulation.

It is not an exaggeration to say that a new financial system is
emerging in the United States, Japan, and probably the world. It

may take five to ten years or more to finalize, but these and other structural changes guarantee that the status quo will not endure.

For more than two generations, U.S. banking and other financial institutions operated smoothly under a fairly rigid system designed to correct problems rooted in the Great Depression. Financial institutions were restricted to rather explicit fields, e.g., commercial banking, investment banking, mortgage banking, savings, insurance, brokerage, etc. Competition was confined principally within each specialized field. Legal barriers created an institutional framework that restricted market expansion across proscribed boundaries.

The erosion of these barriers by accelerating market forces began at least as far back as the late 1960s. Double-digit inflation subsequently caused cracks and then major holes in the statutory walls of finance. The crux of the matter was that bank depositors became increasingly dissatisfied with below-inflation-rate official interest ceilings for their deposits and moved more and more funds to nonbank institutions that could and did pay more generous rates.

Brokerage houses, retailers, and many other nonbank institutions also innovatively created higher-paying financial instruments to attract funds. They aggressively adopted many banking functions that had been considered off-limits to them for decades.

In retaliation, many banks have expanded their own range of services while making significant cutbacks in older, expensive delivery facilities and functions. Bank service expansions, however, have been slower than nonbank competition because of lingering regulatory and statutory restraints, reinforced by numerous challenges in the courts.

The U.S. legal-political process characteristically lags behind economic change. Resistance to the formal opening of specialized financial fields virtually to all comers predictably has been strong and still persists. But the forces of economic change and fair competitive opportunity simply cannot be denied for long.

"Financial services" have already succeeded in replacing "banking" in describing the multiproducts of newly created or expanded U.S. banking and financial organizations. These changes and developments have been materially facilitated by major technological breakthroughs ranging from automatic teller machines to satellite communication systems. The critical economic dimensions of the new technology are (1) significant reductions in unit transaction-service costs; (2) development of new computer systems primarily from outside banking and finance, thus placing traditional banking institutions at a disadvantage over some new entrants; (3) investment of substantial capital and training, which are required to make extensive use of the new equipment and systems; and (4) significant turnover and placement of personnel and administrative organizations.

The emerging system will be more competitive, customer-oriented, technologically advanced, low-cost, market-priced, fast-paced, and devoid of giveaway frills than what is now in place.

The U.S government's role in this overall process of change to date has been largely to ratify *de facto* market changes and formally break down old barriers.

Some new or modified regulatory problems for government, however, are rising, such as protection of the public from undue new concentration of power, interstate operations and control, deposit insurance coverage and cost, consistency in regulatory standards and coverage, and others. Thus U.S. banking and finance now face a slow and complex process of fitting into a new regulatory environment as well as a new financial system.

Adjustments in Japan's Financial System

Scholars have searched for years for the key to Japan's economic success—the Japanese economy being now in a position second only to that of the United States in the Free World. A professional consensus is forming that the wellspring of Japan's initial post–World War II economic surge was sheer necessity, aided by a strong cultural desire to come from behind and reinforced by concerted policy actions to achieve substantial growth—in the absence of equity funds—through heavy debt leverage.

To do so required a reliable source of funds in the form of savings, and some insulation of business borrowers from high and volatile interest rates. Not surprisingly, a banking and financial system with these characteristics emerged under the primary direction of the Japanese Ministry of Finance. Very strict rules were established to govern the capital markets. The credit and tax systems were utilized to help specific industries and firms.

In subsequent years, financial regulations have been liberalized very slowly. The Japanese have followed their traditional approach: avoiding politically and economically painful policy changes until domestic and foreign pressures can no longer be resisted and dictate action.

Nevertheless, Japan's tightly managed financial system has faced its own structural changes in recent years, and many more seem inevitable. The fundamental causes are: (1) Japan's persistent economic success has relentlessly undermined the rationale for pursuing many earlier banking and financial control policies that contributed to it; and (2) distinctly slower economic growth in Japan has drastically shifted funding requirements from the private to the public sector.

Japan's major competitors have widely lost patience with Japanese claims of weakness in the face of very apparent strength. In fact, the fear of rising anti-Japanese trade and other restrictions in Europe and the United States clearly has been a principal force prompting Japan to relax some controls over banking and finance during the past year or two.

Despite economic prowess, however, Japan currently is having difficulty in making adjustments in banking and finance to a combination of structural changes and markedly reduced growth, particularly since 1979. Long-standing saving and investment policies are out of balance with more limited growth trends and prospects. Japanese business executives as well as ordinary savers also have become very sensitive to interest rates. Not only are projected Japanese government tax revenues lower, but at the same time political support has increased for larger government spending policies.

The resultant budget deficit has grown appreciably, foreshadowing eventual debt financing and refinancing problems as well as upward inflationary pressures and higher interest rates. The official Japanese government budget deficit is sizeable, although still smaller (4 percent) relative to gross national product than in the U.S. (where it is about 6 percent). Moreover, it also constitutes a large part of the government's annual budget.

Slower economic growth has cut the external financial needs of many Japanese corporations. Against traditionally strong banking and capital market policies designed to channel savings into highly leveraged and undercapitalized corporations, the new realities are that many of these same companies are now more creditworthy and highly liquid, and thus able to find funds to meet their own major capital and credit requirements overseas as well as at home. In addition, they seem eager to move away from their former very heavy dependence upon, and control by, Japanese banks. In fact, many Japanese corporate treasurers have now become heavily involved in making investments with surplus funds after years of specializing in borrowing.

The Japanese Ministry of Finance confronts a special problem in financing new government budget deficits plus the rollover of accumulated national debt. This is because the tight control policies of the past were not designed to cope with recent and current fiscal developments. Beginning in 1974, the budget deficit has been financed principally by selling bonds allocated at dictated rates — heavily weighted with 10-year maturities — to banks, investment companies, insurance firms, and similar financial organizations. These bonds will soon begin to mature and thus complicate the fiscal management problems of the Japanese government.

The Cost of Capital

Measuring comparative capital costs among nations is always difficult and frequently inconclusive. However, most foreign banking and financial specialists agree that Japanese companies rather consistently have benefited from somewhat lower capital costs than those found in the United States and generally among major industrial countries (see table 1).

Table 1
Indications of Capital Costs
in the United States and Japan (1981, 1983)

	United States		Japan	
	1981	1983	1981	1983
Short-term money market rates	16.38	9.45	7.69	6.86
Government bond yields	13.72	11.82	8.66	7.54
Wholesale prices (1980=100)	109.10	113.50	101.40	100.90
Consumer prices (1980=100)	110.40	121.70	104.90	108.90

Source: International Monetary Fund, *International Financial Statistics* (November 1983).

The underlying Japanese government policy of keeping interest rates comparatively low reflects a much higher degree of debt than equity financing. The substantial increase in the Japanese government's own public debt during the past decade has reinforced the urgency of keeping borrowing costs in Japan as low as is economically and politically possible. Equally important, Japanese companies have benefited from longer maturity funds.

The Japanese contend that their nominally lower (1 to 3 percent) capital costs result mainly from their far-better-than-average control of inflation and the great strength of their savings programs. They also remind Americans that the United States has long had the best organized capital markets in the world for its companies, in contrast to the struggling development of capital markets in Japan. Interest rates are set by market auction in the U.S., but are commonly negotiated in Japan.

Close study of international interest rate patterns reveals limited direct coordination of Japanese rates with those in other world financial centers. High rates of general domestic and international inflation also have not influenced Japanese interest rates as in the United States. Even more than other countries, Japan seems to pursue policies designed to keep interest rates relatively lower during recessions, no doubt to cushion economic shocks and to encourage faster recovery.

These conclusions seem to hold whether the comparisons are made in real or nominal interest rates. Lower real interest rates have sharply different impacts on borrowers than on savers. In both Japan and the United States there have been periods of negative as well as positive interest rates during the past decade. From an economic point of view, negative after-tax and after-inflation interest rates tend to encourage more borrowing but discourage saving and investment. This phenomenon has been rather easily identifiable in the United States banking and financial markets, but less so in Japan.

The Japanese tax system is not generally seen as the major determinant of the level of savings or investment, or of the success of the national economy. Nevertheless, tax strategy is more directed than, and strikingly different from, that in the United States. There is rough balance between nominal revenues from corporate and personal income taxes in Japan, in contrast to a

five-to-one ratio in favor of personal (to corporate) tax revenues in
the United States.

Institutionalized savings have remained much higher in Japan
than in the United States. In part, this reflects the Japanese
government's policy of promoting savings in support of the capital
markets through almost tax-free savings returns for individuals
with average incomes. Income from savings deposits, government
bonds, postal savings, and individual retirement funds are not taxable up to certain fairly liberal amounts. Other key elements supporting higher savings are cultural prudence and the economic
need to finance a major portion of personal retirement costs
because of inadequacies in the government's social security programs. There has also been a striking increase in consumer credit
during the past decade. Yet Japan's ratio of consumer credit to
disposable income (10 percent) is only half the U.S. ratio (20 percent). In part, this is because interest is not deductible for tax purposes in Japan as in the United States—so there is considerably
less incentive for individuals in particular to borrow.

The question of how effectively the Japanese employ their
capital must also be addressed, particularly in view of their
government's policy of protecting corporations from uncertain
and volatile world financial markets. Precise measurement again
is not readily attainable. The record, however, confirms the existence of a fairly determined Japanese strategy to employ capital
heavily and persistently, especially in industrial investments
through the years. Far less attention is given to short-term
returns compared with the United States and most other industrial nations.

For the past twenty years Japanese investment expenditures
relative to gross national product (33 percent) have been roughly
twice the size of those in the United States (17 percent). This investment policy results in high efficiency of capital as long as real
economic growth is also high and expanding. However, the productivity of invested capital obviously falls sharply when overall
growth slows, as has been the case for Japan in the past few years.

Many American businesses have long tended to restrict their
capital investments because of excess capacity, foreign competition, low returns, and high financing costs. Accordingly, a greater
amount of output and financial return per invested dollar actually

has been achieved in America than in Japan during the past two or three years.

New Policy Directions in the United States and Japan

The power of internal and external structural changes as well as relentless competitive pressures in savings, lending, investment, and foreign exchange markets have necessitated new policy directions in both the United States and Japan. The details are still obscure and incomplete, but the eventual outcome is beginning to come into focus.

For the United States the current era of strong deregulation is likely to lead to more consolidation of private and public institutions, followed by a new period of reregulation as the impact of ongoing changes on the public interest becomes apparent.

For Japan, the process of freeing market forces to function more openly in the credit and capital markets will proceed slowly but steadily. Through government guidance, Japan will continue to resist full exposure to domestic and international market vagaries, but it is coming increasingly to recognize the critical linkages among freely functioning finance, economic growth, and political and social stability.

Here is a closer look at the policy tools in use in the United States and Japan.

The United States. The absence of powerful overall national goals or objectives has not deterred the U.S. government from using an array of economic and financial policy tools affecting banking and finance. In practice these tools influence specific markets and institutions unevenly, are not well coordinated, and at times are inconsistent. Their basic purpose is to allocate the country's financial resources, to a considerable degree for political purposes. Currently they seem to be designed to encourage domestic saving and investment but to discourage offshore lending by U.S. banks.

- *Monetary policy* is controlled by the Board of Governors of the Federal Reserve System in its efforts to promote sustained growth. Here, in fact, is the principal source of stop-go instability in the U.S. economy, as the Federal Reserve peri-

odically tightens or loosens its grip on the nation's money supply and credit markets. "Fed watchers" continually monitor
Federal Reserve actions and policy statements and directly or
indirectly shift enormous flows of funds in anticipation of, or in
response to, such policy changes.

- *Fiscal spending and taxing policy* is controlled at the federal
  level by the U.S. Congress, acting on budgetary initiatives from
  the president. Substantial tax cuts have sought to raise the low
  U.S. saving rate and to contribute to the revitalization of American industry. Record high federal budget deficits, however,
  reinforce public expectations of more inflation and persistently
  high interest rates ahead. The tax credits that have been
  enacted offer many incentives, e.g., for capital investments,
  new ventures, stock purchases, small business growth, etc., but
  obviously they also cut revenues. The deductibility of interest
  favors borrowing, discourages equity investments, and shrinks
  government income.

- *Direct government financial programs* number in the hundreds
  and encompass such items as loans, guarantees, interest and
  other subsidies, market supports, credit insurance, domestic producer price preferences, and emergency "bail-out" assistance.

Economic market forces remain more pervasive and effective in
the United States than elsewhere, but many, if not most, of the
nation's financial transactions are regularly and continually
shielded, blunted, or diverted by government for economic, political, and social reasons. Overall U.S. national policy objectives for
banking and finance may not be clear-cut, but banking and financial transactions are affected every minute by some agency of the
federal government. This is also true to a considerable degree at
the state and local government levels.

Recent international banking and finance problems have attracted widespread public attention in the U.S. and around the
world. Concerns have arisen in the Congress and throughout
government about actual or potential damage to American banks
and the U.S. financial system. Nearly a majority of voters in polls
have expressed at least some doubt about the wisdom of American
banks' making future loans overseas.

Pursuit of an inward-thinking international banking and finance policy can only be highly counterproductive for American workers and citizens generally in today's increasingly interdependent world. However, this conclusion is not readily understood and will take time to be demonstrated and win widespread public support. Efforts by the United States to limit or stop overseas lending inevitably must aggravate loan repayment problems, cut export sales, and invite retaliation from abroad.

All multinational official financial instititutions draw on member governments for their financial resources. Accordingly, the U.S. Congress must vote periodically to appropriate more U.S. taxpayers' money for these critically important and vastly underestimated international bodies. For the United States not to meet its full quota of new funds would definitely help to undermine the global financial system, especially the flow of needed funds to developing nations. These countries have 3 billion people potentially or actually prone to social unrest; potential problems include the threat of mass migration across borders, including to the U.S., and stepped-up worldwide anti-American feelings and actions.

Late in 1983 the Congress narrowly passed the IMF quota-increase legislation, but not without adopting many regulatory provisions constraining lending activities of U.S. international banks. Political analysts are convinced that the Congress would not have approved the IMF quota increase without its "pound of flesh" in the form of new controls over bank lending abroad.

The current tendency of U.S. government agencies to intervene in the international lending policies and practices of American banks appears in marked contrast to the relentless pace of deregulation in domestic banking and finance.

Nearly 200 U.S. banks must now file official country exposure reports so that federal banking authorities can more thoroughly evaluate foreign country loans. The underlying reason for this official call for more detailed information is to determine the *adequacy of bank capital*. New minimum levels of capital are being set as well as requirements that capital be added in amounts bearing some clear-cut relation to country lending exposure. In effect, new reserves are being called for in a fairly blunt form.

Banking laws, including disclosure, capital requirements, and definitions, differ substantially across the world. The American laws are as comprehensive as most. In particular, "hidden bank-

ing reserves" (i.e., understated values) are accepted in many nations, but not by the United States regulatory authorities. The new
surveillance measures together with other long-standing constraints threaten the future ability of U.S. international banks to
compete with banks abroad.

U.S. banking agencies now are also directed by the Congress to
consult more intensively with supervisory authorities of other nations to increase review and presumably control of worldwide
lending practices.

The managements of banking and other financial institutions
understandably are now heavily preoccupied with new plans and
programs to cope with the substantially changed economic, social,
and political environment within which they are operating. Com-
partmental market regulations over United States banking and finance gave little incentive for innovation in domestic markets.
However, domestic deregulation has only now opened many opportunities for new products and services. In contrast, international
banking and finance were marked for many years by substantial
innovation, mainly because of the far greater freedom of action
permitted offshore; but recently stepped-up regulation of international banking already has slowed development of new products
and services and caused some phasing out of other services, with
consequences yet to be determined.

The net change in the United States' regulatory environment in
recent years has tended to place established banking and finance
management on the defensive—against government, new entry
competition, shareholders, market analysts, and employees. What
had been long considered a low-risk business, in fact, has now
been labeled a much higher risk field. Security of assets and job
can no longer be taken for granted. Risk reduction and enhance-
ment of earnings are now beyond question managements' top
priorities.

The hallmarks of the past—size and volume of business—have
become far less important to all participants. Capital restraints
simply will not permit high-volume transactions at very low profit
margins. Higher interest rate volatility increases exposure and demands much more attention to matching rates and terms of assets
and liabilities. Off—balance sheet business to earn fee and related
revenues has become more and more attractive because it contributes needed earnings without requiring capital.

Throughout American banking and finance a consensus is forming that the next several years will be marked by cross currents of innovative expansion and defensive consolidation. The net result will be a reduction in participating institutions. New entrants will continue to come into financial markets, but mergers and acquisitions will accelerate and many institutions simply will disappear. Future U.S. financial markets clearly cannot support and do not require 15,000 commercial banks, 20,000 credit unions, 5,000 insurance companies, 4,000 savings and loan associations, 3,000 security dealers, 3,000 finance companies, 800 mortgage bankers, 700 mutual funds and money market funds, 500 mutual savings banks, and a host of pension funds and other financial institutions.

This impending consolidation of financial institutions is certain to stir up political debate and calls for special government intervention, especially whenever voters feel threatened or sense some unfairness in the process. To some degree, foreign financial institutions and capital will be linked to shrinking the U.S. banking and finance participants. Hence, it is likely that more governmental inquiries into the plight of disappearing financial institutions will be held. Some protectionist measures already have been proposed to slow the transition; but the strong economic forces of innovation and consolidation simply will not be stopped.

Japan. Despite the rather consistent official overtone of direct government guidance throughout the Japanese banking and financial system, policies are more flexible than often believed. The Japanese are fundamentally pragmatists. Yet the key policy objective remains fairly clear: aggressively to help the Japanese nation meet its challenges at home and abroad.

Japanese pragmatism will be tested in the period ahead as the government confronts a major dilemma in finance that is not too difficult to visualize. Policies have to be altered delicately to find ways to keep strong pressures off the capital markets, which are a crucial instrument of Japanese management of the economy; appease dissatisfied government bondholders into renewing their investments without pushing up interest rates; further liberalize Japanese capital markets to satisfy domestic and foreign critics; and manage the undervalued Japanese yen without seriously jeopardizing the competitiveness of products moving into export markets. No doubt the Japanese will find many pragmatic answers—including some temporarily severe constraints on government spending—but policymaking cannot be expected to adhere strictly to open market principles, although the trend will be in that direction.

One of the more important policy matters in Japanese relations with the rest of the economic and financial world is the value of the yen, relative in particular to the United States dollar. For some time the weakness of the yen has been a contradiction of the overall good general performance of the Japanese economy, measured by inflation, trade balance, and current account.

A number of explanations given for the relatively weak yen seem to have substance: (1) The interest rate differential that has persisted between Japan and the United States for several years, (2) the preference of Japanese investors for U.S. dollar assets for portfolio-balancing purposes, (3) the Japanese monetary authorities' decision to relax exchange control regulations and permit capital flows from Japan, and (4) the strong worldwide demand for U.S. dollars as an asset haven for economic and political security, which indirectly serves to weaken the yen.

There is some consensus among foreign exchange specialists that the current yen-dollar equilibrium rate is about 190–210 yen to the dollar. The trading range for the dollar during the past three years has been between Y203 and Y270, with the year-end 1983 close at Y232. Political pressures from the United States as well as other industrial nations have led to some official attempts to reduce the Japanese demand for U.S. dollars while increasing the international demand for yen. Some progress is being made and more is to be expected, but many long-standing domestic and international relationships and practices will have to be altered before the process can accelerate. Japan definitely seems to be a continuing capital export country for a considerable period ahead.

Japan now has a savings surplus beyond its own immediate financial requirements. This has led to a substantial *outflow* of capital since 1981, helping to weaken the yen. At a time of economic and political uncertainty across the world, the economic strength and general political stability of Japan also insure some fairly large investment *inflows*. Obviously, the yen is caught between these divergent flows. Nevertheless, the general expectation is that in due course the yen value must return more closely to the fundamental equilibrium rate, with or without the full support of the Japanese government.

Any new appreciation of the yen could signal lower interest rates, further dampen inflation, and touch off still more yen appreciation. The Japanese government, however, is likely to take whatever policy measures it can to limit the rise in the yen because of the adverse impact on manufactured exports.

Inevitably, more interest rates in Japan will have to be set by the market. Government bond issues increasingly will have to be sold at auction. This policy change necessarily will erode more of the Japanese government's financial control systems, especially over long-term interest rates.

The Japanese effectively monitor global banking and finance regularly to keep Tokyo up-to-date on overseas developments. Seldom are the Japanese unaware of new ideas, processes, or markets, all of which are intensively researched for their importance to Japan. Accordingly, the Japanese are keenly competitive participants in the world's financial markets. They usually take full advantage of opportunities to maximize short-term gains and hedge against losses. In the longer-term overseas investment field, however, the tendency is to be more cautious and to pursue policies that fundamentally minimize risk and preserve capital. The Japanese investment emphasis is more on underlying *real* growth over time, and less on financial return as pursued by most American business managements.

Recently the Japanese observed the growing power of U.S. venture capitalists in marshaling funds to finance promising new firms, particularly in high technology. Not surprisingly, the Japanese have now started a venture capital program.

The Tokyo stock market behaves differently from the New York stock market because participants, support measures, underlying economic values, profit-reporting systems, and government influences vary widely. Japanese securities market operations are large and unusually volatile. The recent rise of common stock prices in both countries has improved debt-equity ratios for both, but seems to have helped strengthen the financial position of U.S. companies most.

Japan adopted the principle of open capital entry in 1980. Direct investment from abroad is eagerly welcomed and some upturn can be noted. The Ministry of International Trade and Industry (MITI) reports that American firms account for about half of new foreign direct investments in Japan in recent years. Joint ventures and foreign affiliates are also increasing. In banking and finance, it should be noted, despite the announced open entry policy, no Japanese bank has yet been acquired by a foreign bank or other overseas investor.

Complexities of the Japanese legal system, low returns, administrative inertia, and costly cultural features still impede rapid expansion of direct investment. The Japanese always emphasize the competitiveness of their domestic markets as a major factor slowing foreign entry and delaying profitable growth.

The Japanese government is well aware of its problems and the pressures that are mounting from within as well as from outside to increase interest rates and liberalize capital markets much further. These steps would tend to equalize capital flows, strengthen the Japanese yen, and reduce the Japanese trade surplus—all in the long-run interest of Japan.

Since the Reagan-Nakasone negotiations in Tokyo in November 1983, further official discussions and some policy changes have occurred. The United States has pledged to review the unitary tax issue that requires Japan (and other nations) to pay U.S. *state* taxes on a formula that involves a foreign company's worldwide operations. The U.S. Supreme Court, however, subsequently has upheld the unitary tax, making it necessary for congressional legislation to eliminate this economic irritation to Japan. The United States has officially welcomed the sale of Japanese government bonds in the American capital markets; reaffirmed its determination to reduce government spending and the federal budget deficit, which would lower interest rates; and agreed to lend continuing funding support to official multinational financial organizations.

In turn, the Japanese have pledged to accelerate study of, and action on, measures to increase freedom in the foreign exchange market and to introduce new financial instruments that will widen the use of yen by foreign investors and in Japan's trade transactions. Currently only 40 percent of Japan's exports and 2 percent of its imports are denominated in yen.

Many additional suggestions for U.S.-Japanese policy changes are being proposed: yen security purchases by the Federal Reserve for open-market purposes; Japanese government conversion of some of its large dollar reserves into yen; more Japanese overseas borrowing immediately converted into yen; removal of Japanese administrative rules limiting foreign exchange activities; elimination of Japanese interest rate controls on deposits and government securities; increased yen-dollar swaps; termination of Japan's withholding tax on nonresident interest earnings; greater encouragement for Eurobond issues; development of Japanese offshore banking facilities; increased flow of Japanese savings into domestic housing and infrastructure projects; and more cooperation by the U.S. and Japan to encourage other central banks to hold much larger portions of their reserves in yen.

These and other steps, whenever enacted, can be expected to ease some of the financial tensions between Japan and the United States; but no rapid or completely satisfactory decisions are likely soon. The Japanese financial dilemma and the United States' budget deficit do not lend themselves to quick action or dramatic results. But, again, powerful forces are demanding change.

The Issue of Financial Leadership

The global financial system has functioned impressively well during a decade of change and crisis. Leadership from official multinational institutions, the United States, and other countries has held together well through periods of enormous strains and stresses. In my view, there is every reason to expect the same performance over the years ahead.

Agreement on this point is by no means unanimous. Worldwide attention is focused in large part upon the future leadership roles of the U.S. and—increasingly—Japan in global finance. Just as there are rising doubts in many of the world's capitals about the ability of the United States to ensure political stability and peace, there are also widespread concerns about the role the United States will play in helping to achieve more global financial and economic stability in the years ahead.

The future leadership of the U.S. in global banking and finance is clouded in particular by the rising provincialism evident in recent U.S. public policy discussions and decisions. The economic size and power of the United States and the American dollar's role as the principal international currency ensure a large measure of *de facto* U.S. leadership indefinitely in both domestic and international financial affairs. However, most U.S. financial leaders and institutions, caught in an era of massive change, seem primarily concerned with specific domestic market objectives and the need to respond to public criticism—rather than to help achieve even vague national objectives and strategies, or to reinforce U.S. global leadership.

Leading analysts in the many different specialities within the overall field of U.S. banking and finance now tend to emphasize their differences rather than what they have in common. These adversarial feelings are deeply rooted in long years of legal protections for markets that are now crumbling. Antagonism is often apparent between small and large banking institutions, domestic and international, and commercial and noncommercial investment bankers. U.S. financial leaders are usually politically astute but slow to compromise and unlikely to reach clear-cut agreement on major public policies affecting banking and finance. Concerted action in government relations by major U.S. institutions across the field of finance, therefore, cannot be readily accomplished.

The self-correcting forces in the United States' political and economic system, especially when confronted with crisis, can successfully revitalize U.S. domestic banking and finance, and similarly reaffirm U.S. international leadership as well. But, as suggested, considerable time will be required, during which the absence of new non-American leadership will increase the urgency for the U.S. to accelerate its domestic changes and overcome its provincialism.

For Japan, the problem of accepting more global leadership in banking and finance will be difficult but unavoidable if economic growth and well-being are to continue to meet the desires and expectations of the Japanese people. The issue will not be capability or capacity, but rather governmental unwillingness—reinforced by cultural reluctance—to take on the responsibilities of greater leadership, including more initiatives based on mutual interests. The traditional Japanese fear of shocks, their frank recognition that their domestic banking and financial system is ill-prepared to service truly open capital markets, and the absence of an agreed-upon national and international goal of financial leadership are all strong deterrents to fast action.

Nevertheless, the signs of breakdown of the Japanese regulatory system in banking and finance are unmistakable and irreversible. Japan faces a considerable task both to catch up with the fast-changing standards of U.S. banking and finance and to make the adjustments necessary to assume a global financial market role in yen more commensurate with its economic accomplishments and stature in U.S. dollars.

The most decisive factor is that Japan seems to want the benefits of strong leadership while avoiding the risks that would accompany either its own policies and actions or its efforts in concert with others. It already seems clear that many Japanese leaders know that the policy choice ultimately revolves around their practical ability to pursue opportunities for profit at home and abroad. Their long-standing priority for economic gain and advantage points in the direction of greater—not lesser—Japanese leadership in banking and finance, with the reluctant policy support of government.

The Forces of Change

Banking and finance do not readily lend themselves to inclusion in the current industrial policy debate in the United States because they are traditionally already heavily linked to government policy and regulatory influence, if not control. Yet any consideration of public policy changes to revitalize the U.S. economy cannot logically omit the vital role of banking and finance. In Japan, banking and finance are an integral part of industrial policy.

National and international financial markets are now engaged in deep and continuing structural as well as cyclical change. Governments cannot be aloof to these changes and have little choice but to ratify the legal and institutional changes dictated by them. In the United States, government is responding to market developments with some misgivings but reasonable speed. This is much less evident in Japan and some other major countries where preserving the status quo has a higher priority. The emphasis in America paradoxically is now upon domestic *deregulation* but stepped-up international *regulation.* The response of official government policy in Japan is also toward deregulation, but at a much slower pace. Japan confronts an inevitable role as a full participant in the world's financial and capital markets, despite its strong preference to avoid the risks and responsibilities involved.

The forces of correction are hard at work in banking and finance in both the United States and Japan. The compartmentalized American financial system of the past is rapidly crumbling and forcing a reduction in excessive delivery capacity among competing institutions. The firmly guided Japanese banking and financial system is also gradually breaking up through regulatory reform dictated by pressure from dissatisfied participants in the domestic and foreign markets. Japan is no longer finding it possible or even necessary to pursue protective policies for Japanese companies and institutions as much as earlier. Accordingly, the cost of capital for Japanese enterprises seems certain to rise.

Both Japan and the United States retain enormous financial strengths, the former because of determination, high savings, and high productivity; the latter because of greater private sector ability and willingness to change, rising confidence and a new spirit of revitalization, and the power to attract money and management from abroad.

It is difficult to judge which nation faces the most severe adjustments ahead in banking and finance as well as in other fields. In recent years clouds of doubt have hovered mainly over the future of the United States. It is becoming increasingly clear, however, that Japan faces many formidable problems and that its forthcoming domestic and international changes will be by no means small or painless.

In these uncertain times, the need for the United States and Japan to find and maintain more dynamic cooperation and understanding will be paramount. Yet the clash of cultures and systems will not make this easy. No merging of two distinctly different approaches to policy is to be expected, although a richer blend of the best of both is a worthy and reasonable goal, not only in terms of mutual interest but also to help assure the economic and political stability of the world.

Both the United States and Japan have major adjustments ahead to ward off international confrontations. For the United

States in particular, the principal task will be to reduce the federal budget deficit; for Japan, the urgent need will be to move more promptly to open its capital markets to enlarge Japanese lending abroad and foreign borrowing in Japan. Both nations need to work harder to achieve agreed-upon goals of slowing the demand for U.S. dollars and accelerating the demand for Japanese yen. Neither the United States nor Japan can hope to prosper if confronted with a faltering international banking and financial system or protectionist trade wars.

Industrial policy in the final analysis means finding the changing optimum mix of government and private profit-sector contributions within each nation's particular cultural, economic, social, and political environment. Across international boundaries, however, industrial policy can have meaning only insofar as it draws attention to what nations have in common in order to reduce and offset what they have at variance.

10

PAUL SEABURY

Industrial Policy
and National Defense

As the American economy edges toward recovery, national attention is beginning to shift: preoccupation with the immediate
effects of economic policy on inflation and unemployment is giving
way to a broader concern about the underlying health of the nation's industrial base. Unemployment remains high—most visibly
in such basic industries as automobiles and steel—and pleas for
protection of these industries are gaining in appeal. Such calls,
coming chiefly from Democratic presidential hopefuls, ring loudly
in the country's industrial heartland. They challenge the basic
principles of three decades of American trade and industrial
policy. Taken seriously, they could help precipitate a worldwide
drift toward protectionism—leading to the collapse of valued economic partnerships and even of critical alliances.

The appeal of protectionism during recessions is not to be shrugged off. Jobs are involved, although a serious breakdown in trading relations could cause harm to many more than the currently unemployed. Concern about jobs is likely to diminish with economic recovery. But even with a very strong economic upturn, the deeper issues raised by current calls for "industrial policy" will not go away. It is now almost certain that a prosperous America, restored to its familiar habit of growth, will nonetheless contain a very sick automotive industry, a very sick steel industry, and others in similar shape.

This circumstance makes it almost inevitable that some administration—whether Republican or Democratic—will soon be forced to address the problem of the nation's industrial future in a comprehensive fashion. America's chief industrial trading partners, not to mention the Soviet Union, have long made this subject one of unremitting concern. They do not assume the relation between business and government to be adversarial. Nor do they presume that market considerations should dictate the future course of their economies.

Indeed, in light of the deteriorating state of its basic industries, the United States has a clear need for a coherent industrial policy—but for reasons wholly unrelated to those usually offered. The necessity for a U.S. industrial policy arises not from domestic economic considerations—however large these may currently loom—but rather from strategic military concerns. As the only genuine guarantor of security for both itself and the Free World as a whole, the United States simply cannot afford to allow its industrial base to wither away. Thus far the debate between reindustrializers and "Atari Democrats," between neomercantilists and free-traders, has completely ignored this central dimension of the problem. In the process, the advocates of industrial policy— and their opponents—have framed an agenda totally unsuited to the strategic circumstances of the United States.

It should be clear, for example, that strategic concerns obviate the usefulness of Japan and Western Europe as models for U.S. industrial policy. Even if it were economically advisable to do so, America would be in no position to emulate its allies and trading partners. Our strategic burdens are fundamentally different. In framing economic policy, we must consider not only our economic rivals (who are also our political friends) but also our strategic rival, the Soviet Union. To concentrate on commercial challenges from the former could be to neglect the military-industrial challenges from the latter. Japan and Western European nations remain sheltered under U.S. strategic guarantees. They are not great powers. *It does not lie in the capacity of Japan or Western European nations to envision their economic policies as preeminently strategic, as we must.* Severally and individually they are not strong enough, save in an alliance framework, to address the security question as the U.S. can and must.

Japanese and Western European economic concerns pertain (as do ours also) to jobs, to peacetime prosperity, and to competitiveness within the Free World international economy. But American perspectives, unfortunately, necessarily go far beyond such considerations and must be worthy of a great power. Japan, for competitive reasons, could today foreswear even its domestic steel industry as the price of allocation of resources to more profitable undertakings—and this would not seriously damage its current security position. Others could act similarly; the U.S. cannot. The American industrial base constitutes the strategic core of Free World defenses. Those who, whether in the interests of free trade or a "high-tech" boom, are content to remain untroubled by the demise of U.S. basic industry would do well to remember Solon's stern warning to Croesus: "Sir, if any man hath better iron than you, he will be master of all this gold."

The "Postindustrial" Myth

Already America's economic troubles are raising doubts about the rosy picture that some had painted of the "postindustrial" society. Long before the current recession, "everyone" seemed certain that, thanks to international competition and rapid technological changes, the character of the American economy was quickly changing. Changes to be observed in the composition of the American work force, even in the 1960s, showed such significant shifts from labor-intensive to capital-intensive industries—and from industrial to service occupations—that the idea of a postindustrial America entered our discourse, with all of its mystifying sociological possibilities.

What is of equal interest is that, as this tendency proceeded, fewer young Americans opted for careers in jobs that involved "building things." At the same time, American public education began its long era of benign neglect of basic skills such as mathematics and the sciences. One result is that today many an American engineering school fills its classrooms with foreign students or first-generation Americans—Asians in particular.[1] The once guiltily deplored "brain drain," the siphoning off of human talents and skills from backward nations such as India and Iran and from other parts of Asia, actually may have made possible the survival of America's strength in industry and high technology today.

The same period saw the disappearance of certain once-important consumer industries in the U.S. that were overcome by foreign competition—most conspicuously textiles, shoes, radios, televisions, consumer optics (cameras in particular), bicycles, motorbikes, and so on. Less noticed, because less conspicuous, was the decline of major basic industries, chief among them the U.S. shipbuilding industry,[2] the steel industry, and now the automotive industry.

These tendencies would have manifested themselves without the assistance of U.S. multinational corporations, but the latter helped, hastening the overseas diffusion of America's manufacturing competitors. Clearly also there was the famed "hidden hand" at work, assigning commodity manufacture location in accordance with the whims of what economists term "comparative advantage." Observing this, optimists could remark that in postindustrial America what would remain competitive would be capital-intensive; the labor-intensive industries would migrate abroad, seeking low-wage host nations.

Thus a decade or more ago it was still possible to argue that such changes would be acceptable and even welcome in the aggregate, so long as the U.S. retained its position on the cutting edge of technological change and in the development of new industries and new products, and kept its undisputed lead in important sectors such as the aircraft industry and agriculture. Furthermore, the arguments ran, it would be scandalous to subsidize industries "obviously" incapable of holding their own in the face of tough foreign competition. The American future, the optimists assured us, should be at the forefront of economic change, where the "real action" lay. This future seemed assured by the advent of the "ages"—the atomic age, the space age, the computer age, the technotronic age, and so forth. Through aeronautics, space technology, seabed technology, computers, microchips, biochemistry, and modern agricultural technology, America would retain an unchallenged leading role in the world economy. Thus the shoes in which Americans jogged could be made in Taiwan, for all anyone cared.

An essential element in this line of argument was, oddly enough, mercantilist, since continuing advances required incessant attention to research and development and to quality at the critical levels of scientific research. At the same time, there had to be careful defense of high technology against leakage, theft, and industrial espionage. Thus, in a certain sense, the case for faith in frontier industries relied less on the idea of comparative advantage than on the vision of an energetic fostering and subsidization of the process of innovation itself—as in government defense-related programs in the space industry and elsewhere. But market forces were also seen as hastening these developments. In this view, a good recession might even accelerate the pace at which old-line industries would shuffle offstage, replaced by ones at the forefront of technological progress.

By now this vision has firmly taken hold. As the executive editor of *Forbes* recently observed in an article entitled "The Molting of America," "Are we in a depression? Or a recession? Neither. The economy is throwing off old skin and growing a new one. The implications are favorable for the future."[3] His simple answer was the "high-tech" one—an idea that soon caught the attention of the president himself.

This idea comes as no suprise to economic observers. The earliest consequences of it were marked well over a decade ago by sociologist Daniel Bell in his observation that America was on its way to the postindustrial era and was remorselessly becoming chiefly a "service society"; blue-collar America was on its way out, along with "industrialism," as part of the American way. In short, long before the present recession supervened (and in fact before OPEC began its depredations), this "molting of America" was already well under way. Now many economists see these changes as a secular trend, persisting through inflation, deflation, recession, and recovery.

But to continue with the editor of *Forbes:* "The simple fact is that a given standard of living no longer requires the same amount of iron and steel, labor, energy, rubber, glass as it once did."[4] That sounds plausible, just as would its corollary that a rising standard of living should not require the same mixture of material ingredients it once did. The logic could be carried even further, based upon fortunate experiences of the past three decades: the same given standard of living surely does not require the same amounts of such basic commodities to be located, developed, sustained, used, and renewed within the confines of the American nation or, for that matter, in areas immediately adjacent to it; or to take the logic yet a step further, the very industries that make use of such primary resources do not necessarily have to be located within the confines of North America. All very plausible.

Trade and the "Pax Americana"

The logic of these secular shifts and their ensuing benefits to consumers would seem obvious if one were content to view the American economy as part (a major part, admittedly) of a large, secure, Free World economy, which blossomed after the Second World War and was conditioned upon America's strategic preeminence. In such an environment, it could be argued, the doctrine of comparative advantage could be safely allowed to permit the diffusion of the productive components of an international economy according to its own laws. It would thus not matter particularly where, geographically, the components were, so long as the American portion of the whole sufficed to guarantee Americans their profitable share in the international production and consumption of wealth. It would not particularly matter if in this process some American industries fell behind, or even died out, as long as the whole U.S. economy, on balance, flourished. The ease with which other nations, such as Japan, gained access to American technology, capital, managerial skills, and markets, and the eagerness with which U.S.-based multinationals embraced the logic of economic interdependence, were simply aspects of a larger, mutually beneficial process. The American national interest might judge the worthiness of interdependence on the basis of aggregate "unsubstantive" criteria—balance of trade, levels of employment, balance of payments, rates of aggregate economic growth, per capita income, and so forth—rather than criteria concerning the unique characteristics of the components of the American economy as such.

The migration of U.S. capital overseas was defensible when viewed in the context of a "Pax Americana," with its worldwide security systems, military bases, and friendly allies. That this process of capital and technology expansion (branded by Marxist-Leninists as "imperialistic") had important corrosive effects on the character of the *internal* American economy was less remarked. In fact, the development bore a disquieting resemblance to what occurred in Britain much earlier, in the nineteenth and early twentieth centuries, as capital migrated overseas and the British industrial base corroded. A British observer recently has reminded us of this unpleasant parallel:

> It was this erosion of an industrial lead that was the long-term cause of the end of the "Pax Britannica," just as it is the poor U.S. economic performance in the past two decades that ultimately explains the eclipse of the "Pax Americana." Military might and global influence always need to rest on strong economic foundations. When the latter weaken, so, too, does one's real power in the world.[5]

This parallel can be stretched too far; but there are elements of truth in it, especially with respect to the indifference once fatally displayed by Britain to the internal character of its economy. What should the interior nature of a great power's economy actually be?

Prosperity vs. Security

Even if the logic of comparative advantage is followed and the results prove beneficial by the test of prosperity, still the contrast between the claims of prosperity and the requisites of strength must always be borne in mind. The doctrine of comparative advantage never has been a respecter of the security of nations, as Adam Smith himself recognized. To be sure, some nations that seek comfort rather than security in their policies can repose their destinies, with reasonable hope of safety, in the hands of others more powerful than they (as does Canada today, the size of whose defense outlays makes Japan seem a military superpower by comparison). A great power cannot afford this luxury. When Alexander Hamilton wrote his *Report of Manufactures* in 1791, he offered observations that bore on the destinies of all states that were, or aspired to become, major powers. But he directed them at the new United States. In Hamilton's words:

Not only the wealth but the independence and safety of a country appear to be materially connected with the prosperity of manufactures. Every nation, with a view to these great objects, ought to endeavor to possess within itself, all the essentials of national supply. These comprise the means of subsistence, habitation, clothing, and defense. . . . The possession of these is necessary to the perfection of the body politic; to the safety as well as to the security of the society. . . . The extreme embarrassments of the United States during the late war, are still a matter of keen recollection; a future might be expected again to exemplify the mischiefs and dangers of a situation to which that incapacity is still . . . applicable, unless changed by timely and vigorous action.[6]

Indeed, it could be argued that an essential precondition for current thinking about America's industrial future should be a comprehensive report on manufactures, imitative of Alexander Hamilton's in attending above all to the industrial security requirements of the United States.

It should be emphasized that Soviet strategic planners are under no illusions as to the primacy of strategic policy in governing overall economic resource policy and allocations. As the Soviet theoretical journal *Kommunist* has stated:

The USSR now represents a mighty power in economic and military respects. The scientific-technological revolution currently taking place substantially influences the development of military affairs. In these conditions *the military-technology policy of the CPSU* [Communist Party of the Soviet Union] *is directed toward creating and maintaining military superiority* of the socialist countries over the forces of war and aggression.[7] [Emphasis added.]

If the United States has a military-industrial complex, the Soviet Union (in the words of Robert Conquest) *is* a military-industrial complex. "Our unified military-technical policy," Soviet Deputy Defense Minister Shabanov recently has written,

serves us well in maintaining the technical equipment of the armed forces at the level of modern requirements. The unified military-technical policy . . . ensures the alliance of industry with science in the interest of creating highly efficient models of weapons and hardware.[8]

Shabanov's remarks have been echoed by Chief of Staff Ogarkov:

> Coordination in the mobilization and deployment of the armed forces and the national economy *as a whole,* particularly in using manpower, transportation, communication and energy, and ensuring the stability and survivability of the country's economic mechanism is needed now more than ever. . . . The close interconnection among the mobilization readiness of the armed forces, the national economic and civil defense is a very important condition for maintaining the defense capability of the country as a whole.[9] [Emphasis added.]

Declining Defense Sector

New Hamiltons, conceivably, may pop up, like the mythical warriors that sprang from the soil when Cadmus sowed his dragon's teeth. If they do, they surely will be a race apart from the recent generation of no-growth environmentalists whose fame came from the anti-industrial success of the 1960s and 1970s—the Clean Air Act, the Federal Water Pollution Control Act, the Wilderness Act, the Federal Land Policy and Management Act, the Surface Mining Control and Reclamation Act, and others, the considerable costs and benefits of which all of us now pay for, and some of us enjoy.

The Hamiltonian perspective, by contrast, emphasizes growth and industrial strength. Until recently this perspective has enjoyed little public favor. Now there is something of a resurgence, though observable differences among today's neo-Hamiltonians are worth pointing out—notably the difference between those who call for a renaissance of the Northern industrial base and those would accelerate a transition from "sunset" to "sunrise" industries. Despite this important disagreement, both views would agree on the basic principle of industrial planning. The question is whether the criteria employed by either of them adequately address the question of the character of an industrial base for American security requirements. Recently, General Alton Slay injected this dimension into the controversy: "It is a gross contradiction to think that we can maintain our position as a first-rate military power with a second-rate industrial base. It has never been done in the history of the modern world."[10]

A glance at a few sectors of the American defense industry would suffice to ring alarm bells, but the general picture is even more problematic. In 1980, according to *Aviation Week,* the Defense Science Board (DSB) reported that the defense industry—before the current budget increases—was hard-pressed to meet even the then–relatively modest procurement goals of the armed services. The DSB concluded that the industry's ability to exceed existing levels of defense production was "extremely limited" and possibly nonexistent.[11]

Aside from its "high-tech" sectors, much of America's defense industrial base is old and outmoded. Sixty percent of equipment now used to produce military hardware is more than twenty years old, a proportion far in excess of the average for all U.S. industry in this age bracket. Furthermore, as the defense industrial base has shrunk, so has the lead time lengthened for crucial parts and subassemblies of weapons systems.[12]

The definition of what the defense industry is must naturally take into account not merely current and end-product industrial performance and time schedules for procured weapons, but also the nature of an industrial base that must exist at all times for the undertaking of large-scale, bold, and swift strategic mobilization. *Such an industrial base cannot be regarded as identical with an industrial base designed for the most effective competitive industries in a world market, nor with one largely conceived so as to maintain supremacy in futurist high technology.* Such a base should be understood to include domestic industrial assets readily fungible in case of major international crises and conflicts, so as to match and exceed Soviet capabilities across a dire panoply of forces, some of which the U.S. has badly neglected in recent years.

There is enough unease already among America's defense planners as to how much money to allocate for the near terms (e.g., for new hardware), without even considering the lead time that defense procurement now requires for delivery of end products. This latter question, independent of defense budget size, is very troublesome. To cite several examples: from 1977 to 1980, the time span for military aircraft landing gear delivery lengthened from 52 to 120 weeks. Incredibly, the air force currently requires 41 months for delivery of military jet engines—an interval of time exactly equal to the length of U.S. involvement in World War II from Pearl Harbor to V-E Day. Even high-tech procurement appears impaired. Between 1978 and 1980 the delivery span for integrated circuits more than doubled, from 25 to 62 weeks. Such procurement nightmares, whatever their causes, are as nothing beside the shrinking of the industrial base necessary for surge capabilities in the event of clear and present danger—even of a possible war of quite finite duration (see table 1). It should be noted that many production bottlenecks are the consequence of federal environmental, health, and safety regulations; the closing of hundreds of foundries has been attributable to these. Nearly 30 percent of U.S. machine tools, essential to the industrial base, are currently imported. In 1980, only one U.S. company was engaged

Table 1
Imports as a Percentage of Apparent U.S. Consumption

	1970	1981
Passenger cars	15.2%	27.3%
Trucks	4.0	20.0
Steel	13.8	19.1
Textiles/apparel	10.0[a]	15.0
Nonrubber footwear	30.1	50.7
Luggage	5.0	27.8
Handbags/purses	14.0	39.1
Machine tools	12.1	29.2[b]
Farm machinery	8.0	19.0
Food processing machinery	1.0	23.0
Textile machinery	37.0	44.0
Construction equipment	2.6	9.2
Semiconductors	10.9	38.7
Computers	4.0[a]	8.0
Calculating and accounting machines	20.0[a]	39.0[c]
Radio and TV receiving sets	32.0	60.0
Ball and roller bearings	7.0	15.2
Valves and pipe fittings	3.2	8.6
Refined copper	6.0	16.5
Slab zinc	23.0	69.0
Tires and inner tubes	5.0	14.8

[a]1972 data, first year available.
[b]1981 results based on first-half data.
[c]1980 data.

Source: U.S. Department of Commerce trade association data, from *Industry Week*, June 14, 1982, p. 64.

in the casting of tank hulls and turrets. Only two were manufacturing gun mounts. Import penetration into specific industrial sectors, as a recent report has indicated, "suggests an unacceptable
dependency on foreign sources for key elements of defense production."[13] A recent Department of Commerce report on this subject
also recognized the increasing problem of overseas industrial
dependence:

Some of our basic metal processing industries are facing declining output, as high costs and low world prices cause plant closures. However,
defense and civilian needs for the products of these industries will be
met, *albeit at the cost of increased imports and dependence on foreign
sources of supply.*[14] [Emphasis added.]

The fact that manufactures critical to U.S. defense needs may be
made more cheaply abroad is small comfort to anyone who would
commonsensically conclude that the resulting dependence would
entail unacceptable risks. The forfeiture of a North American
steel production capability to powerful overseas competitors would
be a certain consequence of current projected trends. One might
assume from the standpoint of comparative advantage that South
Korean steel facilities, elegantly efficient, would be preferred to
our own dilapidated ones, but one would wonder how dependable
these would be, situated as they are only hours away from massive
Communist tank forces.

By the same logic it would be folly to imitate the overall
Japanese model, which is almost exclusively devoted to commerce
and which is resigned to a hapless dependence upon foreign
sources of energy and raw materials and upon American protection. The United States has no superpower to guarantee its
security, and its industrial system must reflect that fact.

Some conservative economists particularly bristle at the thought
of a national industrial defense policy, since it would lead to more
onerous government regulation and intervention in the national
economy, and risk also the pork-barrel politicization of the market.
Such concerns are legitimate, but it should be pointed out that excessive governmental regulation for purposes other than defense
bears much of the blame for the accelerated flight of manufactures
from American shores, as well as for the dangerous U.S. dependence upon distant, foreign critical raw materials. In 1982, a White
House report to Congress itemized twenty-one major existing

federal regulations of industry having severe impacts upon the U.S. mining industry, as well as upon defense manufactures.[15] Land-access, safety and health, and environmental regulations, many of them products of the purity crusades of the 1970s, in combination have imposed severe compliance costs upon industry so as to force U.S. production abroad.

The same processes at work in manufactures of defense equipment thus are to be seen in mineral extraction and refinement. While American dependence on overseas sources of minerals long has been recognized as a serious defense problem, this dependence is increasing rather than stabilizing or lessening. But further, as one student of this subject has recently suggested, barring some change in federal regulatory policies, the *processing* as well as the mining of raw materials will likely emigrate overseas for reasons of cost.

Compounding the restrictions barring exploration for minerals in this country are the costs associated with environmental and occupational safety and health laws. As these nonproductive costs are compounded by the rising cost of energy in the United States, pressures to move the processing plants to the source will increase, particularly with respect to South Africa and the developing countries of sub-Saharan Africa.[16]

This in itself is a sobering prospect; for even today the principal suppliers of raw materials critical to defense industries (aside from important dependable sources like Canada) are located in countries and regions of dubious reliability—Thailand, South Africa, China, Zaire, the Philippines, Guinea, Suriname, Zambia and, of course, the USSR, to name a few. Peacetime stockpiling of unprocessed ores is easier to contemplate than measures to deal with the strategic condition of lacking the means to convert them to industrial use.[17]

One less visible feature of the sorry plight of American's defense industrial base is to be seen in the shadowy world of sub-contractors and component suppliers. The world of major defense contractors is fairly well illumined if only because it receives public and congressional attention, at least for cost-overrun scandals. Not so the subcontractors' labyrinth, wherein dwell the gnomes who make, amass, and distribute the small parts of things from which the wholes are made. Here, in this gloomy basement, the classic aphorism applies particularly: "For want of a nail, a shoe was lost." Mundane objects such as screws, nuts, and bolts (known collectively as "fasteners") are a good case in point; semiconductor devices for U.S. products are another. Both sorts of devices now are produced in faraway places like Malaysia, Singapore, Taiwan, the Philippines, and Hong Kong.

A good horror story can be spun from the fasteners industry. According to a recent study,[18] a 20 percent shortfall of these commodities during a projected mobilization year and the first three years of a conventional war would have a multiplier impact of $240 billion in lost defense industrial capacity. (Consumer-durable output would be nonexistent.) Yet in recent years this critical industry has fled the U.S., as boat people fled Indochina. In 1969, standard nuts consumed in the U.S. were produced at home and abroad in equal quantities; in 1982, 90 percent were imported. Most imports now are from the Far East.[19]

Barriers to Discussion

Two factors today paralyze serious public discussion of defense industrial policy. The first—essentially a political impediment—is the current cleavage between dominant conservative and liberal, Republican and Democratic, schools of thought on economic and national security matters. The second has to do with conventional wisdom concerning the relationship between defense mobilization plans and U.S. strategy.

The first impediment contributes to a policy stalemate: conservatives and Republicans by and large now favor a strong defense policy after a decade of neglect; such a policy requires significant increases in U.S. nuclear and conventional armaments, and of course considerable budgetary increases to pay for them. Prominent liberals and Democrats today call for détente, defense cuts, disarmament, and arms control. But prominent conservatives and Republicans at the same time reject any U.S. industrial policies that augur intensified government regulation and control of industry, while liberals and Democrats, contrariwise, see in the idea of a national industrial policy the hope for federal protection of endangered industries and jobs. (Oddly enough, on this latter subject we see a strange reversal of traditional party perspectives with respect to U.S. international trade policy and investment policy. Republicans, including key members of the Reagan administration, stress the still-conventional wisdom of trade interdependence; Democrats move toward protectionism.) Any considered defense industrial policy, in consequence of these polarities, falls between two stools. It is a political orphan.*

The second impediment arises from a far more intractable question that goes to fundamental issues of national security policy. Political polarizations such as I have described above reveal profound uncertainties and disagreements about issues of war and peace in what many now call the "nuclear age."

In its starkest and most problematical form, it is now argued by many that *one can have the capability to deter aggression without having a war-fighting capability at all.* With its huge arsenal of nuclear weapons, the U.S. can display a credible capability to inflict tremendous (and "unacceptable") pain and devastation on its Soviet adversary without displaying, in addition, an ability to defeat its military forces in battle. This view assigns, if not the exclusive, then the dominant, priorities of defense policy to deterrence rather than to *war-fighting as such.* While no serious U.S. defense planners accept this extreme view, it is a view that colors the thinking of many Americans; not only nuclear war, but *any* war directly between ourselves and our Soviet adversaries, is unthinkable. Deterrence is all.

A less stark and more widespread and fashionable view envisions a future war as being *short;* the confrontation, according to this conception, would bring about a strategic decision within weeks. In consequence, the logistical and human determinants of the outcome would be forces-in-being, not potential forces. Such potential forces, as those to which a national mobilization plan should address itself, would therefore play no role in the outcome. (This short-war scenario is present in countless NATO battle scenarios, in particular those that stress "flexible response.")

---

*These generalizations require qualification: important Reagan administration officials are quite aware of the sorry state of the defense industry's vulnerable reliance on foreign suppliers (this was true, also, in the last phase of the Carter administration). Important Democrats, such as Senator Glenn, acknowledge the need for a strong defense buildup. The polarization is by no means total.

The short-war mind-set is further reinforced by an assumption that potential industrial assets are subject to the same vulnerabilities as forces-in-being. In World War II, the American "Arsenal of Democracy" was immune to complete devastation, but now, it is felt, such immunity no longer exists in any strategic sense.

A quite opposite view of potential assets reinforces the complacency that this Armageddon scenario oddly inspires. In this Pollyannaish vision, no serious attention need be given to the neglect of present-day industrial mobilization plans, since in a long war, it is felt, U.S. and Free World assets would come to greatly exceed those of the Soviet Union. (Japanese industrial productivity now may exceed Soviet productivity.) By 1943, in World War II, the American "Arsenal of Democracy" accounted for 40 percent of the industrial production of *all* belligerents, friend and foe alike. We did it before, and we can do it again, the argument goes. Why worry about long-term mobilization more than short-term mobilization? Things will put themselves together, as they always have.

This sanguine outlook offers no comfort whatsoever if one assumes that Soviet nuclear-cum-conventional forces prove superior in the short term and if, in short-term fighting, U.S. conventional forces were to run out of supplies. In such a circumstance, a war would be over *before* Detroit could spew out its vast panoply of new tanks and planes. Then, too, no national industrial policy for defense would be needed!

At all times there is great uncertainty as to what bearing military potential may have on particular contingencies. The nature, length, and location of future wars and crises are matters about which none but soothsayers can speak with conviction. (What Americans dreamed, in 1945, that the next major U.S. war would occur in *Korea,* of all places!) Absent such certainties, the logistical requirements of war entail intelligent conjectures of common sense. In this regard, there should be a distinction drawn between the limited concept of *war* potential and the broader conception of *military* potential (broader in that it addresses the question of strength both in war and in no-war-no-peace conditions). This concept of military potential has lost none of its significance on account of the new military technology. As Klaus Knorr has remarked of it:

Nations become military powers of consequence, globally or within a region, because they have a superior military potential, which even with a moderate rate of mobilization generates commanding ready military strength, or because, though endowed with a moderate potential in terms of manpower and other resources, they mobilize to a greater extent than do states of comparable military potential.[20]

This is a valid observation when we hold in mind two essential facts—that such considerations have a supportive bearing upon general deterrence credibility, and upon U.S. credibility in regions where the likelihood of nuclear confrontation can be greatly lessened by the known capacity to project conventional forces. Military potential also bears upon the capacity to export arms to allies and others, especially in urgent circumstances.[21]

There is yet another argument against programming long-war resources. Not too long ago, some military planners were able to argue plausibly that superior U.S. strategic resources would be used before conventional forces-in-being were exhausted. The role of conventional forces then would be to create a "pause" or "fire-break" until the Soviets would pull back from the brink of nuclear war. Obviously, this argument no longer holds; its plausibility disappeared when the U.S. lost its nuclear superiority.

A cynic once remarked when many American fire departments relaxed their physical standards (including height) for hiring, in order to meet affirmative action goals, that it was now necessary to legislate smaller fires. The same sort of thing could be said of the short-war concept. As one observer has written recently, this notion

has tended to become the basis for establishing requirements, rather than the rationale for allocating fiscally constrained resources against an unconstrained requirement. . . . This circular reasoning results in the short war becoming the requirement. National goals fade from the equation.[22]

An intellectual precondition for addressing the question of industrial capacity for war of indefinite duration is to dispel the mistaken notion that either deterrence or the short war is the exclusive strategy. To hold to either doctrine, ironically, also erodes the validity of either. Each doctrine requires the bodyguard of strength that a visible, known surge capacity displays. Such a surge capacity requires an American economy equipped with its *own* industrial assets, rather than dependent upon distant, and therefore problematic, suppliers.

Soviet Maritime Threat

All this is especially troubling in light of the staggering growth of Soviet naval power in the past fifteen years. This growth, which continues, has many strategic implications for the United States. The one most pertinent to the present subject is the expanding Soviet capability to interdict sea lanes in critical regions—now including even the Caribbean. A subordinate consideration is the spread of actual Soviet political land control in key strategic locations. This startling new development presents U.S. naval strategy with a historically novel problem. There have been precedents in the American experience for such naval threats to vital Free World maritime lanes—witness the "battles of the Atlantic" in World Wars I and II. Never before in U.S. history, however, has such adversarial naval capacity displayed itself on such a vast scale. This consideration alone should give pause to anyone who pays unqualified homage to doctrines of comparative advantage and international economic independence, as these affect U.S. vital interests.

When the U.S. after World War II abandoned its historic protectionism and embraced the idea of international economic interdependence, American naval power absolutely and relatively occupied a position attained heretofore by no naval power in history. In 1945, the combined fleets of all other maritime powers could not possibly rival it—least of all the Soviet Union, which then was still a giant landlocked behemoth.

At that time, the U.S., with its combined military and commercial maritime capacities, commanded naval power with a truly global reach. Intentionally or not, the seas then were an American *mare nostrum*. A liberal America presided over the reestablishment of a giant liberal market economy extending from Japan, in East Asia, to Central Europe, from the Arctic to the Antarctic. The American maritime guarantee of this huge zone of liberal commerce has served as successor and surrogate to the liberal British maritime supremacy, which in its time was the major guarantee of the global trading order of the nineteenth century. In effect,

America in this respect restored the global commercial order of the Victorian era. The situation of 1945 dramatically confirmed the ideas of Alfred T. Mahan, even though few at the time credited him with this accomplishment. It was Mahan who had insisted upon the intimate relationship between global maritime capacity and commercial *order,* as these affected America's prosperity and its destiny.

Since then, America's chief allies and trading partners have benefited from this new order of sea power, which can be seen in the giant mercatorial band of intimately associated open-society economies. One central assumption of this relationship has been that the seas are truly free. Today, however, the seas are also occupied by forces that challenge this freedom. The era of unchallenged American naval supremacy is threatened from the most improbable source—Russia—once regarded as the classic landlocked power of the international state system. The USSR, now an enormous naval power, is committed to the destruction of this two-century-old trading-commercial order that Britain first, and then America, sustained in sequence. This is the underlying challenge to America's position in the global international economy, though few people see it this way.

This strange new maritime situation must be viewed in historical perspective. The pre-Napoleonic maritime rivalries of the European powers—involving Britain, Spain, the Netherlands, France, and so on—differed greatly from the present maritime rivalry. Their contentions reflected national ambitions and rivalries, to be sure. But all these powers were primarily concerned with the capture, control, and exploitation of overseas wealth for purposes of national enrichment. Those maritime struggles came to an unambiguous end in 1803, in the final defeat of French-Napoleonic maritime forces. Because of historical coincidence, control of the seas then passed into British hands at almost the same time as Britain embraced the doctrines of free trade and the philosophy of Adam Smith. British naval supremacy for a century after served as the global umbrella of the world trading community, being both liberal and hegemonial at the same time.

The contemporary East-West rivalry for mastery of the seas differs radically from its seventeenth- and eighteenth-century predecessor. Like that of the British in the nineteenth century, the present American interest in sea power lies in the strategic objective of sustaining a large, far-flung trading community, and in the protection of its own interests and those of its allies. But the Soviet challenge to this maritime order can in no way be explained by mere economic ambitions. The Soviet empire does not expand to enrich itself materially (on this I am sure all Sovietologists can agree). To the contrary, the Soviet economy benefits marginally more from the advantages it gains from its relation to the Western industrial order than it does from its costly imperial conquests in Eastern Europe, Asia, Africa, and now Latin America. By a purely economic calculus, the USSR currently has a vested interest, not in these vast and costly imperial adventures, but in the intimate and profitable economic connections that it cultivates with the Western industrial democracies.

The small comfort that can be drawn from this gloomy situation thus consists in the fact that Soviet imperialism clearly is not moved by a craving to seize wealth and pelf. It is not visions of gold and other riches that inspire the Soviet threat to the U.S.-sustained international trading system; the Soviets indeed pay out their gold and other riches to sustain their expansion. The distress that we can derive from the situation is actually of a more serious order. It is "merely" the quest for total political hegemony that animates the Soviet challenge. In any event, this quest now threatens, among other things, the fundamental basis of America's vision of a vibrant international trading community and the relation of that community to America's most basic strategic interests.

Need for Reassessment

It might be objected that the recognition of these facts offers little comfort to those who wish to focus attention upon America's declining international competitive position in trade and its lagging performance as a consumer-oriented economy. To raise the issue now of the defense industrial base, at a time of rising public objections to defense spending, would seem to some the height of folly. To dwell upon the issue, it will furthermore be argued, would be to suggest that national industrial priority be given to precisely those parts of the economy that are performing most poorly —

hardly an attractive idea even in the best of circumstances. And, of course, any immediate program of industrial action that reflected such concern would nurture well-founded suspicions abroad that the U.S. was commencing a withdrawal into Factory America.

But these objections, serious as they may be, certainly cannot dissipate genuine concerns for the future. Whatever results from the present debate over the U.S. economy, it now seems almost certain that the United States will face an inescapable need for a national industrial policy. Nearly all of America's commercial rivals in the Free World have one, as a means of guiding their economies through an uncertain international future. And if America's strategic rival, the Soviet Union, has one (to put it mildly), why should America permit its own industrial future and its security to be at the mercy of chance events, the autonomous decisions of individual corporations, the vicissitudes of the international market system, and the holy grail of full employment?

In any event, a modest first step, prerequisite to any action with respect to America's industrial future, must be a major, across-the-board inventory of what the current and emerging character of America's industrial plant now amounts to—in itself, in relation to the world economy, and in relation to survival in a strategic contest with the Soviet Union.

"National industrial policy" is an alarming shibboleth to those who smell in it a patriotic excuse for government protection and subsidization of industrial inefficiency. There is good reason for such suspicion. But if critical defense-related industries are allowed to continue to migrate abroad, for whatever reason, this should be a matter of grave public concern.

It would be insouciant to rely upon market forces to determine the geopolitical location of essential American industries, when this may mean location in far distant and/or politically and militarily vulnerable places. Ever since World War II the United States has had an industrial policy with respect to internationally dispersed raw materials. The same prudent logic should apply to basic industrial defense assets. In the case of raw materials, *nature* is the arbitrary tyrant to be dealt with; but nature need have no final say in the location of industries. Certain crucial assets must be located within reasonably secure confines.

A prudent defense mobilization policy, among other things, should inspire a thoughtful inventory of what these essential assets are and how they can be prudently husbanded by federal policies.

11

YOLANDA KODRZYCKI HENDERSON

Tax Reform: An Item for Any Industrial Policy Agenda

The point of an "industrial policy"—as proponents of this apparently new idea often stress—is to increase economic growth and real incomes in the long run. The United States, however, already has an implicit industrial policy, in the form of government expenditures, for example, on infrastructure and defense equipment, on regional economic assistance, and on research and development.[1] A key part of this implicit industrial policy is the way the tax system treats income from capital. Tax laws have an important influence on the growth of the nation's overall capital stock as well as on the allocation of capital across industries and assets. The pattern of capital formation, in turn, plays a significant role in determining how much growth is achieved in the long run.

The 1981 and 1982 Tax Acts attempted to remove some obstacles to growth. Prior to the enactment of this legislation, effective tax rates on capital in the United States were perceived to be high as a result of inflation and in relation to those of other countries. Also, it was felt that the U.S. tax system was artificially encouraging some types of "nonproductive" investment and discouraging some types of "productive" investment. Some observers were particularly concerned that investment in housing was being promoted at the expense of investment in business plant and equipment. To predict the effects of the recent changes in tax law designed to remedy these perceived problems, however, is not a straightforward task. The revisions in the code were substantial and included changes in the allowable basis for depreciation, in tax lives, in depreciation formulas, and in the investment tax credit. Furthermore, these changes were imposed upon an already complicated tax structure. This paper examines the shortcomings of our tax laws and compares them to commonly held beliefs about these provisions.

It is important to realize that one can feel a need for reexamination of the tax system regardless of one's attitude toward centralized planning. Tax reform may be a goal in itself. Some people—and I lean toward this view—advocate tax reform as an *alternative* to "industrial policy" in the new sense of this term. But tax reform may also form part of an overall industrial policy program. The U.S. tax system is already creating "winners" and "losers" among investment projects and industries. Additional measures such as federal subsidies for employment or federal financing of private capital projects may offset or reinforce existing distortions. It is imperative at least to understand what already is in place in order to determine whether we would wish to help industries that already receive favorable treatment, or whether further measures would offset policies affecting currently disadvantaged industries. In addition to clarifying the effects of existing policies, simplification of the tax code would leave industrial planners with a cleaner slate on which to write their blueprint.

After reviewing criteria that economists use to measure the efficiency of a tax system, this chapter will discuss existing investment and saving incentives in the United States, to examine how they measure up against what is perceived as a desirable tax policy in terms of growth. Even with the changes made under the Tax Acts of 1981 and 1982, the tax code falls short of efficiency in many respects. The problem of inefficient allocation of capital across assets and industries is at least as significant as under-provision of investment incentives. I reject the view that we have tried all we can using the traditional methods, and that the solutions must lie outside the realm of tax reform. The next section briefly compares our tax treatment of capital income with those in foreign countries. In the final section of the paper, I offer suggestions for tax provisions that would promote economic growth and higher real incomes.

Efficiency and Taxation

The taxation of income from capital can promote economic growth in two ways. First, it can encourage investment by taxing capital income at low rates. Second, it can encourage the efficient allocation of that investment by specifying appropriate rates of tax for different projects.

The first point is generally well understood. By interposing, in effect, a wedge between gross return and net return on an asset, taxes reduce the incentives to save and invest. If the tax rate is 50 percent and a 5 percent net rate of return is expected, an investment project will be undertaken only if it provides a gross return of 10 percent. Economists refer to this phenomenon as an "intertemporal distortion." That is because the reward for diverting current income away from consumption and into saving is lower than it would be in the absence of taxation. *Taxes tilt the balance in favor of consuming now as opposed to adding to the capital stock and thereby providing for higher sustainable consumption possibilities in future years.*

The second effect of taxes on growth, however, is less often considered in discussions of policy. That is the effect of taxes on capital allocation. Yet taxes play a critical role in choices between housing and industrial capital, between long-lived structures and short-lived equipment, between the automobile industry and the pharmaceutical industry, between the Rust Belt and the "Dust Belt," and so on. The question is, with regard to these various possibilities, what are appropriate relative tax rates?

If there were no taxes, investors would tend to seek out the most profitable investments and combine them efficiently. The U.S. tax system, on the other hand, produces high effective tax rates on some investments and very low rates of tax or even subsidies on others. Investors are attracted to lightly taxed investments at the expense of highly taxed investments, and the otherwise efficient allocation of capital is disrupted. Tax differentials tend to change the allocation of capital away from that which would produce the highest possible output level. These sorts of effects are termed "interasset" and "intersectoral" distortions.

Take, for example, the interasset distortion resulting from tax treatment of structures and equipment. In a recent study, Don Fullerton and I measured the effective pre-tax rate of return needed on various asset categories for investors to obtain a 5 percent real rate of return after all corporate, personal, and property taxes.[2] Two assets considered were general industrial equipment and industrial buildings. We estimated that current law imposes a 41 percent total effective tax at the margin for industrial buildings, while providing a 5 percent subsidy for general industrial equipment. This disparate tax treatment means that the pre-tax or "social" rate of return on buildings would have to be 8.5 percent to meet our investor's 5 percent net target, while the pre-tax rate of return on equipment would have to be only 4.8 percent. Under these circumstances, projects involving structures are of course less likely to meet the investor's net return criterion than projects involving equipment. Purchases of structures that would add greater than a 4.8 percent rate of return to the corporation's gross real sales are not undertaken because of the 8.5 percent hurdle. This foregone corporate output translates into foregone national output, jobs, and income. *The tax system thus encourages the purchase of some assets whose contribution to national output is low and discourages the purchase of other assets whose contribution to national output is high.* In short, the tax system is already picking winners and losers, and doing so badly.

In the absence of special motivating factors, the most appropriate set of effective tax rates is one where all are equal. Lower effective tax rates on some investment projects can be defended only if they are judged to have external social benefits beyond those that can be measured by the increase in the sales of the industry that undertakes them. Special incentives for capital expansion in the steel industry or the computer industry can be justified not by pointing to advantages to these industries, but by finding advantages to other industries that would not be included in the firm's usual cost-benefit calculus.

Much of the source of differential tax rates across industries turns out to be due to differential tax treatment of purchases of different types of capital—equipment vs. structures vs. land vs. inventories—which in turn are normally used with different intensities in different industries. For example, the agricultural sector is land-intensive, while the motor vehicle industry is equipment-intensive. There is no easily identifiable reason, however, for favoring equipment over land under the social benefit criterion that I have outlined. A neutral tax policy toward various assets would be the most efficient. It turns out that there is also differential tax treatment of debt and equity financing of capital projects, with debt-financed projects generally receiving more favorable treatment. Again, this is not easily justifiable. The encouragement of debt finance has resulted in a financial structure that is vulnerable to the risk of bankruptcy, since a firm is committed to meet interest payments regardless of its profitability. It is hard to imagine a social benefit criterion that would support this policy. As it turns out, there are disparate categories of firms that use equity finance to a disproportionate degree. New or "start-up" firms tend to rely heavily on equity. But so do firms in very cyclical industries such as construction. The relative treatment of debt and equity finance is not motivated by a conscious decision that investment by these firms should be favored over that of others.

Proponents of planning often suggest that certain industries should be targeted for support or protection. They wish to find the equivalent of the 1970s semiconductor industry, or they are intent upon cushioning the structural problems of the automobile industry. But as will be shown, the U.S. tax structure already favors some industries over others by a capricious set of policies revolving largely around asset use and financing. At this level of decision-making, market efficiency and social efficiency coincide. This is simply the wrong place to introduce favored status, if indeed we wish to introduce it at any level.

Tax Provisions for Capital

The most important provisions for capital taxation are of four types: depreciation allowances, the investment tax credit, property taxes, and income tax rates. Although the following review is not comprehensive, discussion of some details of the tax code in each of these areas is necessary to illustrate the wide-ranging extent of the problems.

Depreciation allowances and inflation. Depreciation allowances were originally intended to permit the firm to deduct a legitimate cost of doing business. In terms of this purpose, the tax life of the asset should resemble its actual economic life, and the depreciation formula should match the rate of decline of the asset. Depreciation allowances should also be indexed for inflation, to account for rising costs of maintaining or replacing old capital. Until 1981, the pattern of tax lives approximated the pattern of expected economic lives. But allowances have always been based on original acquisition price, so that the high inflation of the 1970s severely eroded the purchasing power of depreciation allowances. The Economic Recovery Tax Act of 1981 sought to offset this increase in the cost of capital by shortening tax lives. As a result of this legislation, types of equipment that formerly had been accorded tax lives of between 7 and 15 years are now depreciated over a period of 4.5 years. Buildings, which had lives ranging from roughly 20 to 50 years, now have tax lives of 15 years. (This was the so-called 15-10-5-3 plan, which would be more accurately termed 15-9.5-4.5-2.5. The 9.5-year life went to certain public utility property, and the 2.5-year life to certain short-lived equipment such as automobiles.) When this accelerated depreciation was criticized as being excessive, Congress passed the 1982 Tax Equity and Fiscal Responsibility Act, which introduced "half-basis" adjustment: firms could base their depreciation allowances on the purchase price *minus* one-half of the investment tax credit.

The decision to shorten tax lives produced higher-valued depreciation allowances and thus reduced the cost of capital. This reduction was even greater for structures, which were not subject to the half-basis adjustment. What about the rationale for these reforms? While it is true that lower cost of capital tends to promote higher investment in the long run, the shortening of lives is not as appropriate a response to distortions as indexing allowances for inflation. Because depreciation allowances are still based on original purchase price, the cost of depreciable capital will still tend to increase with inflation. A rise in inflation will tend to deter investment in these assets relative to investment in inventories or owner-occupied housing.

More recently, a sharp fall in the inflation rate from the levels of the late 1970s, combined with the tax life adjustment, has caused a fall in the relative cost of business capital. (I am setting aside for a moment changes in interest rates brought about by other policies.) It would be a mistake to see the 1981–82 reform of depreciation allowances as a fully successful measure, however. It is tempting to fall into the trap of seeing business-fixed investment as more worthy of promotion than owner-occupied housing. Some observers currently see housing as less productive because it does not produce tangible goods with which to compete in international trade. Alan Blinder, on the other hand, recently argued that this view "makes sense only if, for example, services produced by the housing stock are of less social importance than video games produced in factories." He added: "My house and I resent the implication."[3] Different observers attach different social values to production of housing services and production of other goods. I am willing to bet that the truth lies in between the extremes, and that we should therefore let the tax system be neutral in the choice between housing and industrial capital. Currently housing is undertaxed relative to most business investments, but we can do better than having the relative cost of capital and therefore the relative investment in these two assets be determined by the inflation rate. Indexing depreciation allowances for inflation would lead to a more efficient allocation of our resources than shortening tax lives.[4]

The investment tax credit and inefficiency. The second major feature of the business tax code is the investment tax credit (ITC). For qualified investments, firms may subtract a fraction of the purchases from their income tax liability. When it was first introduced in 1962, the ITC was 7 percent and covered most equipment. After a series of repeals, reinstatements, increases, and extensions, the ITC is now 10 percent, except for equipment in the three-year class, which receives 6 percent. Property purchased by public utilities is eligible for the credit, but other structures do not qualify.

An immediate 10 percent reduction in tax liability has a sizeable impact on the cost of business capital. There are problems, however, for firms having insufficient profits to take advantage of this tax break. Joseph Cordes and Steven Sheffrin have found that of the tax credits earned in 1976 by manufacturing firms, only 70 percent were applied against that year's tax liabilities. For public utilities, the ratio was 58 percent.[5]

The impact of this deductibility problem is likely to be felt by several different types of firms: new ventures that are still not profitable, rapidly expanding firms, capital-intensive firms in general, and firms in industries adjusting to falling demand. From an efficiency standpoint, our concern should be that a prospective investment project that would satisfy the rate-of-return criterion in an otherwise profitable business would not satisfy it in an otherwise unprofitable or insufficiently profitable business. To some extent, then, projects are being judged not only by how much they are expected to add to output, but also by the improper criterion of the profitability of past investments. These past investments determine the size of the firm's current profits, which limit the size of claimable credits. Investments that are profitable at the margin should be undertaken even if they are being considered in declining industries. They should also be undertaken in new ventures, which have not yet generated any income.

The law does have some provisions designed to offset this deductibility problem. Under the Tax Act of 1981, the investment tax credit may be carried forward or back fifteen years. This is an improvement over prior law, which allowed unused credits to be carried back three years and forward seven years. A further adjustment might be to allow the investment tax credits carried forward to accrue interest, in order to compensate firms for not receiving these deductions at the time they are earned. Finally, we might reconsider capital leasing policies. The now-repealed Safe Harbor Leasing program allowed firms with insufficient tax liability in effect to sell their investment tax credits and depreciation deductions to other firms. The program was introduced in 1981 but abandoned in 1982. New provisions might well be designed to address the problems that the Safe Harbor Leasing program was addressing.

Another issue regarding the investment tax credit is that it is available only for purchases of equipment. The ITC in fact is a major reason for the large discrepancy between the effective taxation of structures and equipment. In the study by Don Fullerton and myself (cited earlier), for example, the total effective marginal tax rate for structures purchased by corporations was 38 percent, while the subsidy for equipment was 4 percent. I have reestimated the structures tax rate on the assumption of a 10 percent investment tax credit. This change alone would reduce the tax rate for structures to 24 percent. Thus, a large share of the tax differential between assets is due to the investment tax credit. Although the ITC may appear to be a desirable policy tool from the standpoint of lowering the effective taxation of capital, it is a major factor in promoting inefficient allocation of capital.

Property taxes. This third feature of the tax code for capital income is often forgotten. Property taxes, however, do form a major part of the total tax rate on capital. We tend to ignore the role of property taxes because they are levied by tens of thousands of jurisdictions. It is not easy, as a result, to consider reforms in this tax that would have a nationwide impact.

In the absence of promising proposals, I will briefly outline a couple of facts about property taxes that typically go unnoticed. Property taxes are levied as a percentage of the assessed value of capital. When one adjusts for the discrepancy between the actual tax base and the market assessment, it appears that on average for the nation the tax is between 0.8 and 1.6 percent of the market value of various industrial assets. If the pre-tax real rate of return to business capital is about 7 percent, this tax translates into between 11 and 23 percent of the gross return to capital. The first fact, then, is that local property taxes are a sizeable part of the total tax burden on capital. The second fact concerns the importance of the tax in the residential sector. Nationwide, these taxes amount to about 1.8 percent of the market value of owner-occupied homes, a higher fraction than in the industrial sector. The common view of owner-occupied housing as being "untaxed" — and maybe this view is held by members of my profession only

— is just plain wrong. My research indicates that housing is still taxed lightly relative to business capital, but the extent of the misallocation of capital between these two sectors has probably been exaggerated.

Income tax rates: corporate vs. personal, debt vs. equity. The final area of investigation of the tax code is the tax rate on capital income. The discussion of depreciation allowances focused on a deduction from sales revenue that is made in order to compute taxable income. The investment tax credit is then taken as a reduction after the basic tax rate is applied. I have saved the issue of the tax rate for last because it involves the complexities of both the corporate and the personal income tax systems and their interactions.

Corporations with earnings above $100,000 pay a tax of 46 percent of taxable income. For partnerships and sole proprietorships, the rate depends on the owners' marginal tax brackets, which may be as high as 50 percent under the current law. Both corporations and unincorporated firms may deduct interest payments in computing taxable income. Thus these tax rates represent the taxation of shareholders. Debt holders are taxed on interest receipts at their personal income tax rate.

For corporations, however, the corporate income tax is just the beginning of the story of the tax treatment of equity. Shareholders face personal income taxes on their corporate earnings. There is a further distinction within equity capital, depending on whether the earnings are paid out in dividends or retained by the corporation and eventually paid out as capital gains. Except for a small exemption, dividends are taxed in full. Capital gains accrue without personal income taxation, and are subject to taxation on 40 percent of the amount when paid out. These gains are not adjusted for inflation. Thus one distortion occurs in the fact that the income generated by debt-financed corporate capital is taxed once while the income generated by equity-financed corporate capital is taxed twice. Another distortion occurs because corporate and noncorporate firms are treated differently.

How do these provisions affect long-run growth? First, the personal income tax discourages capital accumulation. *From the standpoint of the total burden of taxation of income from corporate capital, the personal income tax accounts for most of the burden and the corporate income tax for very little.* What about the $55 billion paid in corporate income taxes in 1983? These payments largely reflect tax liabilities on old capital, purchased before the tax reductions enacted in 1981. Expected tax liabilities on future investments are very low.[6] The remaining role of the corporate income tax is mostly in misallocating new capital formation. The personal income tax also discourages capital formation in addition to misallocating capital.

Second, the tax structure is not neutral with respect to inflation. Debt finance becomes more attractive than equity finance in times of high inflation. Corporations are able to deduct nominal interest payments in computing their taxable income. Although individuals must pay tax on their nominal interest receipts, their marginal tax rate is, on average, lower than that of corporations. On net, debt finance is subsidized for corporations, and that subsidy grows with inflation. Returns to equity, on the other hand, are taxed at a positive rate, since both corporations and individuals pay taxes on this portion of their income. Capital gains taxes are applied whether or not there is an actual real gain. A rise in nominal returns means an added real tax burden. The impact of this nonneutrality means that, in times of high inflation, investments in industries that are more able to maintain high debt-capital ratios are favored. These industries are usually those that have a steady earnings stream, and therefore are less susceptible to the risk of bankruptcy. Historically, these industries have included utilities, finance and insurance, and services. Once again, the problem is that there may be some investments that would add more to output than those that are undertaken. In inflationary times, high-yielding investments in industries that do not have good access to bond markets are overlooked.

Finally, many of the supposed saving incentives under the personal income tax are not awarded in a way that would actually increase saving.[7] The total dividend and interest income exclusion is capped at $400. A family already saving more than this limit has no tax-based incentive to increase its saving. The 1981 Tax Act expanded the amounts that may be saved through an Individual Retirement Account. For these projects, the personal income taxes described above may be deferred until retirement. While this obviously lowers the cost of capital significantly, the expansion of IRAs is not contingent upon increasing saving and the capital stock. Some individuals may simply transfer funds from taxable to nontaxable accounts to take advantage of the tax deferral.

In summary, our sampling of features of the tax code has revealed many areas for potential improvement. Indexing depreciation allowances and capital gains for inflation would lower the pernicious role of inflation in allocating capital. Equalizing the investment tax credit for different assets would reduce artificial deterrents to investing in structures. Improving refundability of the tax credit would put industries undergoing rapid growth and industries undergoing structural decline on a more appropriate footing relative to industries that are growing moderately. Equalizing the tax treatment of debt and equity would reduce the handicap that corporations in cyclical industries face in inflationary periods. The list of possibilities for removing obstacles to a growth-promoting allocation of resources is lengthy. In the next section, I examine further evidence on our tax system by comparing it with those in other countries.

High Tax Rates vs. Unequal Tax Rates

The focus of much of this article has been on the role of taxes in misallocating capital. I have pointed out, for example, the favorable tax treatment of equipment as opposed to structures. I have mentioned several ways in which inflation distorts decision-making. There has been relatively little mention of the problem of excessive taxation of capital income. In fact, I have argued that the corporate income tax system adds very little to the overall tax rate on capital. The disincentive to capital formation lies in the personal income tax and the property tax.

It is interesting to look at whether our overall taxation of capital is high relative to that in other countries. In light of the complicated features of the tax code, this question is difficult to answer. Fortunately, a careful study of the tax policies of the U.S., the United Kingdom, West Germany, and Sweden was undertaken recently at the National Bureau of Economic Research.[8] Researchers in these four countries used identical methodologies and found that in fact the United States does not tax corporate capital at an unusually high rate. This study found that the marginal effective total tax rate in the U.S. around 1980 (considering the corporate income tax, personal income tax, and property tax) was 37 percent, compared to 48 percent in Germany and 36 percent in Sweden. The rate in the U.K. was a low 4 percent. On the other hand, the variability of the tax across assets, industries, and owners and under different inflation rates was very high. Furthermore, the 1981 and 1982 reforms have reduced this overall tax rate without lowering the variability of tax rates.[9] This evidence suggests that the issue of tax-caused misallocations of capital should no longer take a back seat to the issue of underinvestment.

Of course, currently there is considerable interest in the "miracle" of the Japanese economy rather than the performance of Western European countries. The research on relative taxes in the U.S. and Japan has not been as systematic or as detailed as the NBER study. The evidence I have seen suggests that any advantage that the Japanese have lies in their increased use of debt finance, which is also cheaper than equity finance in Japan.[10] The role of the Japanese tax system in promoting the efficiency of investment has not been documented to my knowledge.

The Possibilities for Tax Reform

Tax changes under the Reagan administration have decreased the taxation of corporate capital significantly. But tax reform still should be included in our industrial policy agenda. The most pressing reason for reform is that our system of capital taxation masks the real winners and losers among potential investment projects. Equal treatment of alternative investments is a goal that has not yet been achieved. Several proposals that have received the attention of economists are worth exploring. Some of these—the indexation of depreciation allowances and capital gains taxes for inflation, improved provisions for capital cost recovery for firms with low profits, and more equal treatment of debt and equity finance —have been mentioned in the text. These are all steps in the right direction. My own favorite, however, is a more sweeping reform: replacement of both the personal and corporate income tax systems by a consumption tax.

The mechanics of running a consumption tax have already been investigated in a 1977 Treasury Department document called *Blueprints for Basic Tax Reform*.[11] The current income tax system discourages the postponement of consumption by taxing the return to saving. And, as has been pointed out, the tax treatment differs widely depending on the uses of these savings flows. The consumption tax can be implemented as a modified income tax. It could be run in the following manner: tax wage earnings and inheritances, but ignore any returns to further saving from these sources. It turns out that this may be simpler to administer than the theoretically equivalent method of allowing individuals to subtract saving from their taxable income, which is the current treatment of IRAs. Tax rates under the consumption tax could be graduated, in order to maintain progressivity.

What are the advantages of the consumption tax? First, it would eliminate the corporate income tax, which is the source of so much of our inefficiency in the allocation of capital. Most economists—liberals and conservatives alike—have been critical all along of taxing the corporate entity rather than the ultimate owners of the corporation. Corporations are merely a channel through which earnings pass on their way to shareholders. Apart from this equity-based argument for eliminating the corporate income tax, we now have a strong efficiency-based argument. With the recent expansion in the provisions for capital cost recovery, we have been left with a corporate income tax that probably reduces output by more than it raises in revenues.

Second, the introduction of a consumption tax would remove the inefficiencies associated with inflation. The 1981 Tax Act provided for indexed personal income tax brackets starting in 1984, and therefore addressed the issue of tax rates that would otherwise rise with inflation. This adjustment did not address, however, the pervasive problem of taxable *income* that rises with inflation. Although it is theoretically possible to adjust depreciation allowances, capital gains, and interest rates for inflation in computing taxable income, these adjustments would raise the costs of administering our tax system. We should not be too quick to adopt a reform that raises the amount of time needed to fill out income tax forms.

Finally, a consumption tax would lower the overall taxation of returns to capital, and would therefore promote increased capital formation. With the 1981 and 1982 Tax Acts, the tax rates paid by corporations have been reduced about as far as they can be. Our concern with high budget deficits removes serious possibilities of introducing lower tax rates in the context of the current tax system. Further incentives for growth must involve a restructuring of the relative incentives for consumption and saving. The consumption tax would introduce a revision of the tax code in the personal income tax, where the effective tax rates on capital are high, and would do so in a way that deals with the marginal cost of saving.

Talk of industrial planning has forced policymakers to widen their horizons as they discuss methods of promoting economic growth. Incrementalism is being challenged. In this chapter I have outlined the case for reform of our taxation of income from capital. The problems in our tax system are pervasive. A quick fix such as lowering personal or corporate tax rates is not an effective solution. A basic reform such as the introduction of a consumption tax is not as radical a measure as introduction of industrial planning, but it is a larger step than we are used to taking. Because the scope of the industrial policy debate has expanded, however, policymakers may now be ready to devise solutions that deal with the broad range of intertemporal and intersectoral inefficiencies that our tax system has created. The evidence strongly supports a comprehensive reform of our tax code.

V

Conclusion

12

CHALMERS JOHNSON

Conclusion

If the papers in this volume demonstrate nothing else, it is that the United States *needs* a continuing debate about its economic and industrial policies. Dichotomies, distinctions, definitional problems, and deflations of quick fixes exist on almost every page. Wildavsky points out that although (or because) 61 percent of the American public blames the government for the nation's recent poor record on productivity, there is as yet no visible public groundswell of support for any version of industrial policy. In his discussion of Japanese industrial policy, Ozaki implicitly introduces the distinction between big government and strong government: the U.S. is burdened with big government, one that cannot resist the demands of any significant interest group, whereas Japan enjoys a strong government that nonetheless imposes the lightest public sector burden of any advanced industrial democracy. Krauss, Ozaki, and others pinpoint the acute danger that industrial policy is merely the latest pseudointellectual cover for old "beggar thy neighbor" policies of protectionism.

Bartlett and Weidenbaum and Athey all acknowledge real problems of American industrial performance but find the explana-

235

tions to rest primarily in contradictory and unsound macro-economic policies. They rightly emphasize that microindustrial policies without a reordering of both priorities and performance at the macro level constitute a prescription for disaster. No writer in the book believes that industrial policy is a panacea, and many of them are concerned above all to puncture claims that industrial policy can restore American industrial competitiveness without disturbing the spendthrift public priorities to which Americans have become accustomed.

Krauss and Seabury go beyond the purely economic realm to remind us of the moral and political objectives that the economic system exists at least in part to fulfill. "'Fashionable fascism,'" writes Krauss, "is an accurate term for . . . neoliberal economic thought." Seabury stresses that "the United States has no superpower to guarantee its security, and its industrial system must reflect that fact." No one wants fascism, fashionable or otherwise, and I am sympathetic to Krauss's timely reminder that big government is not just economically inefficient but also has been known to usher in what Friedrich Hayek identified forty years ago as *The Road to Serfdom*. But today we need a whole series of "road" books, rather like the old Hope-Crosby movies. These should include *The Road to Bankruptcy, The Road to Revolution,* and *The Road to Scientific Mediocrity*. Seabury has powerfully emphasized that in avoiding one path to serfdom, we could be embarking on a shortcut to the same destination, since not only do our commercial rivals have industrial policies but "America's strategic rival, the Soviet Union, has one (to put it mildly)." Classical theorists of the market also understood Seabury's point: the state is only one of several institutions that might fulfill welfare functions for a society, but it is the *only* institution that can fulfill the defense function. Even in theory the writ of laissez-faire never extended to the realm of defense.

There is surprising agreement among our analysts on one point: there is no such thing (in Wildavsky's words) as *not* having an industrial policy. We have an implicit one in America, and it is not a good one. Henderson demonstrates that if our tax system is not picking winners and losers, it is certainly creating them. The system "encourages the purchase of some assets whose contribution to national output is low and discourages the purchase of

other assets whose contribution to national output is high."
Hoadley concurs and zeroes in on why this is so:

The absence of powerful overall national goals or objectives has not
deterred the U.S. government from using an array of economic and financial policy tools affecting banking and finance. . . . Their basic purpose is to allocate the country's financial resources, to a considerable
degree for political purposes.

Even Murray Weidenbaum, although he ultimately concludes
that in light of political realities the optimum change in the public
policy mix might be zero, lists as things that should be done: tax
simplification, regulatory relief, lower deficit financing, and curtailed government lending. Weidenbaum's caution may reflect important insights from inside. Another former chairman of the
President's Council of Economic Advisers, Herbert Stein (adviser
to President Nixon), has recently given us a devastating portrayal
of the routine subordination of economic analysis to short-term
political objectives within the American government.[1]

What is wrong with the American industrial policy that is
already in place and working? Several writers point to incoherence, lack of coordination, and simple inertia—for example
Henderson: "The remaining role of the corporate income tax
[since it does not raise much revenue and imposes double taxation
on equity investments] is mostly in misallocating new capital formation." My position on this issue is mixed. There are without
question inefficiencies that derive from uncoordinated governmental functions—and the tax system is probably the largest
single source of them—but the economies to be obtained through
managerial reform of the government are often overstated. For
example, the 1984 report of the President's Private Sector Survey
on Cost Control (known as the Grace Commission after the name
of its chairman, Peter Grace) makes for both amusing and alarming reading.

The problem is not really governmental slackness and inefficiency; the fact is that the U.S. government is often extremely efficient and effective at doing the wrong things. Governmental antitrust interventions against mergers in the steel industry, to name
a recent example, have blocked what would surely be a more effective way than bankruptcy to restore some competitiveness to the
industry in the face of foreign competition. Until maintenance of

global rather than purely domestic competition becomes the explicit criterion of antitrust policy in America, the unintended effect of traditional antitrust policy will be to reduce competition by feeding the political demands for protectionism. As Ozaki shows, one of the paradoxes of contemporary economic life is that in Japan the government proposes mergers and the private sector resists them, whereas in America it is a beleaguered private sector that wants mergers and the government that blocks them.

The probability of governmental incoherence in doing the right things and utter coherence in doing the wrong things highlights another issue on which all our writers seem to agree: the likely politicization of a new industrial policy unless public consensus and political leadership intervene to prevent it. Wildavsky details the numerous if remarkably frivolous proposals for industrial policy that have been introduced in the Congress in recent years. At best virtually all of them contain an escape clause for some electorally or monetarily mobilized constituency; at worst they constitute disguised nationalizations of parts of the private sector, as in the draconian laws against runaway factories that are being proposed by the same interests that earlier created the incentives to run away. Similarly, Bardach's telling scenario of the likely prospects of a new Agency for Industrial Policy distills the accumulated wisdom of students of public policy implementation in America in recent years. His warnings, including his explicit conclusion that "putative *alternatives* to protectionism would almost assuredly become *adjuncts* to it," must be heeded. Bardach's essay points up the real value of the debate surveyed in this volume: the United States needs an industrial policy, but only one that is pragmatic, rational, and long-term in outlook. Unfortunately, the political system is geared up to produce one that is ideological, bureaucratized, and short-term. Economic reform is thus impossible unless it is accompanied by political reform.

In my view the United States cannot afford either to fail in its industrial regeneration or to undertake the long learning process that Japan experienced in developing its own industrial policy. This book thus can be read as a kind of primitive social science experiment analogous to what in the field of high technology is called computer-aided design. Just as the design of an advanced semiconductor involves so many theoretical and practical decisions that only a computer can keep track of all of them at once, so the design of an American industrial policy involves so many alternatives as to require the kind of clash of opinions displayed in this book.

The situation is similar to that described twenty years ago by Albert Wohlstetter in the field of the control of atomic testing:

Two illustrations will suffice to show how, in the case of the test ban, each of the two principal factions [among atomic scientists] has found it hard to deal with countermeasures, except where these support a point of view it is propounding anyway. First, Edward Teller: Dr. Teller in my view has performed an important service in helping to develop a test ban with adequate controls, by thinking ingeniously about the possibilities of evading the various control systems that have been proposed. [And yet Teller was blind to enemy countermeasures against defensive weapons such as anti-missile missiles he proposed to develop through continued testing.] . . . Next, Hans Bethe: Dr. Bethe has been the symmetrical opposite of Dr. Teller on this matter as on others. [He was uninterested in possible evasion of the test ban by the Russians.] . . . On the other hand, when it came to evaluating the military worth of weapons that might be developed with the aid of testing, such as anti-missile missiles, Dr. Bethe could frequently think of nothing except enemy countermeasures [e.g., masses of decoys] that would reduce their military worth to zero.

Wohlstetter, the strategist, concluded that his mission required the services of *both* Teller and Bethe to produce sound public policy on this issue. He also noted, quoting the early Bertrand Russell, "The opinions that are held with passion are always those for which no good ground exists; indeed the passion is the measure of the holder's lack of rational conviction."[2]

I believe that the United States must move in the direction of industrial policy, for reasons that I shall try to make clear in a moment. But I also recognize that sabotage via political partisanship, or bureaucratic vested interests, or statism as in some European examples, is as great a danger as failure in the main effort. That is why discussion of these booby traps is included here and why this book differs so markedly from other analyses of industrial policy, either for or against it.

Why should the United States move in the industrial policy direction? Why wouldn't a resolution of the incoherent fiscal and monetary policies that have prevailed in the United States in recent years do the job? As the *New York Times* put it editorially:

The real issue is how best to cope with structural problems in the economy. But no industrial policy can compensate for the current disarray in fiscal and monetary policy—the amazing budget deficits that are causing inordinately high interest rates. These policies are already clearly government responsibilities—and it is not meeting them. What reason is there to think it would do any better carrying out an "industrial policy"?[3]

This question is perfectly reasonable. The problem is that it implies that industrial policy is something to be "carried out" even before it is formulated. Unfortunately, some political partisans of industrial policy—last year's so-called "Atari Democrats" (until the Atari Company shifted most of its manufacturing to Taiwan) —do want to try to implement an industrial policy before they have thought it through. My contention is that industrial policy is first of all a mode of thought, a new form of economic analysis—in short, a *policy*—and only after the hard work of understanding and consensus-building has been accomplished *might* it be implemented through a bank, or new tax legislation, or preferential public loan guarantees. Bardach lists ten functional areas for his hypothetical Agency for Industrial Policy: trade, export promotion, recessed industries, R&D, education, antitrust, industrial infrastructure, investment risk-sharing, taxation, and governmental procurement. This seems logical enough but, as Bardach shows, it is actually a prescription for bureaucratic muddle and ineffectiveness.

Real industrial policy is by definition contingent on the particular problems of an industrial economy at a particular time and in a particular economic environment. It has its theoretical roots in the concept of dynamic comparative advantage and in the application of the theory of the firm or household to a national economy. As Bruce Scott puts it:

Our competitive problems are with countries which have strategies more competitive than our own. . . . The essence of these strategies is the promotion of factor mobility [that is, orderly change on the supply side to produce technologies and exports that are competitive in the world economy], not the substitution of governmental choices of "winners and losers" for those of business managers.[4]

Regis McKenna's discussion of industrial innovation illustrates this analytic point of view. Contrary to the widespread belief that "research and development" is best measured by percentages of gross national product assigned to research budgets, commercially relevant innovation is a highly differentiated and contingent process, one that differs widely from industry to industry, within industries according to the size of enterprises, and among products in terms of the stages of their product cycles. According to McKenna:

R&D itself is a misnomer; far more appropriate is the term "product creation," which encompasses the several stages involved in moving from scientific advances to product manufacturing that bring a new commodity successfully to market. The product creation process is a complex interweaving of universities, the government, and companies of various sizes involved in sponsoring and performing basic research, applied research, product development, and manufacturing/marketing. There is no monolithic R&D process.

Nowhere is a strategic, goal-oriented understanding, combined with finely tuned policies, more necessary to competitive success than in public support for industrial innovation.

Industrial policy is thus a viewpoint, one similar to that of the coach of a football team who has to work both on fundamentals in training his men and on producing a game plan for each individual contest. An industrial policy viewpoint is indispensable to a revision of macroeconomic fundamentals, but a grasp of fundamentals alone will not produce a game plan. Industrial policy can never be a substitute for the reform of fiscal and monetary policy; it is the indispensable complement to them—the mode of analysis of how to reform them and what to do with them when they are in good shape. Let us consider one well-known aspect of America's industrial decline: the overvalued dollar is a serious handicap to American exports and one that must be corrected. But a weaker dollar would not necessarily solve all problems. The dollar was undervalued during 1977–79 without reversing the decline of American competitiveness. The American merchandise trade balance was positive from 1893 to 1970 and has been negative and getting worse since 1971. This is a long-term problem, not one to be explained by any single factor, including the price of oil or the price of the dollar.

There is no way to reduce the value of the dollar except to reduce demand for it, which means cutting the American government's fiscal deficits, thereby lowering interest rates and reducing capital inflows. Deficit-cutting is not conceptually difficult: it requires either indexing for inflation of contributions as well as benefits for all social programs or ending the indexing of benefits alone. Either of these reforms would also necessitate a greater equity in the allocation of burdens. But even then the dollar may remain internationally overvalued—it may be permanently overvalued—because of the safe-haven aspects of investment in the American economy. If that is the case, then the United States must learn to compete with a handicap, just as the East Asian capitalist developmental states have learned how to overcome the handicap of a dearth of natural resources. Reducing the value of the dollar in international trade is no more a panacea for what ails the American economy than is industrial policy when that is understood merely as a quick fix.

The United States must move to ameliorate the broad macroeconomic constraints on its competitiveness, but it cannot wait for this to occur, particularly since there is a very good chance that it will not occur fast enough or to a sufficient degree to make a difference. Given the requirements of national defense and the interdependence of the advanced industrial democracies, fiscal and monetary policy are today close to being beyond national control. But industrial policy is not beyond national control. It is oriented both to trying to leverage a better macroeconomic environment *and* to identifying a winning game plan within a given set of macroeconomic handicaps.

In a major econometric analysis of U.S. manufacturing industries, Otto Eckstein and his associates (much like Weidenbaum and Athey in this volume) conclude, "Investment in U.S. manufacturing [over the past three decades] was 'normal' in relation to our own previous historical experience." But, they add, "it was grossly inadequate in terms of the challenges posed by other countries, particularly Japan."[5] Just how inadequate was suggested by President Reagan's Council of Economic Advisers in 1983:

The share of U.S. gross domestic product devoted to net fixed investment during the last decade was only 34 percent of the comparable share in Japan and 56 percent of the comparable share in Germany. No other major industrial nation devotes as small a fraction of total output to new investment as does the United States.[6]

Here, then, are the real tasks for an American industrial policy, regardless of the macroeconomic discrepancies among nations: bringing down the cost of capital for American manufacturing industries; making it easy to shift more industrial financing into debt rather than equity; curtailing incentives to shift savings into nonmanufacturing assets; helping to commercialize inventions; merging declining industries to produce concentrations on a par with the competition; and eliminating such root causes of inflation as protectionism. There may be a role for industrial targeting but not as large a one as industrial policy enthusiasts or denigrators believe. Such targeting could probably be left to a reorganized National Science Foundation in which commercial and engineering concerns would have a voice equal to those of pure scientists. The model here might be Japan's Agency for Industrial Science and Technology, an integral part of MITI.

Actual policies to achieve some of the above goals are already quite familiar. They include tax simplification—leading logically toward a consumption tax, as advocated in this volume by Henderson. The tax base would be household consumption, defined as income minus saving, and it could be taxed at either flat or progressive rates. It is time that the criterion of "progressive" taxation were shifted from absolute levels of income to the rate of saving. A really progressive tax system would ensure jobs both today and tomorrow and would put the financing of the present and the future on a sound basis.[7] Much of the alleged "myopia" of corporate decision-making in America—that is, its fixation on short-term profitability as the only criterion of good management—is a reflection of an institutionalized incentive structure that makes any other form of management irrational. This can be changed, but such a change requires an industrial policy perspective and intensive analysis.

Regulatory reform is also necessary, but this is probably more a matter of curbing the American penchant for adversarial relationships than of regulatory relaxation. As Eckstein et al. observe, "The traditional hostility between business and government made the learning process [concerning regulation] particularly costly. In countries with a tradition of business-government collaboration, the amount of regulation was probably just as great, but the damage to business was less."[8] As the Tokyo joke goes, when Japan and the United States both mandated emission controls on automobile exhausts, Japanese businessmen hired engineers and American businessmen hired lawyers.

And how might such a seemingly culturally determined response be influenced? Perhaps by stopping to think of it as cultural. Here, it seems to me, some private sector initiatives are needed. There is less of an adversarial stance between government and business in Japan at least in part because Japanese business is well organized, powerful, and internally coordinated. The United States simply has no equivalent of the Japanese Federation of Economic Organizations (Keidanren), and certainly no American business leader commands the respect and attention of the president of Keidanren when he speaks on issues affecting industry. Instead, we have an endless array of vertically oriented policy organizations, political action committees, and trade associations that never coordinate their policies or priorities and all of which directly lobby the government. If the government is being asked to put its house in order and to speak with one voice on the economy, it seems no less important that industry should try to do the same—or at least should produce majority and minority opinions. Japanese industry is certainly not monolithic, but it gets its viewpoint across to the media, the labor federations, consumers, and foreign competitors in a way that is unknown in America. Thus there is ample room for reform in America, even if the government does nothing.

Paul Seabury tells us that it takes forty-one months in this country to deliver a jet engine to the air force, the exact length of time between Pearl Harbor and V-E Day during World War II. Something is wrong. And there are plenty of Americans who have equally frustrating tales to tell—of ineffective government, jobs lost to foreign competitors, unreliable and overpriced products, and entrenched political incumbents who do nothing but run for office. But the challenge of international competition is also having another effect: it may turn out to be the best thing that ever happened to the American economy. For this competition has reopened the debate in America about a vast range of policies and procedures that most of us have long taken for granted. The 1980s are thus likely to be a time of American domestic initiatives and reform. This is not only desirable but necessary, since a decade from now it may well be too late to solve many of the problems addressed in this book.

Notes

Contributors

Index

NOTES

1. Chalmers Johnson: "Introduction: The Idea of Industrial Policy"

1. Charles L. Schultze, "Industrial Policy: A Dissent," *The Brookings Review* (Fall 1983): 7; Richard B. McKenzie, "National Industrial Policy: An Overview of the Debate," Heritage Foundation *Backgrounder*, no. 275 (July 12, 1983); and Melville J. Ulmer, "The War of the Liberal Economists," *Commentary*, October 1983, p. 55. Incidentally, Schultze, a very distinguished economist himself, begins his essay on an ominous note: "These economic theories originated outside the mainstream of professional economic thought." *Caveat emptor.*

2. Hiroya Ueno, "Industrial Policy: Its Role and Limits," *Journal of Japanese Trade and Industry* (July– August 1983): 34.

3. Cato Institute, *Policy Report*, Washington, D.C., November 1983, p. 9.

4. U.S. Congress, House Committee on Foreign Affairs, *Government Decision-Making in Japan: Implications for the United States*, 97th Cong., 2d sess. (Washington, D.C.: U.S. Gov. Printing Office, 1982), p. 92.

5. Jimmy Wheeler, Merit E. Janow, and Thomas Pepper, *Japanese Industrial Development Policies in the 1980's* (Croton-on-Hudson, N.Y.: Hudson Institute, 1982).

6. Miyohei Shinohara, Toru Yanagihara, and Kwang Suk Kim, "The Japanese and Korean Experiences in Managing Development," World Bank Staff Working Papers, Washington, D.C., 1983, p. 28.

7. Louis J. Mulkern, "U.S.-Japan Trade Relations: Economic and Strategic Implications," *U.S.-Japan Economic Relations* (Berkeley, Calif.: University of California, Institute of East Asian Studies, 1980), pp. 26–27.

8. Sol C. Chaikin, "Trade, Investment, and Deindustrialization: Myth and Reality," *Foreign Affairs* (Spring 1982): 845.

9. Semiconductor Industry Association, *1983–84 Yearbook and Directory*, San Jose, Calif., 1983, p. 18.

10. Testimony before the Committee on Governmental Affairs, U.S. Senate, June 24, 1983.

11. See Robert B. Reich, "Making Industrial Policy," *Foreign Affairs* (Spring 1982): 877; J. Mark Ramseyer, "Japan's Myth of Non-Litigiousness," *National Law Journal* (July 4, 1983): 13; and Steven Schlosstein, *Trade War: Greed, Power, and Industrial Policy on Opposite Sides of the Pacific* (New York: Congdon and Weed, 1984), p. 227.

12. See R. C. Longworth, "Debate on Industrial Policy," *Chicago Tribune*, December 4–6, 1983.

13. See T. J. Pempel, *Policy and Politics in Japan: Creative Conservatism* (Philadelphia: Temple University Press, 1982), and Chalmers Johnson, *MITI and the Japanese Miracle* (Stanford, Calif.: Stanford University Press, 1982).

14. Cato Institute, p. 3.

15. "'Reaganomics' Held Responsible for Japan's Surplus," *Japan Economic Journal* (December 27, 1983): 4.

16. Press conference, Tokyo, April 18, 1983.

17. Edward A. Feigenbaum and Pamela McCorduck, *The Fifth Generation: Artificial Intelligence and Japan's Computer Challenge to the World* (Reading, Mass.: Addison-Wesley, 1983), p. 223.

18. Charles H. Ferguson, "The Microelectronics Industry in Distress," *Technology Review* (August–September 1983): 24–37.

19. David F. Prindle, *Petroleum Politics and the Texas Railroad Commission* (Austin, Tex.: University of Texas Press, 1981), pp. 187–89, 205.

20. "Research and Development: Sharpening America's Competitive Edge," *Du Pont Context* 3 (1983): 23.

21. George Gilder, "A Supply-Side Economics of the Left," *The Public Interest*, no. 72 (Summer 1983): 42.

22. U.S. International Trade Commission, *Foreign Industrial Targeting and Its Effects on U.S. Industries, Phase I: Japan* (Washington, D.C.: USITC Publication 1437, 1983), p. 17.

23. See Richard Pascale and Thomas P. Rohlen, "The Mazda Turnaround," *Journal of Japanese Studies* (Summer 1983): 219–63.

2. Aaron Wildavsky: "Squaring the Political Circle: Industrial Policies and the American Dream"

1. See Charles L. Schultze, "Industrial Policy: A Dissent," *The Brookings Review* 2, no. 1 (Fall 1983): 3–12.

2. This discussion is based on an analysis by William Schneider, "'Industrial Policy': It All Depends on How It Is Sold to the Voters," *National Journal* 15, no. 38 (September 1983): 1916–17.

3. Ibid., p. 1917. Schneider's analysis is based on Harris polls conducted in the United States, Australia, Britain, Japan, and West Germany.

4. Jeremy Bernstein, "Profiles: Allocating Sacrifice," *The New Yorker*, January 23, 1983, pp. 45, 78.

5. Joel Kotkin and Dan Gevirtz, "Why Entrepreneurs Trust No Politician: Who Needs Friends Who Ruin Your Business While Aiding Corporate Dinosaurs?" *Washington Post*, January 16, 1983, pp. B1–B2.

6. See Wolfgang Hager, "Let Us Now Praise Trade Protectionism: It's Free-Trade That Would Bring Disaster Today," *Washington Post*, May 15, 1983, p. B1.

7. Barry Bluestone and Bennett Harrison, *The Deindustrialization of America: Plant Closings, Community Abandonment, and the Dismantling of Basic Industries* (New York: Basic Books, 1982).

8. Walter F. Mondale, Address to the Twenty-First Constitutional Convention of the United Steel Workers of America, September 11, 1982.

9. See, for instance, Professor Paul Seabury's "Industrial Policy and National Defense," *Journal of Contemporary Studies* 6, no. 2 (Spring 1983): 5–15.

10. Charles E. Lindblom, "In Praise of Political Science," *World Politics* 9, no. 2 (January 1957): 240–53.

11. See Lester Thurow's comments in "Do Modern Times Call for an Industrial Policy? A Conversation with Herbert Stein and Lester Thurow," *Public Opinion* 6, no. 4 (August/September 1983): 2–7, 58.

12. William A. Schambra, "Is Robert Reich's Vision the Wrong Stuff for the Democrats in 1984?" *Public Opinion* 6, no. 4 (August/September 1983): 8–11, 56–57.

13. For recent thought and different arguments of this kind by distinguished political scien-

tists, see Charles E. Lindblom, *Politics and Markets* (New York: Basic Books, 1977), and Robert A. Dahl's Jefferson Lectures at the University of California, Berkeley.

3. Robert S. Ozaki: "How Japanese Industrial Policy Works"

1. A definitive study of MITI is now available in English. See Chalmers Johnson, *MITI and the Japanese Miracle: The Growth of Industrial Policy, 1925–1975* (Stanford, Calif.: Stanford University Press, 1982).

2. MITI also publishes English translations of its "visions." See, for example, MITI, *Japan's Industrial Structure—A Long Range Vision, 1978* (Tokyo: MITI Information Office, 1978), and MITI, *The Industrial Structure of Japan in the 1980s (Summary)—Future Outlook and Tasks* (Tokyo: MITI Information Office, 1981).

3. A discussion of MITI's thoughts on industrial policy during the early postwar period is found in Robert S. Ozaki, "Japanese Views on Industrial Organization," *Asian Survey* (October 1970): 872–89.

4. For a chronicle of Japan's trade and capital liberalization, see Robert S. Ozaki, *The Control of Imports and Foreign Capital in Japan* (New York: Praeger, 1972).

5. See MITI, *Economic Security of Japan 1982* (Tokyo: MITI Information Office, 1982).

6. MITI officials' statements on Japan's current industrial policy appear in Shinji Kakukawa, *Features of the Industrial Policy of Japan* (Tokyo: MITI, 1983), and Keiichi Konaga, "Sangyo Seisaku no Arikata to Mondaiten [Industrial Policy: Approaches and Problems]," *Japan Economic Research Center Bulletin*, August 15, 1983, pp. 29–35. See also MITI, *Industrial Policy in Japan: A Question-and-Answer Overview* (New York: Japan Trade Center, 1983).

7. For more detailed comparative statistics, see MITI, *Background Information on Japan's Industrial Policy*, May 1983.

8. Similar joint committees on industrial policy have also been meeting periodically.

9. The share of government financing in government-business joint R&D in Japan is usually 25–30 percent.

10. Ezra F. Vogel, *Japan as Number One* (New York: Harper & Row, 1979); Ira C. Magaziner and Robert B. Reich, *Minding America's Business* (New York: Harcourt Brace Jovanovich, 1982); Ira C. Magaziner and Thomas M. Hout, *Japanese Industrial Policy* (Berkeley, Calif.: Institute of International Studies, University of California, Berkeley, 1980); Eleanor M. Hadley, "Industrial Policy for Competitiveness," *Journal of Japanese Trade and Industry* (September 1982).

11. Philip H. Tresize, "Industrial Policy Is Not the Major Reason for Japan's Success," *The Brookings Review* (Spring 1983); Isaac Shapiro, "Second Thoughts about Japan," *Wall Street Journal*, June 5, 1981; Amitai Etzioni, "Why America Shouldn't Imitate Japan," *San Francisco Chronicle*, December 30, 1980.

12. See, for example, Art Pine, "Industrial Policy? It's No Panacea in Japan," *Wall Street Journal*, September 19, 1983.

4. Melvyn Krauss: " 'Europeanizing' the U.S. Economy: The Enduring Appeal of the Corporatist State"

1. Robert Reich, "The Next American Frontier," *The Atlantic Monthly*, April 1983, p. 107.

2. See Roland Sarti, *Fascism and Industrial Leadership in Italy* (Berkeley, Calif.: University of California Press, 1971).

3. Ibid., p. 124.

4. Ibid.

5. Robert W. Merry, " 'Industrial Policy' Divides Democrats, But Is Seen as a Cornerstone for Election," *Wall Street Journal*, January 9, 1984.

6. Reich, p. 105.

7. The term "welfare state" is best interpreted as union-dominated "corporate state" as compared with Mussolini's employer-dominated "corporate state."

8. Bo Carlsson, "Industrial Subsidies in Sweden: Macro-Economic Effects and an International Comparison," *The Journal of Industrial Economics* (September 1983).

9. Melvyn B. Krauss, *The New Protectionism: The Welfare State and International Trade* (New York: New York University Press, 1978).

10. Goran Ohlin, "Introduction," *Adjustment for Trade* (Paris: Development Center of the Organisation for Economic Co-operation and Development, 1975), pp. 10–11.

11. Reich, p. 106.

12. Alan Whiting, "Overseas Experience in the Use of Industrial Subsidies," in *The Economics of Industrial Subsidies*, ed. A. Whiting (London: Her Majesty's Stationery Office, 1976), p. 51.

13. Ibid., p. 53.

14. Melvyn B. Krauss, *Development Without Aid* (New York: McGraw-Hill, 1983).

15. Reich, p. 108.

16. Whiting, p. 56.

17. K. Pavitt, "The Choice of Targets and Instruments for Government Support of Scientific Research," in Whiting, ed., p. 132.

18. William Safire, "The German Problem," *The New York Times*, January 8, 1984.

19. This section is based on Peter Norman and Roger Thurow, "West Germany Hails Rebound but Worries about Industrial Ills," *Wall Street Journal*, January 9, 1984.

20. Charlotte Twight, "The Economics of Fascism: 'National Interest' Above All," *Perspectives on Public Policy*, Council for a Competitive Economy.

5. Eugene Bardach: "Implementing Industrial Policy"

1. See, for instance, Felix Rohatyn, "Time for a Change," *New York Review*, August 18, 1983, pp. 46–49.

2. John J. Fialka, "Pledges by Mondale Add Up to a Big Bill, An Analysis Suggests," *Wall Street Journal*, January 24, 1984, pp. 1 and 14.

3. F. Gerard Adams, "Criteria for U.S. Industrial-Policy Strategies," in *Industrial Policies for Growth and Competitiveness: An Economic Perspective*, ed. F. Gerard Adams and Lawrence R. Klein (Lexington, Mass.: D. C. Heath, 1982).

4. Charles L. Schultze, "Industrial Policy: A Dissent," *The Brookings Review* (Fall 1983): 8.

5. Robert B. Reich, "Beyond Free Trade," *Foreign Affairs* 61, no. 4 (Spring 1983): 782.

6. Richard R. Nelson and Richard N. Langlois, "Industrial Innovation Policy: Lessons from American History," *Science* 219 (February 19, 1983): 814–18.

7. Cf. Regina Herzlinger, "Costs, Benefits, and the West Side Highway," *The Public Interest*, no. 55 (Spring 1979): 77–98, and Melvin M. Webber, "The BART Experience—What Have We Learned?" *The Public Interest*, no. 45 (Fall 1976): 79–108.

8. Eugene Bardach, "Policy Termination as a Political Process," *Policy Sciences* 7, no. 2 (June 1976): 123–32.

9. Bill Keller, "How Congress Spoils Small Business," *Washington Monthly*, March 1982, pp. 44–49.

10. The main reason is that the SBA does not have enough staff to be appropriately fussy. Cf. General Accounting Office, "Better Management of Collateral Can Reduce Losses in SBA's Major Loan Program," CEO–81–123, July 17, 1981.

11. Charles Walker and Mark A. Bloomfield, "The Political Response to Three Potential Major Bankruptcies: Lockheed, New York City, and Chrysler," in *Toward a New U.S. Industrial Policy*, ed. Michael L. Wachter and Susan M. Wachter (Philadelphia: University of Pennsylvania Press, 1982), pp. 423–52.

12. See Clark Nardinelli, "The Reconstruction Finance Corporation's Murky History," Heritage Foundation *Backgrounder*, no. 317 (December 21, 1983), and Richard B. McKenzie, "A New Reconstruction Finance Corporation: No Cure for U.S. Economic Ills," Heritage Foundation *Backgrounder*, no. 316 (December 20, 1983).

13. Jules Abels, *The Truman Scandals* (Chicago: Henry Regnery, 1956), pp. 72–73.

14. Ibid., p. 74.

15. Eugene Bardach and Robert A. Kagan, *Going By The Book: The Problem of Regulatory Unreasonableness* (Philadelphia: Temple University Press, 1982).

16. U.S. General Accounting Office, "SBA's Pilot Programs to Improve Guaranty Loan Procedures Need Further Development," CEO–81–25, February 2, 1981.

17. The RFC strongly favored large firms.

18. See, for instance, Ira C. Magaziner and Robert B. Reich, *Minding America's Business* (New York: Harcourt Brace Jovanovich, 1982), and Robert F. Wescott, "U.S. Approaches to Industrial Policy," in Adams and Klein, eds., esp. pp. 87–95. Wescott writes: "In the past, the U.S. attitude was that it did not need an IP [industrial policy]. . . . This view is changing, primarily because of the realization that an industrial base will not always take care of itself automatically. If anything, there is growing agreement on one issue—the need for more planning and better coordination of policies that affect industries" (p. 95).

19. See Margaret E. Dewar, *Industry in Trouble: The Federal Government and the New England Fisheries* (Philadelphia: Temple University Press, 1983).

20. Magaziner and Reich, pp. 337–38.

21. Jeffrey L. Pressman and Aaron Wildavsky, *Implementation*, 2nd ed. (Berkeley, Calif.: University of California Press, 1979).

22. Dewar, pp. 71–72.

23. Ibid., p. 61.

24. Eugene Bardach, *The Implementation Game* (Cambridge, Mass.: MIT Press, 1977); Pressman and Wildavsky.

25. Congressional Budget Office, "The Industrial Policy Debate" (Washington, D.C.: U.S. Gov. Printing Office, December 1983), p. 55.

26. Bardach, *The Implementation Game*, ch. 9.

27. *Business Week*, June 1980.

28. See Robert H. Wiebe, *Businessmen and Reform: A Study of the Progressive Movement* (Chicago: Quandrangle Books, 1968) (orig. hardback ed. Harvard University Press, 1962).

29. Energy Policy Project of the Ford Foundation, *A Time to Choose: America's Energy Future* (Cambridge, Mass.: Ballinger, 1974), p. 3.

30. Ibid.

6. Murray L. Weidenbaum and Michael J. Athey: "What Is the Rust Belt's Problem?"

1. The categories are at the two-digit level of aggregation. See U.S. Office of Management and Budget, *Standard Industrial Classification Manual* (Washington, D.C.: U.S. Gov. Printing Office, 1972).

2. The R&D and sales data are taken from National Science Foundation, *National Patterns of Science and Technology Resources, 1982* (Washington, D.C.: U.S. Gov. Printing Office, 1982).

3. Technically, we measured the amount of national income attributed to each industry, without capital consumption allowances, in real terms. The deflators used are taken from the implicit price deflators for major categories of gross national product, 1972 = 100.

4. To determine whether a given industry has been growing or declining, we fit the data to the following equation:

$$Y_{it} = \beta_{i0} + \beta_{i1}\,t + \beta_{i2}\,CUR_t + \epsilon_{it}$$

where: Y_{it} = real income produced by industry i over time
     t   = 0,1,...,12; 0 in 1970
     CUR_t = capacity utilization rate
     ϵ_{it} = random error term for industry i
     $\hat{\beta}_{i1}$ = the estimated trend for industry i over the period from 1970 to 1982

5. To determine this trend the original model is used with full-time equivalent employees replacing real income as the dependent variable.

6. Robert F. Dieli, "Employment: One Year Later," *Continental Comment*, December 30, 1983, p. 1.

7. William H. Miller, "The Phony War Between High Tech and Low Tech," *Industry Week*, October 3, 1983, p. 39.

8. The equation used in this section is similar to the one developed above, except that the ratio of industry income to national income replaces industry income as the dependent variable and CUR_t is not included as an independent variable.

9. A similar position has been reached by Robert Z. Lawrence, "Changes in U.S. Industrial Structure: The Role of Global Forces, Secular Trends and Transitory Cycles," in *Industrial Change and Public Policy,* ed. Federal Reserve Bank of Kansas City (Kansas City, Mo.: Federal Reserve Bank of Kansas City, 1984), pp. 29–77.

10. See Murray L. Weidenbaum, *The Future of Business Regulation* (New York: Amacom, 1980).

11. Murray L. Weidenbaum and Reno Harnish, *Government Credit Subsidies for Energy Development* (Washington, D.C.: American Enterprise Institute, 1976), pp. 15–17; Arthur Denzau and Clifford Hardin, *Why Resurrect the RFC?* (St. Louis: Center for the Study of American Business, Washington University, formal publication no. 62, 1984).

12. Miller, p. 39.

13. John Holusha, "Deere & Co. Leads the Way in 'Flexible' Manufacturing," *Des Moines Register,* January 29, 1984, p. 10F.

14. "Excerpts from Soviet Study on the Need for an Overhaul of the Economy," *The New York Times,* August 5, 1983, p. 4.

15. Ibid.

7. Regis McKenna: "Sustaining the Innovation Process in America"

1. See, for instance, Marge Ploch, "Industry Invests in Research Centers," *High Technology* (May 1983): 15–18, and Aerospace Industries Association of America, *Meeting Technology and Manpower Needs Through the Industry/University Interface,* May 1983.

2. See, for instance, the revitalization and reindustrialization arguments: Paul Blustein, "'Reindustrialization,' a Vague Idea, Means a Clear Profit for Some," *Wall Street Journal,* August 27, 1980, and "The Reindustrialization of America," special issue of *Business Week,* June 30, 1980.

3. National Science Board, *Science Indicators, 1980* (Washington, D.C.: U.S. Gov. Printing Office, 1981), pp. 7 and 9.

4. Those that *Business Week* terms the "adjustors" in industrial policy, in "Industrial Policy: Is It the Answer?" July 4, 1983.

5. National Resources and Commerce, Congressional Budget Office, "Trends in the Consolidated R&D Budget," May 11, 1983.

6. Stephen Rosen, "The Fallacy of Future Shock," *San Francisco Examiner/Chronicle,* July 4, 1976, p. 4.

7. National Science Foundation, *National Patterns of Science and Technology Resources, 1982* (Washington, D.C.: U.S. Gov. Printing Office, March 1982), pp. 25–27.

8. Ibid.

9. Ibid.

10. National Resources and Commerce.

11. Ibid.

12. "The Patent Is Expiring as a Spur to Innovation," *Business Week,* May 11, 1981, p. 44.

13. W. J. Sanders III, "Sunnyvale's High-Tech Heartbeat," speech given at State of the City of Sunnyvale Meeting, April 8, 1983.

14. National Resources and Commerce.

15. Bro Uttal, "The Lab That Ran Away from Xerox," *Fortune,* September 5, 1983, p. 97.

16. *Public Policies and Strategies for U.S. High Technology Industry: Proceedings of the SIA Long Range Planning Conference,* November 22, 1982, Monterey, Calif.

17. Ploch.

18. Uttal.

19. "America Rushes to High Technology for Growth," *Business Week,* March 28, 1983.

20. Tim Dickson, "Why Olivetti Is Promoting the Venture Capital Cause," *Financial Times,* August 9, 1983.

21. James C. Abegglen and Akio Etori, "Japanese Technology Today," *Scientific American,* October 1980, p. J20.

22. National Science Board, pp. 7–9.

23. See, for instance, William J. Abernathy, Kim B. Clark, and Alan M. Kantrow, *Industrial Renaissance* (Basic Books: New York, 1983).

24. *The Effect of Government Targeting on World Semiconductor Competition: A Case History of Japanese Industrial Strategy and Its Costs for America,* SIA, 1983.

25. Erich Block, "Quality: The Need for Joint Action," *Public Policies and Strategies for U.S. High Technology Industry,* SIA Conference, Monterey, Calif., November 22, 1982, p. 65.

26. George N. Hatsopoulos, *High Costs of Capital: Handicap of American Industry,* American Business Conference and Thermo Electron Corporation, April 26, 1983, p. 1.

27. Ibid.

28. Robert B. Reich, "The Next American Frontier," *The Atlantic Monthly,* April 1983, p. 103.

29. "Revitalization and the U.S. Economy," House of Representatives, Subcommittee on Economic Stabilization, Committee on Banking, Finance and Urban Affairs, hearings on September 23, 1981, p. 416.

30. "Is the Cost of Capital Too High?" *Politics and Markets* 9 (July 25, 1983).

31. Hatsopoulos, p. 43.

32. *Industry Week,* November 27, 1978, pp. 119–120.

33. "Revitalization and the U.S. Economy," p. 430.

34. David E. Gumpert, "Venture Capital Becoming More Widely Available," *Harvard Business Review* 57, no. 1 (January/February 1979): 178–92.

35. "The Hunt for Plays in Biotechnology," *Business Week,* July 28, 1980, p. 71.

36. William Pat Patterson, "The Rush to Put Biotechnology to Work," *Industry Week* 210, no. 5 (September 7, 1981): 64–70.

37. Brook H. Byers, "New Biotechnology Companies and Venture Capital," presented at Robert S. First, Inc., Biotechnology Present Status and Future Prospects Conference, White Plains, N.Y., June 1–2, 1981.

38. John E. Donalds, "Managing Biotechnology: Research Contracts," presented at McGraw-Hill Business Opportunities in Biotechnology Conference, New York, October 26–27, 1981.

39. "The Patent Is Expiring as a Spur to Innovation," p. 44.

40. *Drug and Cosmetic Industry,* November 1982, pp. 32–36.

41. Oskar R. Zaborsky, "Biotechnology Patents of 1983: An International Perspective," *Bio/Technology* 1, no. 1 (March 1983): 33.

42. Ibid.

43. Ibid.

44. "Insulin by Biotechnology Expected to Impact 'Gradually' on a $150 Million U.S. Market," *Chemical Marketing Reporter* 222, no. 19 (November 8, 1982): 5.

45. "Impact of Biotechnology on the Pharmaceutical Industry," Strategic Inc. Report, June 1982.

46. Daniel D. Nossiter, "Designer Genes—Biotechnology Is Big in Promise and Pitfalls for Investors," *Barrons* 62, no. 8 (February 22, 1982): 8–9, 22, 24.

47. *Chemical Industry*, April 4, 1983, p. 251.

48. Ibid.

49. Charles Fairley, "Commercial Development of Research," Scottish Development Agency, U.K., presented at Online Conference Ltd., Biotechnology 1983 Symposium, London, May 4–6, 1983, p. 101.

50. Barbara J. Culliton, "Academe and Industry Debate Partnership," *Science* 219, no. 4581 (January 14, 1983): 150.

51. Derek C. Bok, "Business and the Academy," *Harvard Magazine* (May–June 1981): 23.

52. M. Kenney, J. Kloppenburg, F. Buttel, and J. Cowan, "Genetic Engineering and Agriculture: Socioeconomic Aspects of Biotechnology Research and Development in Developed and Developing Countries," Cornell University, presented at Online Conference Ltd., Biotechnology 1983 Symposium, London, May 4–6, 1983.

53. David A. Silver, "Venture Capital at the Corporate Planning Desk," *Planning Review* 7, no. 3 (May 1979): 23–24.

54. M. Burne, "Nothing Ventured, Nothing Gained," *International Management* 34, no. 4 (April 1979): 16–19.

55. Michael Borrus, James Millstein, and John Zysman, "U.S.–Japanese Competition in the Semiconductor Industry," Center for International Studies, University of California, Berkeley, 1980, p. 11.

56. Ibid., pp. 21, 25, 29.

57. Ibid., p. 18.

58. Ian Mackintosh, *Microelectronics in the 1980's* (London: Mackintosh Publications, Ltd., 1979), p. 65.

59. Borrus, Millstein, and Zysman, pp. 28–29.

60. Michael Borrus, with James Millstein and John Zysman, "Responses to the Japanese Challenge in High Technology: Innovation, Maturity, and U.S.-Japanese Competition in Microelectronics," forthcoming, p. 23.

61. Sabin Russell, "See $1B Through Shake-Out Looms as Need for Cash Grows: An Interim Technology?" *Electronic News*, June 6, 1983, p. 1.

62. Borrus, Millstein, and Zysman, p. 25.

63. Russell, p. 46.

64. Leslie Breuckner, "VHSIC: An Analysis of the Department of Defense's VHSIC Program's Potential Impact on the Commercial Semiconductors Industry," Berkeley Roundtable on International Economy, forthcoming.

65. U.S. Senate, Committee on Commerce, Science and Transportation, *Industrial Technology* (Washington, D.C.: U.S. Gov. Printing Office, 1978), p. 91.

66. From interview with Michael Borrus, February 1984.

67. Venture Economics Division, Capital Publishing Corporation, in "Statement of Stanley E. Pratt," Hearings on Revitalization and the U.S. Economy, House of Representatives, Subcommittee on Economic Stabilization, p. 435.

8. Bruce Bartlett: "Trade Policy and the Dangers of Protectionism"

1. U.S. Department of Labor, Office of Foreign Economic Research, *Report of the President on U.S. Competitiveness,* Washington, D.C., September 1980.

2. Listed as members of the LICIT are the following businesses and unions: Bethlehem Steel; Corning Glass Works; The BF Goodrich Co.; Ingersoll Rand Co.; St. Joe Minerals Co.; W.R. Grace & Co.; Westinghouse Electric Corp.; Weyerhauser Co.; the Amalgamated Clothing & Textile Workers Union; the Communications Workers of America; the International Union of Electrical, Radio and Machine Workers; the International Brotherhood of Electrical Workers; the American Flint Glass Workers Union; the Industrial Union Department, AFL-CIO; the International Ladies Garment Workers Union; the United Paperworkers International Union; the United Rubberworkers of America; and the United Steelworkers of America.

3. See Robert B. Reich, *The Next American Frontier* (New York: Times Books, 1983), pp. 176–86; idem, "Beyond Free Trade," *Foreign Affairs* 61 (Spring 1983): 773–804; idem, "Industries in Distress," *The New Republic,* May 9, 1981, pp. 19–23.

4. Stuart Aurbach, "Democratic Candidates Part on Free Trade," *Washington Post,* May 16, 1983; "What about Local Content Legislation?" *Washington Post,* December 19, 1982, p. C8; Howell Raines, "Move to Curb Competitiveness of Imports Rises as Focus at End of Campaign," *New York Times,* October 25, 1982; Walter F. Mondale, "It's Time for America to Fight Back," *Washington Post,* October 23, 1982.

5. Ann Krueger and Baran Tuncer, "An Empirical Test of the Infant Industry Argument," *American Economic Review* 72 (December 1982): 1142–52; see also Robert E. Baldwin, "The Case Against Infant-Industry Tariff Protection," *Journal of Political Economy* 77 (May/June 1969): 295–305.

6. Arye L. Hillman, "Declining Industries and Political-Support Protectionist Motives," *American Economic Review* 72 (December 1982): 1180–87. For case studies, see Morris E. Morke and David G. Tarr, *Staff Report on Effects of Restrictions on United States Imports: Five Case Studies and Theory* (Washington, D.C.: Federal Trade Commission, Bureau of Economics, June 1980). See also James M. Buchanan, Robert D. Tollison, and Gordon Tullock, eds., *Toward a Theory of the Rent-Seeking Society* (College Station, Tex.: Texas A&M University Press, 1980).

7. John S. McGee, "Predatory Pricing Revisited," *Journal of Law and Economics* 23 (October 1980): 289–326; idem, "Predatory Price Cutting: The Standard Oil (N.J.) Case," *Journal of Law and Economics* 1 (October 1958): 136–69; Wayne A. Leeman, "The Limitations of Local Price-Cutting as a Barrier to Entry," *Journal of Political Economy* 64 (August 1956): 329–34; Yale Brozen, *Concentration, Mergers, and Public Policy* (New York: Macmillan, 1982), pp. 330–33.

8. *International Trade, Industrial Policies, and the Future of American Industry* (Washington, D.C.: The Labor-Industry Coalition for International Trade, April 1983), p. 15.

9. John Mutti, "Aspects of Unilateral Trade Policy and Factor Adjustment Costs," *Review of Economics and Statistics* 60 (February 1978): 102–10; Robert E. Baldwin, "Protectionist Pressures in the United States," in *Challenges to a Liberal International Order,* ed. R. Amacher, G. Haberler, and T. Willett (Washington, D.C.: American Enterprise Institute, 1979), pp. 223–38.

10. *Foreign Industrial Targeting and Its Effects on U.S. Industries, Phase I: Japan* (Washington, D.C.: U.S. International Trade Commission, publication 1437, October 1983), p. 1.

11. Ibid., p. 31.

12. U.S. Congress, *International Competitiveness in Electronics* (Washington, D.C.: Office of Technology Assessment, OTA-ISC-200, November 1983), p. 423.

13. Paul Krugman, "Targeted Industrial Policies: Theory and Evidence," a paper presented at a conference on industrial policy sponsored by the Federal Reserve Bank of Kansas City in August 1983.

14. For evidence that the U.S. is not losing ground competitively, see Robert Z. Lawrence, "U.S. International Competitiveness," in U.S. Congress, Joint Economic Committee, *U.S. International Economic Policy in the 1980s*, 97th Cong., 2nd sess. (Washington, D.C.: U.S. Gov. Printing Office, 1982), pp. 68–91; *Economic Report of the President, 1983* (Washington, D.C.: U.S. Gov. Printing Office, 1983), pp. 52–61; *Economic Report of the President, 1984* (Washington, D.C.: U.S. Gov. Printing Office, 1984), pp. 87–111; William H. Branson, "The Myth of De-Industrialization," *Regulation* (September/October 1983), pp. 24–54; Thomas DiLorenzo, "The Myth of America's Declining Manufacturing Sector," Heritage Foundation *Backgrounder* (January 13, 1984).

15. Robert Z. Lawrence, "Is Trade Deindustrializing America? A Medium Term Perspective," *Brookings Papers on Economic Activity*, no. 1 (1983): 129–77.

16. Richard Blackhurst and Jan Tumlir, *Trade Relations under Flexible Exchange Rates* (Geneva: General Agreement on Tariffs and Trade, September 1980); Wilson Schmidt, *The U.S. Balance of Payments and the Sinking Dollar* (New York: New York University Press, 1979).

17. *The Effect of Changes in the Value of the U.S. Dollar on Trade in Selected Commodities* (Washington, D.C.: U.S. International Trade Commission, publication 1423, September 1983).

18. Adam Smith, *The Wealth of Nations* (New York: Random House, Modern Library edition, 1937), p. 625.

19. Bernard Munk, "The Welfare Costs of Content Protection: The Automotive Industry in Latin America," *Journal of Political Economy* 77 (January/February 1969): 95. See also Gene M. Grossman, "The Theory of Domestic Content Protection and Content Preference," *Quarterly Journal of Economics* 96 (November 1981): 583–603.

20. See U.S. Congress, House Committee on Ways and Means, *Fair Practice in Automotive Products Act*, H. Report 98–287, part 2 to accompany H.R. 1234, 98th Cong., 1st sess., 1983.

21. Murray Weidenbaum and Michael Munger, "Protectionism at Any Price?" *Regulation* (July/August 1983): 14–18.

22. Steven E. Plaut, "Why Dumping Is Good for Us," *Fortune*, May 5, 1980, pp. 212–22.

23. Milton Friedman, *Free Trade: Producer versus Consumer* (Manhattan, Kan.: Kansas State University, 1978).

24. William A. Brock and Stephen P. Magee, "The Economics of Special Interest Politics: The Case of the Tariff," *American Economic Review* 68 (May 1978): 245–50.

25. Animesh Ghoshal, "Protectionism and the Auto Industry," *Journal of Contemporary Studies* 6 (Fall 1983): 61–71. See also Clifton B. Luttrell, "The Voluntary Automobile Import Agreement With Japan—More Protectionism," Federal Reserve Bank of St. Louis *Review* 63 (November 1981): 25–30.

26. Milton Friedman, "Protection That Hurts," *Newsweek*, November 15, 1982, p. 90. On the Reagan administration's trade policies, see also Robert E. Baldwin, "Trade Policies under the Reagan Administration," *Recent Issues and Initiatives in U.S. Trade Policy* (Cambridge, Mass.: National Bureau of Economic Research, 1984), pp. 10–32; Murray Weidenbaum, *Toward a More Open Trade Policy* (St. Louis: Center for the Study of American Business, Washington University, 1983), pp. 3–16; Sheldon Richman, "Examining Reagan's Record on Free Trade," *Wall Street Journal*, May 10, 1982; Rowland Evans and Robert Novak, "Politics, Not Free Trade, Gets the Front Seat," *Washington Post*, May 11, 1981; Edward Boyer, "Protectionism, Reagan-Style: The Steel Quotas," *Fortune*, August 8, 1983, p. 55.

27. Art Pine, "How President Came to Favor Concessions for U.S. Textile Makers," *Wall Street Journal*, January 6, 1984.

28. George Cabot Lodge and William R. Glass, "U.S. Trade Policy Needs One Voice," *Harvard Business Review* 83 (May–June 1983): 75–83.

29. Philip H. Tresize, "A New Department We Don't Need," *Washington Post*, June 10, 1983;

Art Pine, "A Department for Restricting Trade?" *Wall Street Journal,* July 7, 1983; Benjamin Zycher, "A U.S. Department of Trade—Or Protection," Heritage Foundation *Backgrounder* (December 1983). For Secretary Baldrige's view on why the new department would not be protectionist, see the *National Journal,* December 31, 1983, p. 2697.

30. See, for example, Treasury Secretary Regan's speech at the University of Kansas on October 15, 1983; Council of Economic Advisers Chairman Martin Feldstein's speech to the Commonwealth Club of California on October 28, 1983; and the statements by Assistant Secretary of Commerce Bruce Merrifield, Deputy Under Secretary of Commerce for International Trade Olin Wethington, and Federal Trade Commission Chairman James C. Miller III before the Subcommittee on Banking, Finance, and Urban Affairs, October 27, 1983.

31. See, for example, U.S. Department of Commerce, International Trade Administration, *An Assessment of U.S. Competitiveness in High Technology Industries,* Washington, D.C., February 1983.

32. Juan Williams and Michael Schrage, "Reagan Names Commission on Industrial Competition," *Washington Post,* August 5, 1983.

33. Barbara Spencer and James Brander, "International R&D Rivalry and Industrial Strategy," *Review of Economic Studies* 50 (1983): 707–22; Paul Krugman, "New Theories of Trade among Industrial Countries," *American Economic Review* 73 (May 1983): 343–47.

34. Richard R. Nelson and Richard N. Langlois, "Industrial Innovation Policy: Lessons from American History," *Science* 219 (February 19, 1983): 817; see also Richard R. Nelson, ed., *Government and Technical Progress* (Elmsford, N.Y.: Pergamon Press, 1982).

10. Paul Seabury: "Industrial Policy and National Defense"

1. See Craufurd D. Goodwin and Michael Nacht, *Absence of Decision: Foreign Students in American Colleges and Universities* (New York: Institute of International Education, 1983), p. 13: "In many graduate programs in engineering, for example, from the least to the most prestigious, 70 percent or more of the students come from abroad. In some cases this proportion approaches 100 percent, and only in a few cases is it below 40 percent. Several engineering deans suggested that without foreign students they would have had to close down their graduate programs in the short run and their whole operations ultimately."

2. One of America's most efficient naval shipyards, the Bath Iron Works in Maine, from the outside—in its ancient industrial plant—looks like a relic of the early industrial revolution (which in fact it is).

3. James Cook, "The Molting of America," *Forbes,* November 22, 1982.

4. Ibid.

5. Paul Kennedy, "A Historian of Imperial Decline Looks at America," *Manchester Guardian Weekly,* November 14, 1982.

6. Henry Cabot Lodge, ed., *The Works of Alexander Hamilton* (New York and London: G.F. Putnam Sons, 1904), vol. IV, 135–36.

7. Quoted in John Caravelli, "Surprise and Preemption in Soviet Military Strategy," *International Security Review* 6, no. 2 (Summer 1981): 237.

8. "We Shall Not Be Surpassed," translated and excerpted in *Strategic Review* 9, no. 4 (Fall 1981): 98.

9. "Ogarkov on Readiness for War Mobilization," *Strategic Review* 9, no. 4 (Fall 1981): 102.

10. *The Ailing Defense Industrial Base: Unsteady for Crisis,* Report of the Defense Industrial Base Panel of the Committee on Armed Services (Washington, D.C.: U.S. Gov. Printing Office, 1980), p. 16.

11. See Loren Thompson, "The Defense Industrial Base: Going, Going . . . ," *International Security Review* 6, no. 2 (Summer 1981): 237.

12. Ibid., p. 238. Eighty-three percent of U.S. dollars spent for the Navy's F-14 fighter go to materials with lead times in excess of two years.

13. *The Ailing Defense Industrial Base: Unsteady for Crisis,* pp. 13–23.

14. U.S. Department of Commerce, Bureau of Industrial Economics, *Sectoral Implications of Defense Expenditures* (Washington, D.C.: U.S. Gov. Printing Office, 1982), p. 8.

15. *National Materials and Minerals Program Plan and Report to Congress* (Washington, D.C.: The White House, 1982), esp. pp. 18–19. *Inter alia,* the report notes that perhaps as much as 68 percent of federal land now is closed to mineral exploration and development.

16. Roderick L. Vawter, *Industrial Mobilization: The Relevant History* (Washington, D.C.: National Defense University Press, 1982), p. 74.

17. Dr. John D. Morgan, "Materials Policy," paper presented at the Applied History Conference, Carnegie-Mellon University, November 4, 1983, p. 28. The countries cited are among those upon whom the U.S. now relies to provide 50 percent or more of specific raw materials needed for current consumption.

18. *Nuts, Bolts, and Large Screws: The Impact of Shortages in a National Emergency* (Lexington, Mass.: Data Resources, Inc. 1978), p. 4.

19. U.S. Department of Commerce, *The Effects of Imports of Nuts, Bolts and Screws on the National Security,* February 1983, Appendix K, Table 7. The Commerce Department takes a complacent view of this. In this view, these supplying countries are "politically reliable," "stable" and "pro-U.S."; their geographic locations make them "reliable in practice, as well" (p. 63). Such comforting thoughts should make Mr. Marcos sleep better at night.

20. Klaus Knorr, *Military Power and Potential* (Lexington, Mass.: D.C. Heath and Company, 1970), p. 21.

21. During the 1973 October War, for instance, the U.S. drew heavily upon short-supply stocks of conventional weapons—notably tanks—in resupplying the Israelis. Robbing Peter to pay Paul certainly makes sense when one's logistical reserve is drained to the bottom.

22. Roderick L. Vawter, p. 87.

11.   Yolanda Kodrzycki Henderson: "Tax Reform: An Item for Any Industrial Policy Agenda"

1. See U.S. Congress, Congressional Budget Office, *The Industrial Policy Debate* (Washington, D.C.: U.S. Gov. Printing Office, 1983), ch. 3.

2. Don Fullerton and Yolanda Kodrzycki Henderson, "Incentive Effects of Taxes on Income from Capital: Alternative Policies in the 1980's," in *The Legacy of Reaganomics,* ed. Charles R. Hulten and Isabel V. Sawhill (Washington, D.C.: The Urban Institute, forthcoming).

3. Alan S. Blinder, "Reaganomics and Growth: The Message in the Models," in ibid.

4. A proposal for indexed depreciation allowances was advanced by Alan J. Auerbach and Dale W. Jorgenson, "Inflation-Proof Depreciation of Assets," *Harvard Business Review* 58 (1980): 113–18.

5. See Joseph J. Cordes and Steven M. Sheffrin, "Taxation and the Sectoral Allocation of Capital in the U.S.," *National Tax Journal* 34 (1981): 419–32.

6. No forecasts of tax liabilities actually show zero corporate tax payments, but this is due largely to corporations' practice of making "voluntary" tax payments. Public sentiment, as inferred from recent policy proposals, favors some minimum tax payment by corporations. Tax payments by the owners of corporations—the shareholders—do not seem to be an acceptable substitute in the eyes of the public. Many corporations could lower their corporate income tax payments by, for example, adopting LIFO accounting for inventories but choose not to. There are also some positive payments because of carryover problems or because of monopoly profits that were not taken into account in my research with Fullerton.

7. For an excellent discussion of these issues, see Harvey Galper and Eugene Steuerle, "Tax Incentives for Saving," *The Brookings Review* 2, no. 2 (1983): 16–23.

8. See Mervyn A. King and Don Fullerton, eds., *The Taxation of Income from Capital: A Comparative Study of the U.S., U.K., Sweden, and West Germany* (Chicago: University of Chicago Press, forthcoming).

9. See Fullerton and Henderson.

10. See George N. Hatsopoulos, Statement before the U.S. Congress Joint Economic Committee, April 28, 1983.

11. U.S. Treasury Department, *Blueprints for Basic Tax Reform* (Washington, D.C.: U.S. Gov. Printing Office, 1977).

12. Chalmers Johnson: "Conclusion"

1. Herbert Stein, *Presidential Economics: The Making of Economic Policy from Roosevelt to Reagan and Beyond* (New York: Simon and Schuster, 1984).

2. Albert Wohlstetter, "Scientists, Seers, and Strategy," *Foreign Affairs* (April 1963): 3–15.

3. *New York Times,* January 23, 1984.

4. Bruce Scott, "American Competitiveness: Problems, Causes, and Implications" (Boston: Harvard Business School 75th Anniversary Colloquium Series, 1984), p. 45.

5. Otto Eckstein et al., *The DRI Report on U.S. Manufacturing Industries* (Boston: Data Resources Inc., 1984), p. 28.

6. Council of Economic Advisers, *Economic Report of the President* (Washington, D.C.: U.S. Gov. Printing Office, 1983), pp. 80–81.

7. Also see Harvey Galper and Eugene Steuerle, "Tax Incentives for Saving," *The Brookings Review* (Winter 1983): 16–23.

8. Eckstein et al., p. 53.

CONTRIBUTORS

MICHAEL J. ATHEY is the John M. Olin Fellow at the Center for the Study of American Business at Washington University in St. Louis.

EUGENE BARDACH is a professor of public policy at the University of California, Berkeley. His many articles and published works include *The Implementation Game* (1977) and *Going by the Book: The Problem of Regulatory Unreasonableness* (with Robert Kagan, 1982); together with Robert Kagan, he also co-edited the Institute's *Social Regulation: Strategies for Reform* (1982).

BRUCE BARTLETT is vice-president of Polyconomics, Inc., a New Jersey–based consulting firm. Previously he served as executive director of the Joint Economic Committee of the U.S. Congress and on the staffs of Senator Roger Jepsen, Congressman Jack Kemp, and Congressman Ron Paul. He is the author of several books, including *Reaganomics: Supply-Side Economics in Action* (1981), and writes frequently for *The Wall Street Journal.*

YOLANDA KODRZYCKI HENDERSON is assistant professor of economics at Amherst College, where her research focuses on the taxation of income from capital and strategies for achieving long-term growth. Her published works include contributions to policy-oriented studies at the Congressional Budget Office as well as development of morale to evaluate tax reform measures.

WALTER E. HOADLEY, a senior research fellow at the Hoover Institution, Stanford University, retired in 1981 as executive vice-president and chief economist of the Bank of America in San Francisco. He is an international author and lecturer, a television economic commentator, and a columnist for *Dun's Business Month,* as well as a contributor to many other publications on economic forecasting, the global financial system, and management decision-making.

CHALMERS JOHNSON is the Walter and Elise Professor of Asian Studies and former chairman of the Department of Political Science at the University of California, Berkeley. He is the author of *Japan's Public Policy Companies* (1978), *MITI and the Japanese Miracle* (1982), and many other books on East Asian politics and economics.

261

MELVYN KRAUSS, a professor of economics at New York University and senior fellow at the Hoover Institution, Stanford University, has taught in eight foreign countries. He has written over fifty scientific articles and is a regular contributor to *The Wall Street Journal.* His books include *The New Protectionism* (1978) and *Development Without Aid* (1983), and currently he is writing a book on the economics of the Atlantic Alliance.

REGIS McKENNA is president of Regis McKenna, Inc., a high-technology marketing and public relations company located in Palo Alto, California. He is also president of the National Commission on Industrial Innovation; member of the Berkeley Round Table on International Economy; advisor to the Advanced Technology Center at Georgia Tech and the University of California, Santa Barbara; and private counsel to the Semiconductor Industry Association. Previously he served as a member of the California Commission on High Technology.

ROBERT S. OZAKI, professor of economics at California State University, Hayward, has written extensively on the Japanese economy and U.S.–Japan economic relations. His latest book is *Keizaigaku de Ningen o Yomu (An Economic Interpretation of Human Behavior)* (1983).

PAUL SEABURY is professor of political science at the University of California. His various writings on international politics and U.S. foreign policy include *The Rise and Decline of the Cold War* (1965) and, with Aaron Wildavsky and Edward Friedland, *The Great Detente Disaster* (1975). He currently serves as a member of the President's Foreign Intelligence Advisory Board.

MURRAY L. WEIDENBAUM is Mallinckrodt Distinguished University Professor at Washington University in St. Louis, where he is also director of the Center for the Study of American Business. He served as chairman of the Council of Economic Advisers in the early part of the Reagan administration and is currently a member of the President's Economic Policy Advisory Board. His works include *The Modern Public State* (1969), *Economics of Peacetime Defense* (1974), *Government-Mandated Price Increases* (1975), *The Future of Business Regulation* (1980), and *Business, Government, and the Public* (1981).

AARON WILDAVSKY is professor of political science and public policy at the University of California in Berkeley. He is the author of *Risk and Culture: An Essay on the Selection of Technological and Environmental Dangers* (with Mary Douglas, 1982), and *The Nursing Father: Moses as a Political Leader* (forthcoming, 1984), and he is editor of the ICS volume *Beyond Containment: Alternative American Policies Toward the Soviet Union* (1983).

INDEX

Labor-Industry Coalition for
International Trade (LICIT), 162,
164, 255n2
Labor-intensive industries
Italy and, 83
Japan and, 56
in U.S., 168, 197–198
LaFalce, John, 93
Land-grant colleges and universities,
18
Law Concerning Temporary Measures
for Promotion of Designated
Industries (Tokushin Ho), 64
Lawrence, Robert Z., 166
Lawyers per 10,000 people, in Japan
and U.S., 15
Leadership, international, financial,
189–191
Learning curve advantages, 142
Liberalization, of Japanese trade and
capital, 57–58, 188
Licensing procedures, 137
Lincoln, Abraham, 18
Lindbeck, Assar, 96, 98
List, Friedrich, 18
Loans
Japanese bank, 22, 57
U.S. (nongovernment) bank,
143–144, 182–184
U.S. government, 29, 30–31, 93,
98–107 passim, 131
Long-Term Credit Bank, Japanese,
57
Losers, *see* Winners vs. losers
Low-technology industries, U.S., 14,
121, 123, 124, 126
Lundine, Stanley N., 39

Machinery and Information
Industries bureau, MITI, 54
Macroeconomic policy, 17, 112,
160–161, 167–169, 236, 241, 242
Macroindustrial policies, 9, 19
Magaziner, Ira C., 65, 107
Mahan, Alfred T., 213
Management-labor relations
in corporate state, 72
Japanese, 52
U.S., 13, 36
Manufacturing costs, 142

Manufacturing output, U.S., 118–132,
167
Manufacturing stage, of product
innovations, 134, 140, 141–142,
146, 155
Marketing, 134, 140–155 passim
Marshall Plan, 5
Matsushita, 65
Maturity, industrial, 155
Mazda Motors, 22–23
McBride, Lloyd, 161
McKenna, Regis, 133–155, 240–241
McKenzie, Richard, 6
Meiji Restoration, 18
Merger plans, in Japan, 64, 238. *See
also* Antitrust policy, U.S.
Merrifield, R. Bruce, 25
Merrifield Plan, 25
Metal industries, U.S., 119. *See also*
Steel industry
Metal oxide on silicon (MOS)
technology, 150, 151, 152
Mexico, 9
Microeconomic policy, 160, 167–169
Microelectronics and Computer
Technology Corporation (MCC),
19
Microindustrial policies, 9, 23, 236
Microprocessors, 150
Military potential, vs. war potential,
210–211. *See also* Defense
industries, U.S.
Mining industries
in Europe, 74, 75, 77
U.S., 207, 258n15
Minish, Joseph G., 31
Ministry of Finance, Japanese, 53–54,
176, 178
Ministry of International Trade and
Industry (MITI), Japanese, 4, 11,
50–70 passim, 171, 188, 243
and business-government relations,
18, 59, 62, 63–64, 66
patent office in, 21
Mitchell, Parren J., 33
MITI, *see* Ministry of International
Trade and Industry, Japanese
Mitsubishi, 52, 62
Mitsui, 52
"Mixed" economies, 50